A GUIDE FOR WOMEN IN RELIGION, REVISED EDITION

A GUIDE FOR WOMEN IN RELIGION, REVISED EDITION

Making Your Way from A to Z

First edition edited by

Mary E. Hunt with Rebecca Alpert, Karen Baker-Fletcher, Valerie E. Dixon, Janet R. Jakobsen, Rosamond Cary Rodman, and Katharina Von Kellenbach

Revised edition edited by

Mary E. Hunt, Kecia Ali, and Monique Moultrie

palgrave
macmillan

A GUIDE FOR WOMEN IN RELIGION, REVISED EDITION
Copyright © Mary E. Hunt, Kecia Ali, and Monique Moultrie, 2004, 2014.

First edition published in hardcover and paperback in 2004 by
PALGRAVE MACMILLAN®
in the United States—a division of St. Martin's Press LLC,
175 Fifth Avenue, New York, NY 10010.

Where this book is distributed in the UK, Europe and the rest of the world,
this is by Palgrave Macmillan, a division of Macmillan Publishers Limited,
registered in England, company number 785998, of Houndmills,
Basingstoke, Hampshire RG21 6XS.

Palgrave Macmillan is the global academic imprint of the above companies
and has companies and representatives throughout the world.

Palgrave® and Macmillan® are registered trademarks in the United States,
the United Kingdom, Europe and other countries.

ISBN: 978-1-137-48573-1 (pbk)
ISBN: 978-1-137-48572-4 (hc)

Library of Congress Cataloging-in-Publication Data is available from the
Library of Congress.

A catalogue record of the book is available from the British Library.

Design by Newgen Knowledge Works (P) Ltd., Chennai, India.

Revised hardcover and paperback edition: November 2014

10 9 8 7 6 5 4 3 2 1

With gratitude to the pioneer women in religion, and with high hopes for the women who will follow.

Thank you to the women who are following and making their own way as they go.

CONTENTS

Acknowledgments   ix

Acknowledgments for the Revised Edition   xi

Editors' Introduction to the Revised Edition   1

Introduction to the Original Guide   3

The Guide from A to Z   9

*Appendix I: American Academy of Religion Sexual
    Harassment Policy*   179

*Appendix II: American Academy of Religion Sexual Harassment
    Grievance Procedure*   183

*Appendix III: Society of Biblical Literature (SBL)
    Ethics Statement*   189

Appendix IV: Making Your Presentations Disability Friendly   191

Appendix V: "Be Brief, Be Witty, Be Seated"   193

Appendix VI: Writing a Successful Annual Meeting Paper Proposal   195

Resources   201

About the Editors   205

Index   207

Acknowledgments

Scores of women too numerous to name shared their experiences as religious studies professionals for this book. Each submission was read and incorporated into this final product. Gratitude abounds for their generosity and candor.

The writing committee is largely responsible for the form and content of this book. Special thanks go to readers who improved the early draft of this book with their astute critiques and helpful additions: Laurie Wright Garry, Julie Kilmer, Rachel Magdalene, Heather McKay, Jacqueline Pastis, Judith Plaskow, Rosetta Ross, Susanne Scholz, Gwendolyn Zohara Simmons, Ilene Stanford, and Kerry Wynn. Jane Webster contributed important material on topics related to the Society of Biblical Literature. Rita Nakashima Brock added the voice of experience on many pages. Shannon Planck brought an American Academy of Religion perspective to bear.

Appreciation flows to Judith Plaskow and Rita Nakashima Brock's Committee on the Status of Women in the Profession of the American Academy of Religion. They started this process more than a decade ago and produced the *Guide to the Perplexing: A Survival Manual for Women in Religious Studies*, the forerunner to this volume. Equal gratitude goes to the current committee members: Rebecca Alpert, Mary C. Churchill, Janet Jakobsen, Sarah Heaner Lancaster, Karen Pechilis, and Gwendolyn Zohara Simmons, who saw the importance of keeping the process going. Special thanks are due to the Committee Chair, Rebecca Alpert, and to Shannon Planck, the AAR Staff Liaison, who shepherded the early part of the process with style.

Publishing colleagues helped to direct this book to its eventual home at Palgrave. Elizabeth Castelli, Pamela Johnson, Frank Oveis, and Gayatri Patnaik provided invaluable expertise. Palgrave editor Amanda Johnson offered smart ideas and effective technical assistance. To all of them a grand thank you for demonstrating that feminist work in religion is worth promoting.

The Women's Alliance for Theology, Ethics and Ritual (WATER) provided the infrastructure for editing this book. WATER's Carol Murdock Scinto and Laura Bernstein edited the book with their usual eagle eyes. The Women's Studies Program at Temple University hosted the writing committee's meeting. Kudos to these small women's groups that make a big difference.

ACKNOWLEDGMENTS FOR THE REVISED EDITION

The new editorial team is indebted to many generous colleagues who evaluated the original book in light of a decade's worth of experience. They suggested new entries, focused attention on needed redactions, and reinforced our sense that *la plus ça change...*

Among those to whom we are grateful are: Rebecca Alpert, Barbara Ardinger, Xochitl Alvizo, Neomi De Anda, Julia Watts Belser, Rita Nakashima Brock, Carol P. Christ, Mary Churchill, Paula Fredriksen, Jacqueline Hidalgo, Jennifer Hughes, Kate Jackson, Mignon Jacobs, Aislinn Jones, Katarina Von Kellenbach, Samantha Kennedy, Kwok Pui-lan, Pamela Lightsey, Kathy McCallie, Gina Messina-Dysert, Michelle Mueller, Judith Plaskow, Robert Puckett, Vanessa Rivera de la Fuente, Emily Ronald, Carolyn Roncolato, Arlene Sanchez-Walsh, Kristi Slominski, Shively Smith, Harvey Stark, Su Pak, Susan Brooks Thistlethwaite, Kate Ott, Emilie Townes, Elizabeth Ursic, Amina Wadud, Renita Weems, and Theresa Yugar.

We also thank Cathy Jaskey and Kate Stoltzfus at WATER for help with manuscript preparation.

Editors' Introduction to
the Revised Edition

Change happens slowly for women in religious studies, but it happens because colleagues collaborate, sharing wisdom and experiences aimed at improving options for all. So we discerned in looking at this guidebook to determine what needed to be done next to encourage even more change.

The earlier version, built on the original publication that served so many women so well, contains a plethora of data and advice. Ten years later, the *Guide* is more than ever the go-to source for women in the field of religion. While we all wish that it needed to be completely rewritten because everything is rosy, unfortunately circumstances have not improved sufficiently for women to warrant a new book. So our team collaborated to bring the current version up to date using the best womanist/feminist/*mujerista* insights. Several recent books and many online resources address the general challenges women face in academia (see our updated **Resources** section). Although some overlap is inevitable, rather than reinvent the wheel we have tried to focus on those elements that pertain particularly to religious and theological studies.

Major changes in the text include integrating technological innovations that have revolutionized how we do our work. From online teaching to blogs and social media, the tools of our trade are now portable, fast, and ubiquitous for those who have access to them.

The access question remains perhaps the most difficult problem. Racism, religion, ableism, economic class privilege, heterosexism, colonialism, and other factors combine to ensure that white, economically advantaged Christian women still outpace others in progress. Our goal is to share the improving context and avoid having women repeat the mistakes of men as they gain increased power.

Another major change is the variety of jobs students of religion can and must pursue. A recessive economy and social values that favor business over the humanities result in a shrinking job market for graduates of most programs. The good news is that the kind of training we receive is easily applicable to many fields. Who else is as able as we to handle texts critically, to look behind the numbers for trends and clues to meaning, to think broadly and systematically from a number of perspectives, to write in clear and compelling prose? It is no wonder that our colleagues are making major contributions to the nonprofit sector, to government, the arts, and business. Our skill sets are enviable and eminently more practical than most of us realize.

Of course the usual and, for many, the preferred route after doctoral studies is a teaching career. But the number of prepared professors far outstrips the number of jobs, and as adjunct teaching and **MOOCs** (Massive Open Online Courses) become increasingly normative, there is good reason to assume that this trend will endure. Hence, our manual assumes what have been traditional career trajectories in religious studies, but embraces the fact that many of our readers will create their own templates as they go.

A third change in the past decades is the gradual but certain maturing of the work force. Our intended audience is everyone from undergraduates contemplating a career in religion to retiring professors wondering how to finish up with emerita status. In between are all of those who are searching for jobs, thinking about a job change, figuring out how to "play the game," helping implement rules that are fair to all. This is a guide to have on the shelf to consult at various junctures as life changes.

One wise colleague advised that we think of our target reader as a woman of color just getting started in her career. Diverse voices and attention to historically marginalized members of the profession are hallmarks of this edition. That all women may flourish in religion and not just a few become presidents of theological schools or luminous professors is our goal.

Maps that are out of date help no one. Likewise, a guidebook needs to reflect the current reality of an ever-changing situation, an impossible task. So we offer this second edition as a springboard for your own explorations. Share with your colleagues, mentor and be mentored with care, expect that the contours of the field will change as you and your cohort give it shape. That is what previous generations bequeath in an enduring effort to amplify women's voices, ensure women's safety, and encourage women's creative contributions to the field of religion.

Introduction to the Original Guide

By Mary E. Hunt

Women are transforming the field of religion in profound and historic ways. There are simply more of us than ever before, though numbers alone do not tell the story. We bring a wide variety of experiences and perspectives to our work. We come from myriad faith traditions or with no personal religious commitment at all. Whether or not we work on women's issues in religion, we are all indebted to the pioneering feminist, womanist, and *mujerista* women who made clear that religion, and, by extension, the study of religion, is gendered activity.

We need and welcome newcomers and students as colleagues who share the challenges, excitement, and fulfillment of working in a field where women are creating new approaches. This guide is intended to elucidate some of the complexities and to smooth the path for those who follow us.

This guide is a collegial project. The writing group looked at how the interstructuring of sexism, racism, Christian hegemony, economic injustice, Postcolonialism, and discrimination based on sexual choices has made work in religion difficult for many women, especially for women from marginalized racial, ethnic, sexual, and religious groups. We agreed that we need to grapple critically with the structural inequalities built into the fabric of the United States and an increasingly globalized world that privilege some at the expense of others. We also need to consider carefully the patriarchal religious traditions that bar women from having access to information and to informal networks where decisions are made. Understandably, many women enter the field lacking self-confidence, searching in vain for the support that their male colleagues take for granted, needing the collaboration with other women that is usually, but not always, forthcoming.

The American Academy of Religion (**AAR**) and the Society of Biblical Literature (**SBL**) are professional societies in the field. Their meetings are opportunities for women to meet one another and develop professional skills. It is inspiring that our senior colleagues, including some who are deceased, were able to work so effectively against long odds that accumulated in the field over the centuries. Women held top leadership positions, including the presidency, of the Academy's predecessor organization, the National Association of Biblical Instructors. For example, the first woman president of the AAR served in 1974. Six of the last ten presidents have been women, and a woman has served as the chief executive for more than a decade.

Some AAR and SBL members started the Women's Caucus of the American Academy of Religion in 1971; it became part of the official program in 1972. In 1986, the Caucus began a series of successful preconference workshops that continue to the present. These are opportunities for women to network, discuss common concerns, and share skills. Many of the themes of the Caucus gatherings are reflected in this guide.

For example, Caucus members and other activist women introduced the idea of childcare at the Annual Meeting. The Committee on the Status of Women in the Profession (**SWP**) made the case and the AAR Board of Directors agreed. SWP developed policies and procedures against sexual harassment, and established the expectation—long since an academy policy—that job interviews be conducted on a safe and level playing field.

Religious feminist pioneers founded the *Journal of Feminist Studies in Religion*, created institutes that focus on women's issues in religion, and developed women's studies programs in their institutions, all the while fulfilling their responsibilities as scholars and teachers. Scholars, most of them women, pushed the theoretical edges of their respective disciplines to ensure that women would not be ignored or left aside in the study of religion, historical as well as contemporary. Behind the scenes, they networked and connected in order to survive and thrive as professionals in a field in which men predominated.

One useful tool these creative women produced was a camouflage-covered book, *Guide to the Perplexing: A Survival Manual for Women in Religious Studies* (Scholars Press, 1992). It was conceived so that successive generations of women would not have to start from scratch to assure their own well-being. "The Guide," as it was fondly known, was the work of the Academy's SWP, under the leadership of Susan Brooks Thistlethwaite, the Committee's first chairperson. Rita Nakashima Brock and Judith Plaskow wrote the majority of the volume with additional material provided by Committee members including Susan Thistlethwaite, Kelly Brown Douglas, Paula Fredriksen, Adele McCollum, and James Poling, in consultation with other colleagues. Many of the themes in the first guide were also agenda items in pre-conference Women's Caucus workshops.

Several scholarly generations found our way in the field thanks to this practical and insightful book. A decade later, the field has changed appreciably, in no small measure because those who went before us took the time to share their wisdom. Moreover, this now sizable percentage of women in the academy has grown older and wiser still! Thus, the SWP decided it was time to publish an updated guide to bring new collective wisdom to public expression in a second version that, we hope, will have a similar impact.

Women are making substantive changes in the field. For example, it is possible to study feminist/womanist/*mujerista* and Asian feminist work in religion on the undergraduate level in many institutions. There are a number of doctoral programs where feminist work, gender studies, and queer theory are part of the mix. Women are now presidents of theological schools and universities, as well as deans and chairs of departments. Of course, many women are also working in the traditional fields of study and contributing from other perspectives as well. The program units of the AAR and the SBL that feature women's work are at the cutting edge of scholarship in religion. Women outnumber men in some seminaries. While this is significant progress, it does not mean that women, especially women of color, have an easy time. Indeed, with the growth in our numbers and in the diversity of our social locations and ideologies, some of the camaraderie of an earlier time has dissipated. Nonetheless, new coalitions are being forged across differences by colleagues who seek to empower those whose voices have been underrepresented in the field.

Unfortunately, some things have not changed at all. For instance, men are still the majority of those teaching on religion faculties. The task of balancing work and family continues to fall disproportionately on women. After some early gains as faculties sought to include at least some women in their ranks, it can be especially hard for women to find jobs in a market that is far more competitive than it was years ago. Women are sometimes pitted against each other on ideological grounds, allowing some institutions to hire women without introducing women's issues into their curriculum or institutional commitments. For example, explicit feminist work is as often punished as rewarded. It is a complex situation, made more so for women who come into religion from other fields and for women who come from countries other than the United States and seek to enter the U.S. job market.

The current AAR SWP, ably chaired by Rebecca Alpert, continues to see the need for a "survival guide," because women are still far from receiving equal opportunity, fair treatment, and equal pay. This time the focus is on women thriving as well as surviving.

I accepted with enthusiasm the Committee's invitation to edit a new volume, with the proviso that the process and the product would reflect our diversity and our commitment to advocate for women in the field. Thanks to the AAR's generous support, I was able to design and implement a process that would bring multiple voices to the task. The writing of this guide began as a project of the SWP. However, its publication is indebted to but independent of SWP and of the AAR.

I issued a call through the AAR and SBL to the various women's groups, including womanist, Asian women, and *mujerista* colleagues, the Feminist Liberation Theologians' Network, and the Women's Caucus. I invited women to share their insights and experiences. Scores of women (too numerous to name) sent valuable, heartfelt information. Responses came from many women, ranging from students to faculty and staff; from US-based women and women living elsewhere in the world; from women representing a range of racial/ethnic groups and sexual orientations; from professors and librarians; from artists and authors. I hope that this guide effectively reflects their insights.

The wonderful writing committee I convened was comprised of Rebecca Alpert, Karen Baker-Fletcher, Valerie E. Dixon, Janet R. Jakobsen, Rosamond Cary Rodman, and Katharina Von Kellenbach. Together we sifted through the replies, conceived of the overall framework, refined the title, and drafted many of the alphabetical entries. I wrote the rest based on the input we received, with occasional help from persons with special expertise.

Our rich conversation was reminiscent of the early AAR/SBL Women's Caucus sessions, proving that *la plus ça change, la plus c'est la même chose*. Issues of scholarship and spirituality abound. Finding one's voice, handling a commuter partnership, paying off student loans, juggling a career and family life, negotiating a contract, building a case for tenure—all of these remain current areas of concern. But there are new issues not found in the earlier volume—choosing an administrative career, teaching online, retiring and moving to emerita status, among others—that simply were not concerns of most women in religion ten years ago, when the average age of women in the field was younger.

Another significant change is that ten years later the increased numbers and participation of lesbian, racial and ethnic minority, Muslim, Hindu, and other diverse women in the academy bring to the fore more questions of multiple layers of discrimination against women. These include racism, sexism, heterosexism, ageism, ableism, colonialism, and more. We now listen to diverse voices in the field and take seriously the complexity of our struggles.

The writing committee had consensus around the fact that each of us is trying to make a life and a living, but we noted the wide range of ways we are doing it. That is why we decided that moving seriatim as in the earlier guide through the undergraduate and graduate years, to the dissertation, first job, tenure, perhaps a second job, and on to retirement, would simply not do. We could not assume that all of us would get or even seek tenure-track jobs. The academic market is tight and other exciting options abound. We developed this guide in light of the structures of academic life, while recognizing that more and more women will not get, and some do not aspire to, academic jobs.

This is both a fresh possibility and a new tension, calling us to balance the "traditional" route with other innovative options. Our view is that work other than teaching can be equally fulfilling and useful. Indeed, graduate education in religion is great preparation for careers in publishing, libraries and information technology, nonprofit organizations, ministry and religious administration, as well as in politics, social work, and health care-related areas. Far from being second-rate options, we see some of our best and brightest colleagues moving in these directions. Nonetheless, the "default" academic assumptions still rule, especially for women students, who, as newcomers to the field, have a priority claim on our attention and wisdom. Let them be heartened by the growing options available to those trained in religious studies.

Many men will find this new guide helpful, as they did the first one. They confront many of the same challenges. They will get insight into what women face in the field of religion and how men can work in solidarity with them. This guide is also essential reading for hiring and tenure committees, academic administrators, and others concerned with equality. We support efforts by colleagues who come from underrepresented racial and ethnic minority groups to develop their strategies as well.

This guide, like its older sister, is not meant to be a substitute for good legal advice. Difficult issues that require legal expertise arise in our work. For example, issues regarding tenure, publishing contracts, and sexual harassment are legally complex. If you need legal help, consult a lawyer. You might also wish to consult the American Association of University Professors (www.aaup.org), Lambda Legal Defense and Education Fund (www.lambdalegal.org), Legal Momentum, formerly the NOW Legal Defense and Education Fund (https://www.legal-momentum.org/), and the National Women's Law Center (www.nwlc.org).

This guide is not intended to take the place of consultation with trusted colleagues or to supersede an individual institution's rules and customs. If you need advice, we recommend that you consult your colleagues broadly, both those within the field and those within the institution where you work.

Use this guide as a ready reference for some of the practical issues you or others you know face while engaged in a career in the study of religion. You may wish to read straight through to get an overall picture, to discern some of the trends and customs, pitfalls, and possibilities in the profession. Or you may wish to take advantage of the alphabetical compendium and the cross listings to focus on a particular theme. Words/phrases in bold are cross-references to other entries for your convenience. You will note that we have chosen a conversational tone in our writing. It reflects women's commitment to share what we have learned, to honor women's informal networks as well as our formal, institutional ties, and to invite you, the reader, to join us.

Consider this guide a compilation of the experiences of many generous women, shared so that our field may become increasingly more just for women and thus for everyone, and more collegial for the doing so. Above all, enjoy your work in religious studies. Thanks to courageous, innovative women and supportive men, the field of religion is now open wider than ever to your creativity and contribution.

The Guide from A to Z

AAR

This lexicon begins fittingly with the AAR, the American Academy of Religion (https://www.aarweb.org/), the professional association for people in religious studies. With nearly nine thousand members (in 2013), it is a key source of information, support, and development. Its peer organization is the Society of Biblical Literature, or **SBL** (http://www.sbl-site.org). The "alphabet soup" of its many aspects and linkages can be found in this guide under their own entries, such as the Status of Women in the Profession Committee (**SWP**). Women make up 38% of those AAR members who identified themselves by gender. (Seven people identified as transgender; the rest as male.)

Most people become acquainted with the AAR through its Annual Meeting (see **AAR Annual Meeting**) where members present and listen to papers, shop for books, network with other members, and interview for jobs. In fact, the AAR has much more to offer throughout the year as a clearinghouse for information and activities in the field. The *Journal of the American Academy of Religion* (*JAAR*) and the online publication *Religious Studies News* (*RSN*) are welcome sources of scholarly work and timely articles about goings-on in the field. AAR also publishes a book series with Oxford University Press, and an online publication for grant news and conference announcements called *In the Field*, as well as numerous e-publications of use to the general membership.

If you make the effort to get involved, the AAR can also become a location for friendship networks, support, guidance, and intellectual stimulation. It is a good place to get a sense of the "big picture" in religious studies, a healthy antidote to isolation in your institution. Attendance at the yearly gathering is a wonderful opportunity for continuing education in the field of religion. Regional meetings are also useful and on a smaller scale so they can feel more doable if you are new to the work.

Once you are ready to move beyond attending meetings and/or presenting papers, the next obvious place to get involved is with the governance of a program unit, which can be small and relatively specialized ("Groups") or large and (potentially) unwieldy ("Sections"). Program units are the backbone of the AAR's structure. They organize most conference sessions. They maintain recommended reading lists that are relevant to their subfields, and they offer the opportunity to work more in depth with scholars in your particular discipline. Of particular interest for women in religion are the Women and Religion Section and the following groups: Feminist Theory and Religious Reflection; Lesbian-Feminist Issues in Religion; Womanist Approaches to Religion and Society; Women of Color Scholarship, Teaching, and Activism; Body and Religion; Religion and Sexuality; and Queer Studies in Religion, among others. You need not limit your involvement to these, however; female and feminist voices are needed (and usually welcome) in all program units.

Each unit has one or two chairpersons and a steering committee of five to seven other members who serve three-year terms. Some program units elect new members to replace those whose terms are ending at business meetings during one of their Annual Meeting sessions; others work things out less formally. If a unit seems right for you, attend the business meeting, introduce yourself, and ask/listen to how they do things. Program unit leaders need not have regular faculty appointments. Graduate students can serve on and even potentially chair committees (usually post-all but dissertation status), as can adjuncts (see **appointments, adjuncts**) and **independent scholars.**

There are numerous opportunities to volunteer to serve as a graduate student or professional member beyond program unit leadership. Graduate students can serve through the new (as of 2013) AAR Ambassador Program. Ambassadors act as points of contact for the AAR in the home departments.

After you have been a member for a few years, you might consider nominating yourself to one of the several committees of the Board of Directors. For example, the Status of Women in the Profession Committee (**SWP**), the group that created *Guide to the Perplexing: A Survival Manual for Women in Religion* and initiated the first edition of this book, is charged with monitoring issues of importance to women colleagues. Over the years, they have worked on matters such as securing childcare options at the Annual Meeting, sexual harassment policies, job equity, mentoring, work–life balance, and making public the contributions of religious feminists. There are similar committees on Racial and Ethnic Minorities in the Profession (**REM**), on People with Disabilities in the Profession (**PWD**), and on Lesbian, Gay, Bisexual, Transgender, Intersex, and Queer Persons in the Profession (**LGBTIQ Committee**). There are also committees on Teaching and Learning and the Public Understanding of Religion, as well as a Graduate Student Committee, all of which do important work for the AAR. Note, though, that although one can self-nominate, the AAR president ultimately selects and appoints committee members; it is not a democratic process, though committee members have striven to make it a transparent one.

For further information on participating in the AAR, consult its website (https://www.aarweb.org/) where you will find the governance structure, information about the committees and the Annual Meeting, and many other activities and publications carried out by the AAR. Find what interests you and volunteer or ask a colleague to nominate you for the task.

AAR ANNUAL MEETING

The Annual Meeting of the **AAR** is held in late November in different cities around the continent (e.g., Atlanta, Chicago, and Toronto) in conjunction with the **SBL Annual Meeting**. Ten thousand people gather for a long weekend of paper presentations and panel discussions, book buying and job hunting, meetings and social events. Though it can be a major expense, the Annual Meeting provides the opportunity to catch up on scholarship in your field and to meet people from around the world who are doing similar work. For independent scholars and those who work in religion nonprofits, the meeting offers a unique chance to connect with far-flung colleagues.

The gathering can be intimidating given its size and scope. Plan ahead by reviewing the online program or app to note what sessions you want to attend. Consult with colleagues about what they are doing so you can find out which sessions might be interesting, even if they are not in your field (keyword searches of the program can help). Make dates with your friends and colleagues before you arrive on site. A refreshing encounter with someone you have not seen in a while can be as productive as attending a program session. You can also reach out before the conference to someone you don't know but would like to meet to ask if she or he is planning to attend and would like to get a cup of coffee. If you are reluctant to simply contact someone out of the blue, ask your advisor, a colleague, or a mentor to introduce you by email. Keep a careful schedule of your commitments and your "free" spots so you can quickly suggest a meeting time when you run into someone on site with whom you want to chat.

It is important to pace yourself as you go through the meeting. Make strategic choices about which sessions to attend. The Annual Meeting includes cultural events, films, local tours, concerts, and the like. These events provide a great way to "rest" while still being stimulated intellectually. They are also good places to meet people with similar interests and appreciate just how rich and diverse our field can be.

Spend some time in the book display, the only place where you actually need your name badge to enter. It is helpful to catch up on the latest publications and to find books for next year's syllabi. It is a great place to run into people, or to track down a publisher with whom you would like to work. Many books are sold at discounted prices. Publishers' catalogs announce forthcoming works and advertise their current lists. This can be helpful as you decide what review or desk copies you wish to request. The program for the Annual Meeting includes a guide to the book displays so you can plan where you want to go in the cavernous room to get the books you want.

Don't be shy about introducing yourself to someone whose work you admire, whose name you've noticed on his or her badge (without staring rudely). Usually, colleagues are grateful for the contact. You can also ask someone whom you know to make an introduction—or, if you know two people who would benefit from connecting, make the introduction yourself.

After a paper has been delivered, it is quite common to present your business card to the author and ask for an electronic copy. Or, if you miss a paper and would like to read it, simply contact the presenter and ask her/him to share it with you. (Many will share; some won't until publication.) This is what it means to work collegially. Since only members can present, anyone who has presented a paper at the Annual Meeting will be listed in the membership directory, available on the AAR website to all current members.

Make sure you have fun at the meeting! Find people to chat with and share meals. Connect with graduate school friends or old colleagues. Take walks, use the hotel health facilities, or go to a movie or museum. Remember to breathe! Do whatever you need to do to keep from running yourself ragged, especially if you are on the job market. Go easy on alcohol at receptions and remember that professional expectations do not end when you have delivered your paper.

The costs of attending the Annual Meeting can be high. Food costs at conference centers can be outrageous; you may want to stock up on healthy, portable snacks and bring a refillable water bottle. If you have special dietary needs, more planning may be required, as well as a stop at a local grocery store. If you have an institutional research or travel budget, use it. Other universities may subsidize the cost for faculty or students who are presenting papers or serving on committees. If you itemize deductions for income tax purposes you can often deduct a portion of your unreimbursed meeting expenses. Ask an accountant for details and save your receipts. Students find these meetings a real stretch financially, so consider buying your students a meal or inviting them for coffee, especially if you can also introduce them to colleagues or publishers.

If you have a disability, you are no doubt aware that official policies requiring accessibility are not always fully implemented. If you will be presenting at or plan to attend particular sessions, it is worthwhile to contact AAR staff in advance to remind them of your requirements and consult the AAR Status of People with Disabilities in the Profession Committee (**PWD**) webpage, which lists accessibility information for the Annual Meeting. If you find persistent obstacles, let someone onsite know so the problem can be fixed or, at the very least, noted and investigated after the fact.

The Annual Meeting can be hard on introverts. So many people, so little silence. Anyone who has been involved in a large institutional structure knows that the best way to survive is to get involved with a small group within that structure. The Annual Meeting provides many opportunities for you to do just that. Some groups at the AAR hold pre-meetings on Friday, before the conference officially begins, including womanist scholars, the Feminist Liberation Theologians' Network, and others. There are events for adjunct faculty and those exploring alternate academic career (**Alt-Ac**) positions. Check them out and find your way.

There are mentoring programs that provide good chances to meet other women. These include a mentoring lunch co-sponsored by the Committees on the Status of Women in the Profession (**SWP**) and Racial and Ethnic Minorities (**REM**). The Committee on the Status of Lesbian, Gay, Bisexual, Transgender, Intersex, & Queer Persons in the Profession (**LGBTIQ Committee**) also hosts a mentoring lunch that is very useful.

These committees also offer Special Topics Forums that address political and professional concerns. There is a student group and an elected student director who serves on the AAR Board of Directors (see **GSC**). The students provide a session introducing the AAR to new members at each Annual Meeting. They have a lounge in which to relax and meet people. There is also a Women's Lounge, and the Women's Caucus provides innovative programming. Many international colleagues attend the AAR/SBL. There are often special events for them as well.

Another important way to make connections is to attend the business meeting of the section(s) or group(s) in your field of study. Through these meetings, you can become acquainted with scholars in your area of interest, and be involved in crafting the topics for the Call for Papers for the following year. Depending on the practice of the group, you might be able to serve on the steering committee, which decides which papers will be accepted for presentation. Like most things, what you put into it will mirror what you get out of the AAR, so consider it a worthwhile investment, especially if professional service is important for your tenure and promotion.

AAR Regions

The AAR is broken down into geographic regions. If you are an AAR member, you automatically belong to a region. Regions vary by size and level of member participation. In some of the larger regions there are significantly more opportunities to present your work and network with colleagues in your subfield. However, do note that not all regions' programming unit divisions match the AAR structure, so you may need to look more carefully at the Call for Papers to see where your work would fit. Each year the regions sponsor conferences, usually in the spring. You can attend, give a paper, or become involved in regional governance and organization. It is usually less expensive and more convenient to go to a regional meeting than to attend the AAR Annual Meeting. It is a good way to accomplish what may be more daunting on the macro level, namely, to meet people in the field and display your work on a smaller scale before you tackle the Annual Meeting (see **AAR Annual Meeting**)

Ableism (see also Disability)

Ableism is the systemic discrimination against and exclusion of people who have physical, mental, sensory, and/or emotional disabilities. Normative assumptions about how bodies and minds work (many work differently) are codified in law, architecture, education, language, and virtually every other sphere of life based on often arbitrary values. Ableism leads to devaluing and disregarding people with disabilities. It is a form of oppression that, when combined with sexism and racism, for example, ensures that women and people of color with disabilities will suffer disproportionately. Many institutions have offices and/or officers who handle discrimination against people with disabilities. Others need them.

Academic Freedom and Risk

Academic freedom is a time-honored dimension of life in the academy. It typically refers to the respect accorded to each one for her/his work and to the expectation that one can articulate possibly unpopular ideas and beliefs in the classroom and in print (and, now, online). What is not always clear is what it means, how far it goes, to whom and how it applies. In fact, an irony is that many of the people who most need **tenure** for the protection of their rights do not get it, sometimes because their ideas challenge the status quo. Worrying too much about the academic freedoms accorded to tenured faculty can also seem misguided in a climate where a significant and increasing proportion of humanities faculty is comprised of poorly paid and badly treated adjunct laborers.

Academic freedom is especially tricky when religious matters are involved since the "freedom" to contradict a religious tradition's beliefs may well result in problems on the job in religiously affiliated institutions, though problems with academic freedom are not limited to such institutions. Many of the trickiest religious issues concern women's bodies and female authority, and job security may be contingent on toeing the line. Learn the local landscape early in one's term at an institution (better yet, ask before taking the job). Make choices accordingly, weighing risks and benefits. Still better advice, if sometimes costly, is to keep your banner high even in religious institutions, since they risk the loss of their reputations when they abrogate a basic tenet of academic life. Academic freedom is for all or none of us.

Activism

Activism and scholarship go hand in hand in a society in which privilege accrues for some and oppression for others. Activism takes many forms, and scholarship can indeed be an important one. Besides, myths of academic objectivity are widely debunked. Without activism, this *Guide* and all of the accomplishments of women in the field would never have taken place.

Some women in religious studies may become full-time activists, making social change outside the academy rather than through teaching in or changing academic institutions. Still others will write and teach their way into social justice work, their scholarship adding to the analysis and strategies needed for a just world. Options abound to make practical use of our sometimes specialized knowledge. Activism is an integral part of our common project.

The relationship between activism and scholarship raises key questions, some structural, some individual. At the structural level, one activist noted that activists are often treated by academics as "objects of study" rather than as "legitimate producers of knowledge" about gender and religion which, although not obtained by typical scholarly methods, is nonetheless valid and valuable.

For any given woman committed to scholarship and activism, one issue is the balance to be struck, the choices to be made. Then there are the logistics of finding time and energy to do both. What are the written and unwritten rules about activism at your institution? What are the possible consequences of your activism for your institution, students, family, yourself? How can one **not** become involved when one has the skills and the expertise to make a difference? How can one learn skills necessary to make a difference? Some academic institutions have a "town/gown" problem. Other communities depend on scholars to provide leadership on local issues as well as to be resources on global ones, including for the media. There are countless ways to be useful.

Women scholars must be especially vigilant not to be lured into so much activity that their scholarship suffers. However, far more common is the tendency to keep one's head down and stick closely to the expected path, especially early in one's career, an approach that can lead quickly to being co-opted. This helps no one. Service learning, sometimes called community-based learning, can be a kind of activism. When professors design courses that require students and/or themselves to work in local settings, they are encouraging community and/or volunteer work that can become a life-long habit. Likewise, using one's position in an academic or other professional setting to leverage ideas and commitments can be a highly responsible use of privilege that the vast majority of the population will never have. These are tough choices, of course, but activism in an unjust climate is crucial to change even if it is at times personally expensive.

Moreover, a career as a social change agent is a great way to put religious studies into practice. "The learned ministry" is one way to think about it. Another way is to see community-based work as a creative way to teach. No matter how you slice it, using our skills for the common good is an integral part of feminist work in religion.

Administration

Women are taking on increasing administrative responsibility in the field of religion, inside and outside of the academy. This is new in recent years and invites critical reflection. In some cases, women are brought in to clean up dysfunctional situations, to raise money where that task has been neglected or unsuccessful, or to try to right a sinking ship. Happily, some of our best and brightest have stepped up to these tasks with great success.

Administrative work used to be looked down upon in academia as if the "rock stars" were those who did research, wrote, and taught, often in that order. But now, especially at higher levels, such positions can be better paid and/or more powerful than many faculty jobs, making them well worth considering.

Women who have been involved in administration find that it has many hidden rewards, both personal and professional. Although at the highest levels administration requires time commitments that are hard to balance with family life and other worthwhile activities, some administrative positions (such as running departments, programs, centers, or organizations) may be more compatible with a lifestyle that allows for leisure or family pursuits because of the flexibility they offer. Reduced or no teaching can be perks of administration even for scholars who once thought that all they wanted to do was teach. Administrative posts can lead to opportunities to affect the quality of life at an institution. Administrators often control budget, workload and pay adjustments, curricular decisions, hiring, class sizes, and, at higher levels, the overall direction and goals of the institution. Depending on women's life-cycle responsibilities, whether (and when) we have had children or other major caregiving responsibilities, we may rise to sufficient prominence to be considered for high-level administration jobs at a time when we are more available than at earlier stages of our careers.

While we have learned from experience that gender does not determine one's ability to govern wisely or justly, the presence of women in administration in general has helped create more humane governing practices and working conditions. But there are notable cases where women in charge have taken the same autocratic approach as many of their male predecessors. The results are complicated to deal with, especially for women faculty and staff, because of unexamined expectations of women leaders. Being a woman is no guarantee of being a good, kind, just and effective administrator. Nor does having a woman boss inoculate workers against employment problems. But with careful preparation and constant support women administrators have the potential to make a real difference in a field that has been male-led for centuries.

To be a good administrator you need a penchant for multitasking. You need to be able to encourage staff and faculty so that they feel they are working with (and not for or against) you. You need an ability to connect with other administrators (both peers and bosses), a keen sense of budgets and other numbers and systems, a commitment to academic integrity and honesty, and a great sense of humor. You need a real dedication to students or other clients who are served by your organization. You will also benefit from acute political antennae, an ability to "read" how you are perceived by others, and, especially, good personal boundaries.

If you are interested in and, more important, have discovered you have an aptitude for administrative work, you might try running an interdisciplinary program such as women's studies or American studies, or the practical curriculum at a seminary, to get a feel for whether it's a good "fit" for you. If you then find yourself hankering to get back to the classroom or suffering from library withdrawal, this might not be your vocation. However, if you like it—the meetings and strategizing, the memos and long-term planning—you might want to start reading the *Chronicle of Higher Education* (see **Resources**), an excellent resource and tutorial, and letting your colleagues know of your interest.

Lots of dean and presidential searches are done through recruiters. Processes can differ, but in general you can expect an invitation to be considered for a job. Then if you agree to be considered you will be called by a third party, not someone from the institution, who acts as a kind of go-between for you and the institution. S/he will ask questions about your interest, and answer questions you might have about the position. Then you will be asked to send of letter of intent laying out your qualifications for and interest in the job. A short list of candidates is chosen for interviews and later an even shorter list for on-campus meetings. Those individuals meet with all of the institution's stakeholders—faculty, staff, students—and mutually discern the fit.

Sometimes a candidate will realize on site that this is not the place s/he wants to bail out of its current problems. Or, the candidate will feel great about the job but the institution chooses someone else. Finally, there is usually someone who feels good about it and about whom the institution feels equally positively and bingo, there is a new leader. It is not an easy or trivial process. But if you don't play you can't win. Give it a whirl if you are interested in administration and see what results. Our institutions need strong, smart, and collaborative leaders.

Your institution might support your attendance at the HERS Summer Institute for Women in Higher Education Administration (http://hersnet.org/) (see **Resources**) where you will learn all about the issues and find out if administration is your cup of tea. For the high atmospheric ranks of presidencies, the Harvard Graduate School of Education runs an excellent summer training session as well (http://www.gse.harvard.edu/) (see **Resources**).

Senior women in the field of religion report a variety of experiences ranging from unexpected fulfillment to unmitigated disasters. However, the key is that administration is an important option for women, and women are important for such leadership posts. Younger colleagues report that on occasion they have been named chair of a department, sometimes before being tenured. While this can look like a plum assignment, it can be way of saddling women with administrative busywork that gets in the way of their own scholarship and professional development. Beware of such offers. Be open to others.

Admissions

If you have determined that **graduate school** is the right next step for you, you have your work cut out for you even before you begin your studies. Applying to graduate school is a major investment of time and energy, with no guaranteed positive outcome.

Some success, as on the job market, connects to factors you can't do anything about: who else is in the application pool, what the fellowship situation at a given school is, who might be on leave and not reading admissions files that year. Other factors are in your control: how well you do on GRE exams, whether the faculty members in your chosen field know you, how polished your application essay and writing sample, as well as **recommendations**, are. Though you do not write recommendations, you control whom you ask. Be sure it is someone who knows you well, not simply someone whose name might impress an admissions committee. You, and not your recommender, want to go to school.

As you consider programs, you may want to ask about and arrange to speak with current and past female students: do they proceed through the ranks at the same rate as males? If you are lesbian, bisexual, queer, or a trans woman, will faculty be supportive or hostile? What about the area where the campus is located? Is it safe? Are there campus resources for post-degree employment? If you are a person of color, and/or with a disability, consider whether to make this obvious in your application materials. Consult people on site to get a feel for how the institution works.

If you are a faculty member surveying applications or participating in admission decisions, speak up on behalf of valuable candidates who might be overlooked by others. Speak up if the top candidates emerging seem consistently to be white and/or male disproportionately to their representation in the pool of candidates. If the pool of candidates is too homogenous, think about why that is, and think about what you can do to make your department/institution a more vibrant and diverse place.

One piece of advice goes for both faculty and applicants: make an effort to reach out to people you are seriously considering working with. If you cannot connect productively before admissions, chances that you will have a strong advising relationship after admission are slight.

Advisor/advisee relationships

One of the great privileges of academic life is the opportunity to work with students, both undergraduate and graduate, whose area of interest is in some way connected to your own. On the undergraduate level, advising usually includes choice and construction of a major field of study, guidance on graduate school and/or job options, writing recommendations, and, if the program requires or permits one, help in writing a senior thesis.

Being an advisor for graduate students comes with a great responsibility to introduce students to the academic world they wish to enter and/or to acquaint them with other opportunities that correspond with their abilities. Advising tasks include attention to writing and teaching skills. The advisor helps students to develop a CV and/or dossier (see **Curriculum vitae**), encourages them to attend and present papers at academic conferences, and to apply for **grants** and **fellowships**. Writing thoughtful, detailed recommendations is an ongoing responsibility even long after a student has graduated. Likewise, introducing your students to your academic colleagues, helping them enter the world of **publishing**, and counseling them realistically on career options, within and outside academia, are all part of the job when it is done well.

Graduate students should try to find an advisor who shares their academic interests, of course, but also who has a reputation for nurturing graduate students while simultaneously treating them as adults. Many women want a woman advisor; many people of color want someone from their community if possible. Given that women/people of color are still in relatively short supply in many institutions, it is best to seek someone who can give the time and energy even if that person is not the preferred fit. Students with children or other significant caregiving responsibilities will flourish best with an advisor who is supportive and understands the occasional need to reschedule meetings or work around day-care. Actually, this flexibility may be required when life throws a curve ball—unexpected illness or disability, a sudden loss or major life change—to someone who entered graduate school relatively unencumbered.

The advisor/advisee relationship can be quite intimate. Advisors often are students' first real colleagues in the field, the ones who see them up close and respect what they seek to accomplish. Beware of any sexualizing of the advising relationship that can undermine the purpose of it, which is for the more experienced person to help in the professional development of the colleague being mentored. Such boundaries on both sides are essential to successful advising, but the professor who has the greater power in the relationship is always finally responsible to avoid such behavior. An inappropriate relationship with an advisor can compromise a student's relationships with other students, the institution, or other members of the field, all of which are important to long-term professional success. In addition, many faculty handbooks prohibit intimate relationships by faculty with students under their direct supervision (see **Faculty handbook**). Err on the side of caution.

AFFIRMATIVE ACTION

Affirmative Action was intended to mitigate the general exclusion of disadvantaged minority Americans and white American women from a broad range of opportunities, including employment and promotion, and admission to formerly all-white and predominantly male universities and professional schools. Its enemies have interpreted Affirmative Action as reverse discrimination, or, even more insidiously, as a covert means of promoting unqualified persons for college admission or jobs. Federal laws bind institutions in this regard, though informal practices vary. For a good list of controlling statutes, including Title VII of the Civil Rights Act of 1964 prohibiting employment discrimination, the Equal Pay Act of 1963 prohibiting discrimination on the basis of gender in the area of compensation, etc. consult the U.S. Equal Employment Opportunity Commission (http://www.eeoc.gov/).

Concerted attacks on Affirmative Action across the United States, especially in the courts, mean some gains made by minorities and white women are being eroded. Of particular interest is the schism revealed in the Supreme Court case of Fisher v. University of Texas where Abigail Fisher, a white woman, sued the University of Texas, claiming she was denied admission to law school in favor of minority applicants. Studies show that white women have been helped by affirmative action more than any other group, yet white women have waged many of the recent legal challenges to Affirmative Action in higher education. The Supreme Court's perspective is still emerging as of this writing and debates over affirmative action as a strategy for increasing diversity in colleges and universities continue. Affirmative Action debates require more than a passing conversation since schisms may play themselves out in faculty governance if minority communities are pitted against each other for access to small slivers of power.

Women, particularly those of color, must be vigilant about increasing resistance to diversifying college and university faculties and student bodies. People on hiring committees must be reminded of the benefit of diversity to faculties and student bodies. Women already on the inside must struggle to get onto hiring and admission committees to advocate for the hiring and entry of qualified minorities and white women. The successes that the opponents of Affirmative Action have made in diminishing and/or dismantling these programs call for increased efforts to maintain programs that ensure diversity of faculty and student bodies.

Aging

One obvious consequence of women thriving in the field of religious studies in large numbers is that many women will age there. There are challenges in moving toward retirement and **emerita** status. There are also simply the inevitable realities of growing old—welcome to the club no matter how old you are—though, happily, diminished energy is paired with increased wisdom. Age is a concern for colleagues who enter the field of religion as a second or third career. Age discrimination in hiring is a real problem even for a newly minted Ph.D. at forty.

Sexism against older women is common. How a woman dresses, whether she uses makeup or dyes her hair can be, against all logic and morality, issues in the workplace. Vigilance is necessary because age discrimination is against the law.

As young colleagues turn into middle-aged professionals, many of the so-called mid-life issues emerge: Am I doing what I want to be doing with my life? Is this all there is? Why are some people seemingly so much better off, happier, more fulfilled than I am? It is important to recognize that people who seem to have it figured out may be equally uncertain or insecure or struggling under the surface. But your questions can lead to a midcourse correction in the form of a job change, perhaps even a career change, a makeover that morphs a longtime professor into the head of a nonprofit organization or that catapults a social activist into a university post (see **Mid-career issues**). Increased life expectancy and the fact that many universities and organizations do not have a mandatory retirement age mean that many senior colleagues are just hitting their stride at sixty-five. This is especially true for women, many of whom are ten years behind their male counterparts in terms of job progression because of years given to care for children or earlier careers in other fields.

Along the way, many women face the "sandwich generation" phenomenon where they are balancing care for children with care for elders. Sane employment policies that recognize these realities often need to be negotiated.

Aging brings economic concerns such as pension funds, 401(k)s, and health insurance that women need to attend to in a culture that renders a high percentage of older women poor. Moreover, student debt can linger long into one's career, making debt payment a financial priority. A financial planner can help, and a visit with your institution's benefits officer is a must. Nevertheless, there is no substitute for forthright conversation with trusted friends who can help clarify options and suggest good choices.

Allies

Finding, being, and developing allies on the job is essential if sometimes difficult work. Women tend to look to one another, often but not always with great success, for help on the job. Nothing is as disappointing as finding out that presumed allies are not, that trusted colleagues are unworthy of trust. Women should support other women, but one should also build alliances where one can—with men as well as women in the department, with colleagues in other areas, in cyberspace as well as down the hall, along and across racial/ethnic lines, and with people of all sexual orientations who share one's perspective and can provide support. Good allies are worth their weight in gold.

The most important people in any institution are not necessarily the ones with names on their doors, but the secretaries, administrative assistants, and custodial staff, most of whom are women, who make the place run. Cultivating their friendship as equals can go a long way toward creating a less hierarchical environment and making institutional life pleasant. The key to being an ally is being consistent in one's support. This does not mean uncritical acceptance of views or behaviors with which one does not agree. But it does mean developing a power analysis of the workplace to understand where structures work against people and colleagues have to work for them.

Alternate Academic Careers (Alt-Ac)

In recent years, the glaring mismatch between the number of humanities PhD graduates and available faculty jobs has led some individuals and institutions to think more capaciously and creatively about what students, advisors, and graduate programs might do to prepare graduates for careers other than faculty jobs. The name alt-ac or "alternative" [to] academic careers suggests that academic careers are standard and anything else a deviation. This is patently not true but, terminology notwithstanding, some institutions and professional organizations are moving beyond treating nonfaculty jobs as a second-rate "Plan B" when a tenure-track job offer does not materialize or a two-body problem cannot be accommodated. In addition to articles in the *Chronicle of Higher Education* (see **Resources**), an online search will turn up numerous useful sites where humanities-trained people discuss, debate, and offer guidance about nonteaching paths they have taken.

Common themes include **entrepreneurship**, the importance of building on individual talents and inclinations, and the power of collective wisdom. Alt-ac advocates have been generous in sharing their experiences and insights. Among scholarly organizations, the American Historical Association has responded most effectively to the transformed job market, helping prepare historians for careers in archival work, museums, the public sector, and even corporate work. Religious and theological studies organizations lag somewhat behind, although one increasingly finds sessions devoted to alt-ac careers at annual meetings and conferences. In addition to **Administration**, nonteaching careers for scholars in religion and theology include publishing, nonscholarly writing, nonprofit work, and work in religious bureaucracies and organizations.

Appointments, Adjunct

Given the increased corporatization of the academy, many academic institutions are cutting corners, taking advantage of the abundance of well-prepared people by trimming their tenure-track faculty rosters, and turning to adjunct hires to teach core courses. This makes good economic sense if you are on the budget committee, but is a mixed blessing, at best, if you are on the job hunt, and a disaster if you are a student. Benefits tend to be minimal (i.e., lack of health insurance, retirement benefits, office space, and teaching support) and course loads often approximate or exceed those of tenured professors. Contingent academic labor is made up of adjunct appointments that may be paid on a per-course basis or by multiyear contracts.

Though the types of adjunct appointments vary, all yield a similar economic reality. Salaries for adjunct teaching are generally a fraction of what one would be paid for the same course offering as a segment of a full-time teaching load. (Per-course payment can be distressingly low, often $2000–3000—sometimes, fortunately, more, but occasionally, shockingly, less.) One advantage of adjunct teaching is that *in theory* one just teaches and has none of the advising, committee work, and the like that go with a full-time position. Of course, students do not make such distinctions when they want to discuss their vocational plans, request a letter of recommendation, or research a topic about which they consider you the world's expert.

Another advantage of adjunct teaching is that it offers academic affiliation and the opportunity to get a foot in the academic door. Yet, it is rare for departments to turn adjunct appointments into tenure-track positions. Teaching for a year or two while one is finishing one's dissertation can be a good idea, or it may be the fastest route to being "all but dissertation" (commonly called ABD) for a long career. Some people actually prefer to teach as adjuncts, particularly if they land in supportive departments, but for most it is not a choice. Women are especially taken advantage of here. When we take primary care responsibilities for children or elders, or pursue other worthwhile endeavors, part-time teaching can help maintain a toehold in academia while still pursuing other goals, but it has swiftly diminishing returns.

After several years of adjunct work, aim to negotiate full benefits and/or to be hired as a half time rather than adjunct professor. These changes are tough to get individually (though it never hurts to ask); consider participating in an adjunct union or organization that is working to organize and gain legal protections for contingent faculty as a collective. Also, try options such as taking on (or inventing) a hybrid position as a director/administrator with teaching responsibilities. Think about a move to a cognate field or to another form of teaching. Writing or media work, for example, may be areas where your skills will be appreciated, and you will not be blatantly used to provide cheap skilled labor in the classroom.

Appointments, Visiting

Visiting appointments are a mixed bag. In some cases, a visiting professorship can be a nice change of pace, a chance to see if the grass really is greener elsewhere, and an opportunity to work with different colleagues. But in many instances, especially for people who do not have full-time tenure track positions, a visiting appointment is just that, a quick visit. It is not usually the prelude to a long-term appointment, so do not go with unrealistic expectations. It can also be a hardship: time away from one's family and usual surroundings, perhaps working in a different language or cultural setting. While many institutions like to have visiting faculty, few know how to welcome and sustain a visitor as part of the community.

Evaluate such offers with care, and negotiate conditions with as much attention as you would for a regular job. Otherwise, it can be a semester or a year wasted. (Some institutions will allow you to contribute to a retirement plan, for instance; you can later roll this over into an Individual Retirement Account or another institutional retirement savings plan.) Be sure that expectations are clear and that there are no hidden demands that will compromise what might otherwise be a good time to get some writing done and/or to try out a new course. Visiting experiences can be the frosting on the cake of a satisfying career spent mostly in one institution. Or, they can be like a trail of breadcrumbs leading nowhere and taking a lot of time to get there. Talk with colleagues at the institution to find out if it is your kind of place, and think realistically about your long-term goals and whether this appointment gets you closer to them or not.

ARCHIVES

Women's papers are important for historical purposes. They allow future generations to see how we lived, what we thought, how we changed a formerly all-male field like religion into one that reflects more accurately the racial, gender, national, and other forms of diversity that characterize it now. Consider archiving your materials.

There are a number of major women's collections: the Sophia Smith Collection at Smith College; the collection at The Arthur and Elizabeth Schlesinger Library for the History of Women in America; the Women and Leadership Archives of the Gannon Center at Loyola University Chicago, to name just a few. Many other institutions have archives that would welcome papers from scholars in religion. Online archives are changing archiving practices, so it is worth consulting someone with expertise about what to keep.

Your work may be just the missing link in a collection's effort to showcase a developing field. Or, you may have created an organization or participated in a project that future scholars will want to study. Do not be modest and decide that your papers have no value. Ask an archivist. Check with someone at your local setting. A professional will be honest with you and history will thank you.

BENEFITS, DOMESTIC PARTNER

Many colleges and universities today offer domestic partner benefits as well as benefits for same-sex spouses. Some do not for reasons of ideology, finances, etc. Others that formerly offered domestic partner benefits but are now in states that permit same-sex marriage may only grant benefits to married partners. It is a fluid situation with little relief expected until the states and the federal government settle the legal matters. Meanwhile, you probably should avoid asking about the policy at your initial interview (along with other questions about benefits that are better handled after an offer has been made). You might want to check with the **Affirmative Action** office at the institution to see if it has such a policy. Some places are discovering that unless they offer equal benefits they cannot compete for the best employees. You could also check out the institution's website for this information. But do check as policies are evolving quickly and institutions that want the best and the brightest find they have no choice but to offer equal benefits to all.

Investigate carefully what is being offered. Some policies include funeral leave, campus privileges (tuition, library, swimming pool, etc.), or inclusion of partners as beneficiaries on life insurance or pension. Some policies allow you to cover your partner on your health care policy, while others provide cash allowances (often subject to taxes) equivalent to some or all of the cost of taking out your own policy. Some policies cover only same-sex partners, while others also cover heterosexual couples. This is an area where movement toward parity is slow but steady. You can help it along by becoming an advocate for equal benefits regardless of sexual orientation or marital status.

Benefits, Leaves (Family)

Federal law mandates that institutions allow people to take leave for illness, the death of someone close, and other life-changing circumstances. Maternity leave is required by law (see the 1978 Federal Pregnancy Disability Amendment to Title 7 of the 1964 Civil Rights Act), so your institution must provide it. Some institutions are generous with leave for female regular faculty who bear or adopt children; paternity leave (or spousal leave for a nonbiological parent), typically of shorter duration, is increasingly common. Women in ministry or religious organizations will have a wide variety of policies. If you think it will be an issue, check out this benefit in the negotiating phase just so you know where you stand. Feel free to push the envelope since U.S. institutions are notoriously stingy in granting time off and women are notoriously reticent. Remember that in Sweden the mother and her partner get a year and a half of paid leave that they can share however they wish.

Other sorts of leave, including that guaranteed by the Family Medical Leave Act, are available for up to 12 weeks during any calendar year. If the leave is for one's own medical needs, it may be compensated; if it is to take care of a dependent, it is typically unpaid. This means, unfortunately, that some women who really need such leave are unable to take it and still ensure that other family needs are met.

BENEFITS, LEAVES (STUDY)

Academic life is considered so demanding and stressful, so lacking in time to keep abreast of developments, that a major concern is when one can leave, bow out for a bit, to refresh. For tenure-track and tenured faculty, **sabbaticals** are coveted parts of the academic benefit package, negotiated furiously to wring the most time away possible. There is a certain irony about the fact that in the flurry to get a job, one is negotiating how to leave!

Some nonprofit organizations have imitated that model and make a paid leave part of the package for their research and/or administrative people. Full-time clergy can also apply for sabbatical programs (e.g., see the Louisville Institute or the National Clergy Renewal Program). Academic leaves of absence, like sabbaticals, can be paid or unpaid, a semester or a year, on campus or off, usually for a specific project and often with the goal of publication in mind. Know what your institution offers and plan accordingly. If you are required to have a book done or a project completed, be sure you comply or the next leave will be that much harder to justify.

BENEFITS, MEDICAL

Most institutions offer some form of health benefits for employees, though the changing conditions of the U.S. health care system dictate that these can range considerably. Too few universities make such benefits available (or affordable) for adjunct or annual contract faculty, though with increased organization on the part of adjuncts, this is changing slowly. Graduate students may have access to campus health services and some will be eligible to enroll themselves and any dependents in a plan. You may have a smorgasbord of insurance choices, all with different costs and benefits. Take time to study your options in relation to your particular health situation and that of your dependents, if any. If you have a chronic illness, physical or mental, or a disability which requires specialized care, some options may be substantially better than others.

If you are considering adding children to your family, investigate prenatal and delivery coverage, fertility services, and/or adoption benefits. A dental plan and vision benefits are important. As you approach retirement, an important consideration is what benefits will carry

THE GUIDE FROM A TO Z ❖ 31

over when you become Medicare eligible. If you are from outside the United States, explore what might apply from your country, and make your choices accordingly.

Don't forget that the best health insurance is preventative care. See if your institution offers benefits in the form of gym or health club access. (For students, mandatory fees usually cover this.) If not, start a campaign so they will (see **Health**).

Benefits, Retirement

In the United States, the social safety net is eroding and the presumption is that individuals should take increased responsibility for their own **retirement** savings. Virtually everyone is required to pay into Social Security, so, at least for the near future, those benefits will be available. Beyond this, every institution has its own retirement policy, though adjuncts and other part-time employees may be excluded from participation. Even those eligible to contribute may be so poorly paid that they cannot afford to defer 10% to retirement savings. Those who are eligible to contribute to retirement plans should do so and try to invest with socially responsible funds. Many institutions have provisions to reserve a certain percentage of one's salary, sometimes matched by the employer, for retirement saving. Those ineligible to contribute to university plans can use Individual Retirement Accounts (IRAs). Given that women often outlive men and earn less during their lifetimes, saving is important to ward off poverty in retirement. Once again privilege determines so much of this that attention to social structural change is a good investment for everyone.

Books

Books are still important tools of the religion trade, even though there is much evidence that people read fewer books, shorter articles, watch television and movies, and surf the Web more. **Publishing** a book, perhaps beginning with the dissertation recycled into a more generally accessible text, is part of the expectation in most religion-related fields, even though this can be hugely difficult for those with heavy teaching loads and no research leave, or those whose fields are bitten by the economic downturn. Not everyone writes well or easily, though people can learn to write better, and writing is not directly parallel to other professional skills. Some fabulous teachers never publish a book, and some well-known authors are disasters in the classroom.

Books still reign despite the fact that most people now get as much information from blogs and other social media. Writing—whether books, articles, or blogs—remains an important component of religious studies work. Urge your students to write, write, write. It is a good bit of what we do in this field, however it gets published. In the academy, individually authored books are preferred over jointly written/edited volumes regardless of their usefulness. This is a vestige of the Lone Ranger approach to scholarship that is rapidly being eclipsed by joint teaching and research projects. But it remains an unfortunate norm.

Once colleagues get academic jobs, or for that matter jobs in information technology, the nonprofit sector, or the like, they are inundated with announcements and catalogs (mostly online now) from publishers advertising their wares. Careful study of selected ones may be useful in helping to develop **syllabi** for courses. Sometimes it is possible to get a free review copy (yes, you need to write a review), an examination copy for a nominal fee, or a desk copy that is free if you adopt the book for a course. Publishers want to promote their books for classroom use, so this is a win-win for everyone. Just do not request books you will not use, as that puts a crimp in the system for all. Electronic books are increasingly popular (some publishers offer online exam copies) and their use is changing the publishing industry. Publishers love them for the profit and ease of delivery that they portend.

The days of campus bookstores are on the wane. If your institution has one, consider patronizing it. Get to know the manager who orders books, as she/he can be very helpful in suggesting titles you may have missed or finding deals for your students on expensive texts. Even if your institution does not have a bookstore, consider using a local one for your course. Rather than simply feeding the Amazon frenzy or supporting other online behemoths, one option might be to post carefully selected excerpts on your institution's course website (taking due cautions about copyrights). This is less expensive for students and more focused than several textbooks. Another option: approach a university press directly and ask if they will offer discounts and free shipping to students who order directly from them; they are generally struggling in the new publishing climate where they must heavily discount books sold through online retailers and university book-stores. If you have a local independent bookstore, you can encourage students to buy books there, but be aware that students receiving book stipends as part of their financial aid may be unable to buy from them. Local booksellers, too, can be helpful in making suggestions on titles you might have missed.

If policy allows, put books on reserve at your library. Some schools do not allow this because they provide financial aid for books and want to support their bookstores. Reserve can be a good way to socialize knowledge without felling more trees. Many students are on very limited budgets so sensitivity to their situations demands being creative about how to share resources.

In some settings, organizing a book discussion group can be a great alternative to a full course on a topic. It can be a way to test interest in a theme or drum up business for a future course. Such groups can also be a way for community people to join those in the academy, as well as to highlight certain materials that would otherwise be ignored.

Consider inviting authors to offer teleconferences about their work. These are a great way to promote a new book and provoke discussion. Online videoconference services or toll-free call-in lines make this free or very low cost, and can expand access to a great education.

CHILDREN

A career in religious studies does not preclude children in a woman's life. To the contrary, this is a field in which passing on faith and knowledge from generation to generation is an all-important task. It is not easy. Unfortunately, women still usually bear more than their share of child-rearing responsibilities. Having children requires finding ways to balance the needs of young people with the demands of a professional job, with accent on the "balance." However, women in academia have some flexibility in hours. With a fully engaged partner or other means of support, especially good childcare, women can often manage to raise children and build a successful career. Women in other fields, like the nonprofit sector, publishing, etc. find less flexibility and more challenges in arranging their schedules to fit the myriad and growing needs of children, but it can be done.

Ways of doing this are as varied as we are. Some women find that planning their children around their career milestones, such as starting a family as soon as the ink is dry on the dissertation, is a good way to go. Many women find that spacing children according to other needs, such as not trying to have a baby around the time of general exams or tenure review, makes sense. However, while there are bad times to have a child, there is no perfect time; moreover, life does not always work on schedule. Others already have children when they enter a doctoral program or take a job. Still others find themselves caring for nieces and nephews or grandchildren at times they never expected. Some women choose to adopt children. Many choose to enjoy other people's kids without full-time personal responsibility. It is important to recognize these differences as the fruit of decades of struggle for choice, and to accord each the dignity and support it requires.

All mothers need a support system—friends, colleagues, partner if you have one, family, neighbors—who can be the "village" the child requires and deserves, especially in the face of inevitable childcare failures. Sage advice from the mothers, grandmothers, and aunts boils down to "make time for the children in your life and get all the help you can afford." It is a balancing act. The urgent demand of a child crying at night or at other hours pleading "Play with me" or "Help me with my homework" is serious competition for any dissertation or book, project, class, or conference. Nonetheless, there are still only twenty-four hours in a day, so some accommodation to supply and demand is required. If you can afford it, having a babysitter at home while you are in your study working can provide some respite. Some women find, however, that they must leave the house to get anything done.

Despite all of our progress on shared childcare, we note that women still do the lion's share, a problem that needs attention. Childcare is costly, and in a field where salaries are not usually high, this often creates a strain. Some academic institutions and some nonprofits provide it at reduced cost, perhaps at a childcare center on campus. Check on the federal tax credit now available to offset part of such costs; adjuncts may be poorly paid enough to claim the Earned Income Tax Credit. Choose your childcare with safety as the foremost concern, with reliability and flexibility a close second and third.

When kids get into school, they often need their parents in different but no less demanding ways than before. Day care options may be harder to find for older children, though you may be able to shift your teaching obligations to be home for school pick-ups. Consider taking your child with you if you have professional travel obligations. It is generally easy to find babysitters along the way; if you have a partner also in the field, you can take turns attending panels and being with kids. For example, the **AAR Annual Meeting** offers childcare by advance reservation. Of course, travel with children is always a challenge. And be sure that their needs are met when you take them along, not just your need to avoid guilt for leaving them at home.

Some institutions offer tuition reduction or reciprocity with another institution for your children as they approach college age. Seek low-rate loan programs that your institution might offer to help with education costs.

Christian Hegemony

Christianity still dominates the field of religious studies despite the many traditions under study. That is hegemony. Increasingly, scholars recognize this dominance as discrimination and also recognize the deleterious effects of excluding some of the more creative and able scholars. But it is far from being remedied even in feminist circles. Christian hegemony, and its cousin the exclusive study of the so-called major religions to the exclusion of, for example, tribal or horticulturally based traditions, is something to eradicate.

Many jobs for scholars of religion are at Christian seminaries or in the departments of religion at church-related schools. Much of the scholarship on various religions is undertaken by Christians who study "other" religions. The majority of members of the **AAR** are Christian. This Christian hegemony is a reflection of both the historical development of the field of religious studies and the longtime dominance of white Protestant Christianity in American social and cultural life. Thus, all kinds of Christians—African American and Asian Christians, Catholics, Anabaptists, for example—may find themselves marginalized by Christian hegemony, even as they may simultaneously enjoy certain of the privileges of Christian affiliation. Feminists of all stripes find out early that many institutions will tolerate, even welcome the study of "women and" their tradition, but explicitly not welcome feminist, womanist, *mujerista* and other approaches that aim to transform the religions or the study of them. Add Wiccan or pagan to your list of classes offered and you will often feel the full weight of Christian hegemony.

There are both conceptual and practical implications to this Christian dominance. Because Christians historically formed the field of religious studies, "religion" also contains Christian assumptions. The category of "religion" itself was taken up and shaped by colonialism. Spiritual and cultural practices were recategorized as "religions" on the model of Christianity. For example, the wide variety of South Asian practices were brought together as variations of the single "religion" called Hinduism.

Certain South Asian texts were translated by British colonists and treated as sacred scriptures analogous to the Christian Bible. Thus, the word "religion" as in the American Academy of Religion, or "religious" as in religious studies can indicate the plurality of "religions" studied in the field. The practical implications range from who is allowed to study which religion, to what types of jobs are available, to the organization of the **AAR Annual Meeting** with its compartmentalized, disciplined approach, to how the field is structured (including such matters as jobs, panels, anthologies, and departments). The **AAR** increasingly has space for the study of "new religious movements," paganism, and other traditions formerly marginal. Some groups, such as Women and Religion or Religion and Sexuality, look thematically across traditions. Too often, however, non-Christian groups are included in only a token way (see **Tokenism**).

While Christians may range widely in their choice of specialization, often those who practice another religion are expected to take up an academic specialization in line with their identity. Those who are not Christian—who practice another religion or who are atheists, or who are conscientious objectors to religious identification—may find their experience of the field alienating. The task of changing that belongs to all of us.

Christian hegemony can mean that even those who are very concerned about diversity may focus on the categories of gender, race, class, or nation, but fail to address issues of religious diversity. Resistance to Christian hegemony requires being able to think through and respond to the crosscutting of issues related to diversity. For women it means conscious efforts to see one another as colleagues across various lines, and even to consciously promote feminist/womanist/*mujerista* scholarship that opens the disciplinary borders and leaves religious differences aside.

Religious diversity and pluralism in the culture means that students preparing for chaplaincy positions, for example, in public institutions like local hospitals, the National Institutes of Health, or community colleges need to be schooled in a variety of faith perspectives in order to do their work. Gone are the days when the Protestant chaplain attended only Protestant patients, for example. So Christian hegemony in its many pernicious expressions is undercutting the quality of education provided to contemporary students, reason enough to consign it to the dustbin of history.

CLASS, SOCIOECONOMIC

Class is a changing, challenging, and tricky problem as questions of money, access, education, race, and culture interweave to form layers of privilege and discrimination. For women in religious studies, it is important to realize that academic institutions and many related settings in publishing, library work, and so forth are organized as if white upper-middle-class ways were normative. This involves everything from who can afford to go to graduate school (or take an internship at a nonprofit doing important social justice work) to what fork to use at a faculty dinner, from what your stationery looks like to whether you can pay back your student loans without taking a state or corporate job.

Women in the field of religion need more frank discussion on such matters. In an economy where women still earn less than their male counterparts and where women often find employment in the lowest paying positions such as contingent faculty work, it is necessary to speak out about class. Yet, it is often easier to address one's sexuality than one's financial status. In the meantime, structural analysis of class-based oppression in a globalized economy should be an integral part of any religious studies program. That means examining our institutions and ourselves to determine how to share resources and recognize and respect substantive differences that result from women's different histories. It also means doing work that is aimed at shrinking the growing gap between people with privilege and those without.

CLOTHING OPTIONS

Some women colleagues worry about religious *haute couture*. What to wear to interviews, what to wear for professional events, what to wear for teaching, how to dress for office hours, and what to take to the **AAR Annual Meeting** (for sure toss in a bathing suit, as many hotels have pools) are concerns. Norms vary by campus and region. There is plenty of advice online and in print about what to wear, especially to conferences and interviews, for trans women and butch lesbians, Muslim women who cover their hair, and women who adopt mainstream female dress styles. Women who look young may want to select more formal clothing to avoid being mistaken for students. Women in ministry may have a range of clothing options accessible as religious authorities, but may also need to invent styles as they go along. Factor the cost of clothes into your budget.

Women's appearance remains unfairly scrutinized. Do clothes make the woman? Sometimes it matters and sometimes it does not. Bottom line: it ought not to matter as long as one is clean and neat. Nonetheless, clothes present messages in a complex social order. Individual style choices are expressions of oneself to others and can be creative, may reflect one's heritage or faith, but should always be dignified. Consensus is to be comfortable in one's clothes and to dress in a way appropriate to the setting. And one bit of advice from a senior scholar: if you wear pantyhose to a campus interview or conference, be sure to carry a backup pair—something men do not have to worry about!

Collaborative Work

Collaborative work is not regarded as highly as the Lone Ranger approach in our field. The gender and race of the Lone Ranger may have something to do with it, but we will save that for another day. For those for whom tenure is a consideration, know that joint publications and collaborative efforts count for less than single-authored work. This flies in the face of all good sense, and passes over the fact that it is often harder, more of a stretch, and therefore more of a growth experience, not to mention often resulting in a better product, to work in collaboration. We recommend collaborative work nonetheless, especially when it comes to interdisciplinary teaching and writing. This *Guide* is a good example. We encourage women in faculty jobs to raise this issue with their colleagues and challenge this outmoded protocol. Increasingly, senior women scholars are collaborating on projects, both with peers and new colleagues, which will help increase appreciation for such work.

One advantage of being an independent scholar is the chance to choose projects, including collaborative ones, without concern for what will "count" in an institutional review. Many colleagues in tenure-track jobs do not have that luxury. A caution: When submitting collaborative work for tenure review, be sure to state clearly your contribution. Do not misrepresent your contribution but do not do what many women do, either, and downplay it.

If you are invited to a collaborative process, give it a whirl even if you are a reflector by learning style and prefer poring over a text to discussing an idea in a group. You may find that the stimulation of working collaboratively (and this includes team teaching) is well worth the occasional aggravation. Beware, though, of collaborators who do not collaborate, that is, the people who are happy to have their names on a product but do not do their share of the work. But otherwise, join the twenty-first century in both business and industry by working in teams. Watching your productivity soar and your enjoyment quotient double. We found that even doing this *Guide*!

COMING OUT

Among the real changes in religious studies is the matter of sexuality. Of course, in many institutions, especially in more conservative ones, it is still a major liability to be an out lesbian, gay, bisexual, transgender, intersex, or queer person (**LGBTIQ**). On the other hand, in a few places it has become so ho-hum that people hardly notice. Some young people consider themselves and everyone else gender queer and cannot understand what all the fuss is about. But for many people, and especially for people of color who already have the injustice of racism to deal with, the price of coming out or being out may be high, higher than some feel they can afford to pay.

You may not be hired at all. If you are a graduate student, you may get clear and distinct signals that you might consider a career in another field that would be friendlier to you. If you problematize queer issues in your work, you will find it even harder in some settings, for example, some more conservative denominational seminaries, to survive. Changing this injustice is a field-wide task, requiring **allies**.

Due to lots of hard work, some graduate programs now offer queer theory courses and a number of institutions realize that some of their best and brightest (faculty, staff, and students) are LGBTIQ persons. Support networks, conferences, and meetings for LGBTIQ students and for scholar/activists in religion exist (including at **AAR**). New centers at several theological schools deal with LGBTIQ issues in religion and ministry and archive materials from LGBTIQ religious groups. For example, there is the Center for Lesbian and Gay Studies in Religion and Ministry at Pacific School of Religion (www.clgs.org). The Chicago Theological Seminary has the Heyward-Boswell Society (HBS), an outreach and support group for the lesbian, gay, bisexual, and transgender community and their supporters at that school (https://www.ctschicago.edu/students/student-organizations). The Lesbian, Gay, Bisexual and Transgender Religious Archives Network (http://www.lgbtran.org/) is a marvelous source of materials and inspiration.

There are prominent professors, directors of organizations, rabbis, and ministers who are out lesbian, bisexual, transgender, or queer women. In many circles, LGBTIQ scholarship is increasingly respected. The landscape has changed enormously in a relatively short time. There is still much work to do to extend the welcome and level the playing field until sexual orientation and gender identity no longer matter (see **Transgender**).

How you position yourself as a student, a job applicant, a young faculty member, an editor, or a religious leader is up to you, knowing that some settings are more open than others. No one should be required to commit professional suicide for the sake of being "out." Nonetheless, the onus is on everyone in the field, not just lesbian, bisexual, trans, and queer women, to recognize LGBTIQ scholarly and activist work for what it is—namely, work—and to evaluate it on its merits.

Meanwhile, the law guarantees your right to privacy. Your right to separate your professional life from your personal life is important. It is illegal for interviewers to base hiring decisions on your answers to personal questions. Most search committees are advised to avoid questions about your private life and marital status (see **Interviewing**). You may offer such information if you choose, but you can politely refuse to answer such questions, gently pointing out that it is against the law to discriminate.

The consequences of staying "in the closet" can be devastating, forcing you to work under stressful conditions. The best advice is to find colleagues who can share their experiences and advise you from their wisdom based on the institutional climate. The AAR's "Ask the Diva" advice column (https://www.aarweb.org/about/ask-the-diva-questions-and-answers) is one place to get answers if you do not have trusted colleagues you can ask at your own institution. In an ideal world, such matters would never arise, but since they do, we should all work to stop the injustice. Transgender people will have an especially hard time until our institutions and surrounding culture catch up with the diversities of gender identities. Since so much about sex and gender is rooted in religious language and imagery, people in religious studies have a special professional responsibility to work to overcome the prejudices that abound. Justice begins at home.

Committee on the Status of Women in the Profession

The Society of Biblical Literature (**SBL**) Status of Women in the Profession Committee, like its AAR counterpart **SWP**, addresses issues that women face in religious studies, specifically in the area of biblical scholarship. A standing committee of the SBL council, CSWP was constituted to assess the status and encourage the participation of women in all professional areas of biblical studies.

In pursuit of this mandate, it works to open the Society to greater participation by women, and to call attention to the ways in which the Society through its various activities speaks to and about women. The CSWP encourages networking and mentoring by sponsoring a breakfast for women members. This breakfast is an opportunity to meet new people and to build relationships, to honor excellent mentors with a "Mentoring Award," and to identify, through speakers, panels, demonstrations, or roundtable discussions, new issues that women face in the profession.

The CSWP also offers an annual student coffee gathering for students, both to enable networking and to introduce people to the complex nature of the Annual Meeting. There is usually a mentoring component where students can engage senior scholars on particular issues. This networking hour also has annual book giveaways and a free annual meeting registration offered each year.

The CSWP also helps administer a travel award that enables women, racial and ethnic minorities, and members from developing countries,

Asia, and Eastern Europe to attend the Annual Meeting. Between meetings, the CSWP keeps members connected through a Web page (http://www.sbl-site.org/SBLCommittees_CSWP_Activities.aspx) and a list serve. Your input is welcome.

Committees

Committees are a mixed blessing in our business. On the one hand, much work is done this way, especially in large departments or organizations. On the other hand, the burden of meetings, reports, interviews, and the like can double your workload in no time whatsoever.

As a first year faculty member in any institution, you will be invited to join a committee or three. Be prudent and know that what you gain in meeting colleagues and establishing your reputation for being a team player has to be balanced against what you lose in terms of time for your own work, your family and friends, and your sanity in general while adjusting to a new place. Some institutions wisely do not expect new faculty to serve on committees until their second year. If your institution has no such policy, limit what you accept to the minimum required during your first year.

Women of color are especially vulnerable in such situations, where institutions are anxious to diversify and see them as the means to that end. While women need to say "no" when they have taken on enough responsibility, those holding power in institutions need to cease and desist from over-inviting them and expecting them to carry more than their fair share. (The obvious solution: hire more women of color!)

Committee work can be fun, a stepping-stone to administrative work, and a diversion from the humdrum of teaching core courses. Committees can yield rich results in terms of shaping an organization or a department. However, like so many good things, a little bit goes a long way. Be sure to check how heavily committee work is weighed in your institution when it comes time for tenure or promotion before committing too much time.

Adjuncts may be invited or even expected to join committees. Some appreciate the ability to help set policy, plan enriching activities, or engage in campus life, but others point out, correctly, that this is unpaid work which unfairly burdens contingent faculty who are paid only for teaching specific courses. This conundrum is for everyone to figure out—how to integrate part-time people into a team without exploiting them.

Commuting

Factor commuting into your decision about employment, your choice of housing, and your allocation of time. In an increasingly mobile society where it seems that fewer and fewer people live near their jobs, commuting is becoming a major issue in quality of life planning.

Be realistic. Know that the trade-off for endless hours in your car or on a subway or bus can be positive—the newspaper read, a chance to listen to a good novel, some time to yourself for a change. Alternatively, it can be negative—loss of research time, a crowded, unpleasant, stressful part of your daily routine. Some of it is unavoidable, such as plane rides if you and your partner/family live in different cities or if you take a visiting appointment for a bit. In that case, try to maximize your time and resources by booking the shortest commute you can afford, getting frequent flyer points, and traveling light.

Commuter relationships are becoming more common, but they have stressors that may impact women more significantly than men. For example, there can be external pressures to maintain the same level of care as when you live full-time in one community. Commuting for employment may require you to be a part of two communities and both will have time constraints and expectations. Set your new normal as a commuter and allow for anxiety, loneliness, and even excitement as you get to know a new area.

Some of the hassle of commuting is avoidable now that telecommuting is possible. If you are a pastor, your congregation will expect you to be available in person, but other sorts of work can be more flexible. If you teach, you might be able to keep your on-site workweek to three or four days, create a home office, and join the fray from the comfort of your own home. Some universities allow administrators to consolidate their workweeks too. Online teaching allows for maximum flexibility. Be creative and ecological in all of this, saving yourself and the environment at the same time. We each get 24 hours in our day so deciding how to spend yours is crucial to your well-being.

COMPETITION

Our field is as competitive as many, though not as cutthroat as some. Recall that at Harvard Law School of old, students were known to cut assigned articles out of journals so their peers could not read them. Happily, there are few reports of such behavior in religion, but we still compete with one another in often subtle and sometimes unjust ways. Our playing field is no more level than anyone else's with young people, those who are the first generation in families their going to college, people of color, queer folks and others living the disadvantages to which we pay lip service.

Graduate school is, by history, culture, and structure, competitive. Getting in is competitive, and once in, some faculty thrive on having graduate students compete with one another for their attention. That is the bad news. The good news is that after coursework and comprehensive **exams**, the drive to compete softens up substantially. Dissertations are so diverse that there is (usually) little worry about having your work appropriated by someone else.

The issue of women in competition with one another in graduate school and in professional positions can be particularly fraught. Cultivating cooperative and mutually supportive relationships is easier said than done in graduate school, since the need to distinguish oneself can make for uneasy liaisons. One of the best ways to see alternatives to the competitive model is just that: to see alternatives to the competitive model. Reading groups and writing groups can be helpful and sanity-producing sites for collegial rather than competitive learning. A mentor might be able to discuss her own experiences. Having friends and colleagues outside of one's primary field is a way to be sure of getting disinterested feedback and unthreatened support.

Professional associations and networks of women are another good source of alternatives to counterproductive competition. At the same time, it is worth keeping in mind that a healthy sense of competition can be enlivening and mobilizing. Just don't overdo it. Keep in mind that virtually all of our progress as women in the field has come about because of cooperative work. This does not mean we cannot survive and often thrive in a competitive atmosphere. To the contrary, it simply means that we know achievement is not a zero sum game. As the women of the Grail movement say, "Together, we are a genius."

Confidence

Many women enter our field with low self-esteem and even less confidence in their abilities. Lack of confidence can plague faculty as well as students, administrators and organizers as well as staff. It shows up in many ways, including jealousies, nasty competition, and undercutting one another. Many women come by our lack of confidence honestly, because we are still discriminated against due to sexual, gender, racial, national, and class prejudice. Trans people may confront greater obstacles to confident self-presentation, especially as they transition. Confidence is hard to instill, easy to undermine. Experience proves that rather than losing or searching for one's academic voice, the problem may be a kind of theological laryngitis, an infection cause by outside factors, barriers erected on the basis of normative white, privileged, maleness that make access by others hard to achieve.

Dominant cultural norms associate maleness with confidence. It pays to be aware of unconscious body language and speech patterns. Try to minimize "uptalk" (in which inflection at the end of sentences turns declarations into questions) and never preface your contributions in meetings with "This is probably a stupid idea, but …" (If you are an undergraduate, now is the time to unlearn these unhelpful patterns of communication. If you are a full professor, it's not too late.) Some manuals aimed at corporate cultures advise women to adopt "power postures"—lean back or stand with hands spread on the table. Even if you choose not to take this advice, at least be aware of what your typical postures convey. Save "I'm sorry" for very special circumstances and instead when confronted respond with "Let's talk about it, " "Here is another way to think about it," and the like.

There is no substitute for the rewarding hard work, the projects completed, the goals reached to increase our confidence over time, but sometimes we cannot see our successes clearly. Women are particularly susceptible to "imposter syndrome"—the idea that somehow we are frauds and we will someday be revealed as unfit for and undeserving of our successes, that everyone else is the real thing but we are just pretending. We measure our insides—our insecurities, our awareness of how our work may not measure up—to other people's outsides—their visible successes.

Ideally, forewarned is forearmed. Scheduled regular meetings with friends and mentors, who are in the best position to assess one's skills, will go a long way toward increasing our individual and collective confidence. The most effective route to self-confidence for women is to instill it early in girls, and reinforce it with every step, something institutions and organizations need to assume as their part in this project called equality. Support and **networking** are good ways to reinforce one another's confidence. In some cases, therapy can help, though the problem ought never to be seen as only individual but always as rooted in the often-unjust culture in which we find ourselves as women.

CONFIDENTIALITY

Confidentiality is understood in many professions as maintaining absolute privacy of privileged information. Realistically, in our circles, it is somewhere between the seal of the confessional and what prisoners jokingly call confidence that you will not use what you know against me. Assume that anything online belongs to the National Security Agency and the world. No email is exempt from the possibility of larger scrutiny than simply that of the intended recipient, especially if you use your institution's computer, or even your personal device on their network; legal precedent upholds their right to snoop. Write accordingly and push the "send" button with care.

Beware of assurances of confidentiality, whether from colleagues or committees, as all too often privileged information finds its way into the public arena. Many women have found their reputations ruined or their trust broken in such situations. There may also be times when the demands of confidentiality serve the needs of the institution and not the greater good, much less your well-being, creating a situation of extreme dissonance and ethical dilemma. Do not agree to keep confidences you know you cannot manage.

At the same time, if you serve on a committee or are in a situation where you are expected to maintain confidentiality, that is, not to spill the beans regardless of what legal fine-tuning may apply, it is considered your professional obligation to act accordingly. Be sure to learn what your institution expects in this regard (e.g., whether you are obliged by law to report illegal activities when you learn of them), then make your choices accordingly. You may decide that serving on a review committee is too stressful or that you know the person too well to be objective. Know when to excuse yourself. Since most correspondence is electronic, exercise extreme caution on personnel matters and other private concerns. Sometimes you are better served by sending a quick note requesting a brief chat by phone than risking an email.

The digitalization of health care records is especially fraught. Be careful of your own records lest someone make a decision on the basis of information to which they have no right. But be especially careful in the handling of other people's records. Just because we can know does not mean we should know certain kinds of personal information.

CONFLICT (SEE ALSO COMPETITION)

Conflict styles vary both culturally and individually. Women's conflict styles can be greatly misunderstood, leaving us especially vulnerable: too stereotypically feminine and you will not be taken seriously; too masculine and you are dismissed as bitchy. Racial stereotypes can also determine what others expect from women. For some people, arguing means you care; for others, arguing means that the world is about to explode into violence. Some people seek to engage in conflict as a means of engaging in relationships, while others seek to avoid conflict for fear that it will destroy relationships. Some people experience any disagreement with their views as disrespect. For others, vociferous argument signals respect for another person's views, showing that one takes them seriously.

Because the United States is dominated by a white, middle class culture that tends toward conflict avoidance, those who are not white and/or middle class and who engage directly in conflict may find themselves disciplined in various ways. On the other hand, this dominant culture is much more accepting of anger expressed by white, middle class men, such that those men become used to expressing their own anger regularly without expecting much response, and can be greatly offended when similar forms of anger are directed at them. This is a recipe for institutional disaster.

As one enters various institutional settings, it is often good to learn to identify one's own style with regard to conflict and that of one's colleagues. As a religious leader or activist, how do I handle conflict with those with whom I am building community? As a student, how do I engage in disagreements with my fellow students and with my professors? As a faculty member, how do I engage with other members of my department, the staff, and administrators around conflictual issues? How do I handle conflict in the classroom setting, where

I am expected to make room for differing views? It may be helpful to acknowledge various styles of conflict directly and to ask the students to identify their own styles, as well as to be aware of gender and racial stereotypes they may impose on expectations of the behavior of others.

CONTRACTS (SEE ALSO **NEGOTIATIONS**)

You did not go to law school, but negotiating a contract is not for lawyers only. Faculty and other jobs typically involve contracts, as do publications, and often paid lectures. Once a job offer has been made, you will be expected to sign a contract that binds you and the institution to mutual agreements. It is a legal matter, so should only be signed after the greatest of scrutiny and, if possible, with someone to help you think through the implications.

For teaching jobs, know the salary range at an institution to ascertain whether what you are being offered is in the ballpark. The American Association of University Professors collects and publishes salary information for many institutions, as well as for regions of the country, annually. Even if you lack specific information for the institution hiring you, you can get a sense of a fair salary for that part of the country. At many state schools, salary information is public and available online. Adjunct pay can vary wildly from institution to institution and even by department.

Salaries can be secrets, but colleagues will often be helpful in orienting you. Insist on having all benefits spelled out in writing, especially when it comes to tenure-track or long-term employment options, leaves and sabbaticals, funding for conferences and equipment, course load, and the like. All of this varies enormously around the country, in small schools and large, for undergraduate and graduate programs, to say nothing of the range in the nonprofit sector or publishing.

The basics are the same: Know that your bargaining power is at its peak when the institution wants you, wants to conclude the search, and wants you to sign immediately. That is the time to call your friendly lawyer for advice and ask the potential employer for your wish list. Most women have not been socialized to ask for what we want or need. As a result, we end up with less than men in comparable positions. This is the point at which your advisor and your friends will be

of great assistance. Then get it all in writing to prevent future problems. Note, however, that anecdotal evidence suggests that there is a
real possibility of backlash if one negotiates too vigorously, or without
finesse or a realistic sense of what is possible. This complicates the picture but do the best you can. It is not just you but many others who
will benefit.

CURRICULUM VITAE

The *curriculum vitae*, or CV as it is known, is an important document
on paper or online that conveys who you are to the world. Scholars
should have one and keep it updated.

Like its cousin, the humble resume (which is what you should use
if you are seeking a nonfaculty position), a CV includes basic information about you: name, address, phone/email, and professional preparation including education and certification. If you have a personal
website related to your scholarly career, list it. The CV showcases your
academic work by listing your dissertation, published articles, reviews
and books, and of course your invited lectures, prizes, fellowships,
and other information that conveys your credentials. In some fields,
it is customary to list language skills. In the digital humanities or for
certain hybrid positions for which tech qualifications will be an asset,
list computer languages too. If you are proficient with online course
platforms such as Blackboard or Moodle, list these. (If not, figure out
how to gain proficiency.)

There are several keys to a good CV. First, it must be scrupulously
honest, not inflating or misrepresenting your accomplishments.
Second, it must be simple in design, easy on the eyes, and accessible
at a glance. Third, it must be up-to-date, with the most recent accomplishments and publications listed first and the rest in descending
order of date. Fourth, it should be proofread carefully, with publications displayed in proper bibliographic form. Some universities have
their own required format, so check with your career planning office,
your advisor, or the dean's office.

Computers make all this easier, but they do not update it for you,
nor select the standard white (or other neutral color) paper (bond, or
in any case a good quality) that you will print it on, if you ever have
occasion to make hard copies. With so much work being done online,
including job applications, it is a good idea to have a nicely formatted

version ready to go at a moment's notice. Resist the temptation to enhance it with graphics, colors, and the like, though you may want to have live links in an online or emailed version, so that readers can click through to documents (e.g., a PDF of an article), audio of an invited lecture, or other materials.

The major questions about a CV have to do with how much information is too much. Personal information such as date of birth, religious affiliation if any, marital status, citizenship, ethnicity, etc., is entirely discretionary. In some countries it is customary to include a small picture, typically a head shot, on the CV; in the United States this is unusual and will invite questions. As you move forward in your career, your CV may get unwieldy. It is perfectly reasonable to keep a shorter version on hand, highlighting your most important and recent publications and lectures.

Have a nicely formatted CV along with a one-paragraph biography that you can email on request. These can also be available on your departmental page, personal website, or page on a professional networking site. You may also find it worthwhile to invest in a professional picture to send along for publicity purposes if you are asked to deliver an academic or public lecture.

Computers allow us to tailor documents easily to fit the circumstances. This means you can highlight certain aspects of your CV depending on the need.

When you are applying for nonacademic jobs, you will need a resume—similar sorts of information, different format. The bottom line is the same—keep it simple, accurate, and up-to-date while highlighting your most significant accomplishments.

Debt

Many students of religion are leaving graduate programs with overwhelming debt. This can condition their job choices, pushing them toward jobs that include debt forgiveness in return for years of work in underserved communities, or propelling them into the private sector for salaries that will whittle down debt faster than most academic offerings. By saddling some graduates with payments for years to come for which the average salaries in our field are not adequate to pay, debt can increase the distance between rich and poor in our field. Those who leave school without debt have more choices than those who are heavily indebted, who will remain economically marginal even if they earn decent salaries.

One way to avoid this problem in the future is to work for equitable financial aid for entering graduate students. Some schools do not admit doctoral students they cannot support. Another way to approach it is with sensitivity to differing personal circumstances, helping young scholars to manage their debt, avoid more, and steer clear of bankruptcy-causing defaults. Think about growing student debt as you put together your syllabi and choose texts for your class. Some undergraduate students may also work full-time so service-learning commitments in your syllabus may be a particular strain, even as they are a key component of broader efforts toward social transformation.

As an employer, provide a living wage. Debt is the new class divide—those who have it and those who do not. The racial/ethnic and class patterns of debt replicate prevailing oppressive structures. That is why the best solution is to provide more support for students to avoid the problem in the first place.

Disability (see also Ableism, Illness and Disability)

Disability can encompass forms of cognitive difference and neurodiversity, as well as mobility, sensory, learning, or communication difference. The Americans with Disabilities Act of 1990 (ADA) defines disability as having, or being perceived as having, a condition that impairs a major life activity. Conceptions of disability are often based on arbitrary social norms for physical, mental, neurological, and perceptual abilities. Women with disabilities often face additional discrimination due to sexist gender expectations and ideals about female bodies.

The middle of the twentieth century saw the beginning of major shifts in the role of people with disabilities within society with the influx of disabled veterans following World War II and the rise of the civil rights movement. The first shift was from medical isolation and marginalization to medical rehabilitation and mainstreaming as a means of normalization. The second shift, brought about through the rise of the disability rights movement, was to abandon the medical model in favor of a social model that emphasizes that social attitudes and architectural barriers limit the life circumstances of people with disabilities. The social model is not meant to deny the reality of impairment. Rather, it aims to highlight the fact that society imposes normative standards that marginalize or aim to normalize people with disabilities. Standards that privilege nondisabled people may be called "ableist" or "normate."

People with disabilities have been entering the academy at all levels in recent years. Civil rights legislation such as Section 504 of the Rehabilitation Act of 1973 and the ADA have opened the doors of higher education for people with disabilities. Institutions are required to provide accessible programming for people with both visible and invisible disabilities. Many campuses have centers or formal support services for students with disabilities.

Religion faculty members will find that they will be called on to make the appropriate accommodations for students with disabilities. This may range from delivering course knowledge through a variety of learning styles, to extended time on exams and assignments, to alternative formats for materials, use of assistive listening devices in lecturing, or working with a sign language interpreter in class. Faculty should become aware of their institution's policies and resources for accommodating students with disabilities. (**Appendix V**, "Making Your Presentations Disability Friendly," is aimed at those preparing to present at the Annual Meeting, but its advice applies to the classroom as well.)

The rights of faculty members with disabilities, like those who work in other sorts of institutions, are also covered by legislation such as the ADA, although the rights of an employee differ to some degree from the rights of a student. Employees with disabilities should become familiar with their rights and the process at their institution for pursuing appropriate accommodations. Faculty should not assume that the campus' student disability service center will provide direct resources for their needs. Typically, faculty needs are addressed by the Equal Employment Opportunity Center (EEOC), while the disability services center can serve as an informal resource. Current practices in disability accommodation should be seen as a transition stage in enabling people with disabilities. Universal Design is a philosophy that calls for the structuring of all facilities, institutions, and instruction in such a way that the range of human ability is addressed rather than accommodation to ableist norms.

The study of religion is a particularly sensitive area for people with disabilities. Care should be taken in identifying ableist attitudes and biases within different faith traditions. Often ableist perspectives arise in the interpretation and translation of sacred texts. Religion often encounters issues of embodiment and normative humanity, such as physical and mental perfection; similar issues arise when elements within traditions view women as inherently inferior or defective. Ableist views often surface when dealing with issues of faith and healing. Ableist attitudes, like sexism and racism, should be dealt with openly and candidly en route to their elimination.

DISSERTATION

Many more women than men in religious studies get through comprehensive exams but never finish the dissertation, a condition coyly referred to as "all but dissertation," or ABD. Much of the explanation is economic and societal in nature, having nothing to do with competence. Writing a dissertation requires uninterrupted time, which is expensive, and it requires overcoming the social conditioning that women have nothing unique and meaningful to say. As a field we have come some distance on both accounts but still have a long way left to go.

Women are getting more financial aid than ever before but should still consider applying for graduate fellowships. Once upon a time it was assumed that men would handle the heavy intellectual lifting and the family income, and thus it was unnecessary to waste money to educate a woman; this is fortunately much less common today. Support groups, women role models, and good colleagues are helping with the conditioning problems. We still are a long way from making the dissertation process user-friendly for most women.

A dissertation is like and unlike anything you have written before. In a way it is akin to books you have read throughout your career. For most students, it is the largest project taken on to date. Graduate school does not teach you how to develop and sustain an idea over the course of hundreds of pages.

A well-thought-out prospectus can be a good roadmap. Consult it often, since you will undoubtedly hit dead ends in the writing process. It will remind you of your core ideas and how they are structured. There is no formula for dissertations. However, most in religion are five or six chapters, with an introduction, a review of the literature, and analytic and constructive chapters followed by a conclusion. Bibliography and the usual scholarly tools are included as well.

A good advisor, a mentor, and a writing group will help you. Only your persistence will get you through it. When push comes to shove, perhaps you only need two things to write your dissertation: a chair and a bucket of glue. Put some glue on the chair. Sit down. WRITE. (An exaggeration, of course, but containing a grain of truth!) Here are some tips:

- Say what YOU want. You have trained too hard to collapse into other people's desires and expectations. This is your unique contribution.
- Allow yourself to share your writing with others—especially your peers, who can give you excellent feedback—before taking your drafts to your advisors.
- Spend lots of time on your thesis statement. The longer and more complicated it is, the harder the writing is. The more crisply stated and brief, the easier the dissertation will be to write.
- Keep writing. Write every day, even if it is only for a brief period.
- Take calculated risks. Your peers and your committee will help you come to terms with the risks that will benefit your project, and the ones that will not.
- Divide the project into blocks. Reward yourself after you have completed each one.
- Write with a wide audience in mind. This will make your rewrite for publication simpler.
- Contrary advice: indulge yourself with footnotes as specialized as you like; given trends in academic publishing, this may be your only chance to comment on abstruse sources for other (potential) readers.
- Be patient, and push yourself.
- Understand that this is not the final word on the topic, but simply, and importantly, your best effort at a given moment.
- Finally, even though the dissertation is copyrighted once submitted, many editors recommend placing it under embargo to give you time to publish it in book form before it becomes widely available.

Editing

The often-overlooked skill of editing is gaining increased prominence. Some women are finding jobs with publishers for which their writing/

editing skills are in demand. Editors make writers look good. If you can, ask someone you trust to edit any major work you make public. Your smart phone will try to edit your texts, often adding words you do not intend, but a good editor will enhance your writing by subtracting mistakes, multiplying meaning, and dividing the work. It is a skill we can share. Editing can also be a kind of collaboration; beware lest your work in serious editing become (uncredited) co-authorship. If you undertake this sort of work for others, it is reasonable to expect reciprocation.

Emerita

Growing numbers of women are working to retirement and seeking emerita status. This is a welcome sign of progress. It means that they have retired officially from active teaching at their institutions. Emerita status usually follows a full professorship. The title is an honorific conferred to signal their accomplishment at the time of retirement.

Depending on institutional policy, it may mean a continuation of certain benefits of the job, for example, an office on campus, library privileges, and, in rare cases, some secretarial help. These need to be negotiated carefully since such benefits can be very valuable as women live longer lives. Beware, however, of efforts to grant emerita status early as a way of putting feminists "out to pasture" prematurely. Do not agree to retire until the particulars are settled and you are ready. Some women discover that withholding the honorific and benefits that go with it is just one last way for an institution to dishonor their achievements.

Entrepreneurs

One wonderful result of women coming into religious studies in larger numbers is that some of us are able to imagine not simply moving into open slots but actually creating new opportunities for others and ourselves inside and outside the academy. These so-called entrepreneurs are responsible for the creation of new departments of women's studies and gender studies that simply did not exist before.

They have created and endowed lectureships and research programs. They have founded journals like the *Journal of Feminist Studies in Religion* (*JFSR*) (http://www.fsrinc.org/jfsr). They have built organizations like the Resource Center for Women and Ministry in the South (http://www.rcwms.org/); the Center for Black Women in Church and Society (http://www.itc.edu/programs-at-itc/black-women-in-church-and-society/), the Women's Alliance for Theology, Ethics and Ritual (WATER) (http://www.waterwomensalliance.org/), the Faith Trust Institute (http://www.cpsdv.org/), as well as many other such accomplishments. Consider joining their ranks so that future generations will have more places to do their work.

Entrepreneurial action takes money and time that most of us simply do not have on our own, as well as varied skill sets. Therefore, such initiatives require intense collaboration, meticulous organization, fund raising ability, and good luck. But we need new centers and new platforms to do our work. Give it a try but not without at least one, and preferably more colleagues. If a project does not "belong" to someone or a few people, chances of it becoming an enduring organization are slim. But if one or two people embrace it as a calling, the sky's the limit.

The downside is that there are also hucksters out there who will commercialize and commodify your work, sell it to the highest bidder, and profit from your labor. These include companies that tape and sell lectures or lecture notes without proper permission, or people who quote work without attribution, or who appropriate ideas without acknowledgement. They are entrepreneurs, too, and their numbers are increasing as business people realize that religion "sells," especially in tough times. Avoid them, as there are many better ways to get your ideas into the mainstream without reducing them to soup or a bad movie.

Ethnocentrism (see Racism, Classism)

Ethnocentrism is one of the many means by which social hierarchy and domination are maintained. Placing a dominant or ethnic group (in the United States, white/Anglo Americans) at the center—of knowledge, of concern, or of activity—marginalizes other groups and reinforces existing hierarchies.

There are any number of ways that ethnocentrism is enacted in the academy. For example, assuming that Euro-American traditions of knowledge are the most important and relegating African American or Asian American traditions to a week or two at the end of the semester is ethnocentric. Christian hegemony falls into this arena.

Even efforts to address race/ethnicity and racism can fall into the trap of ethnocentrism. For example, white parents, in teaching their children to be tolerant, often say that Latino or Native American children are "just like" white children. They rarely say that white children are just like children of color. In this formulation, whiteness remains the center to which "others" are compared. All important questions and problems ultimately revolve around the concerns of white people. Therefore, for example, white people may assume that the study of race/ethnicity and racism is important for the undoing of white racism. While this may be a laudable goal, it misses the value of, for example, womanist study or Asian feminist work on their own terms. Alternatively, when attending meetings and conferences that address race and ethnicity, white people sometimes attempt to focus discussion on their concerns and antiracist attitudes, rather than accepting the marginalization they might feel when people of color are at the center. One simple but too often overlooked strategy for white allies is to *listen*, just as male allies ought to listen to women working for gender justice.

Putting the concerns of nondominant groups at the center does not simply replicate the centering of the dominant group's concerns. Moving "from margin to center" may be a necessary correction to entrenched racism. In other words, white people should think twice before accusing people of color of ethnocentrism or "reverse racism." Such accusations may be just another means of returning white concerns to the center once again.

Ethnocentrism is possible between and among people of color given that there are differences among and within racial groups. In some situations, one of these groups may have an established social dominance and may act in an ethnocentric manner. Ethnocentrism remains a critical problem in the religious academy but a deepening awareness of it and a commitment to eradicate it are the fastest routes to its elimination.

Evaluations, Annual

Annual evaluations are particularly relevant to tenure-track and tenured faculty, but they exist in other organizations as well. In many companies and larger nonprofits, an annual performance review— typically tied to a raise—is standard. In universities, administrators are also reviewed annually and in some places contract faculty are assessed as well. When you take a new position, ask about how evaluations are done and what the standards for measurement are. In a college or university, your department chair or administrator is probably the right person to ask; in a company it will likely be the human resources department, though colleagues can give you an informal perspective on how things are done.

Most schools have well-documented procedures. Often, there is a form that your **curriculum vitae** should follow, and it is best if you begin by formatting it in the prescribed form, then keeping it up-to-date on a regular basis. Some people save materials in a file and update the CV periodically; others find it easier to simply update the document as they give talks or publish papers. Ask about documentation requirements when you are hired.

The most common advice people give is to "save everything." You will need to document your activities. It is not a bad idea to have the **files**, but it also may not be necessary to hand everything in—find out from a trusted friend what the institutional culture requires. If you present a paper at a conference, save the program bulletin. If you receive a note from a colleague or student commending your work, file that as well. You should also be working on a **teaching portfolio**; that means saving your assignments, syllabi, examples of student work, etc. All of this collecting will make it easier to put an annual report together, and those collected evaluations will be a big help when you are ready to put your tenure file together.

When you fill out annual reports listing your accomplishments, this is the time to toot your own horn. Mention the guest lectures you gave in your colleague's classes, the stellar reviews of your book, the contributions you made to advising the undergraduate religion majors' association, and the like. Your chair, who will decide your merit raise, may be vaguely aware of these things but it cannot hurt to bring them to mind. Depending on your institution, it may be viewed favorably to list evening classes you teach at a synagogue or the weekly Qur'an-study circle that you lead for your mosque; some institutions welcome this sort of work and others will look askance at it. Likewise activist work or nonprofit advising. (If you are compensated for outside activities, you may also have to fill out a form listing the fees you received.)

In addition to more or less thorough annual reviews, many institutions have a third-year review, about halfway through the tenure clock, during which progress in publishing will be surveyed and other accomplishments measured. This is a big deal. Milestones for lecturers on contract will differ but some colleges and universities are making separate tracks available, with promotion and other possibilities; here, too, annual reviews are important.

Pay careful attention to the letters you receive from the dean each year renewing your contract. Some institutions give clear recommendations for what you need to do to meet requirements for tenure, including specific information about what the chair or dean is expecting you to complete or areas in which they wish you to improve. If you do not agree with the evaluation, it is also important to commit your response to writing. At other institutions, this sort of information may only be communicated in a third-year review. After your third-year review you may find it necessary to seek delayed tenure review due to circumstances such as child-rearing or medical leave that have slowed your progress. Learn if there such a process and what it entails.

Evaluations, Peer

In the academy as well as other workplaces, you will sometimes be in the position of having to review your colleagues—for example, when they come up for promotion or tenure (see **Evaluations, annual**)—and to be reviewed by them as well. You may also be asked by publishers and journals to do peer reviews of manuscripts, usually once you have published on a topic, or by grant-making associations to review proposals when others seek funding. While reviews are meant to be confidential, reviewing the work of your colleagues can be a source of tension, especially in small departments or organizations. It is helpful if you remember that the critiques of and by your peers (whether of teaching, scholarship, or preaching effectiveness) can be a valuable source of learning and growth. While we may not enjoy being judged or judging, it is part of the learning experience throughout any career, and something we need to get used to.

That said, it is important to remember when doing these reviews that even the harshest criticism can be given gently and with a generous spirit. It is often the tone rather than the content of reviews, whether of a colleague or a manuscript, that inflicts unnecessary pain and breeds ill will. You may find yourself in a situation where your best judgment tells you that a colleague's work does not merit tenure or promotion by the standards your university has set. You need to be sure that you have really thought through the situation, have not been unduly swayed by political pressure, and have come to an honest and ethical conclusion. You also need to consider the institution's makeup and criteria. If this is a place that rejects women and people of color routinely you may need to adjust your own thinking to counter that. It is complicated, but serious reflection is called for. That is all you can ask of yourself. Whatever your judgment, do your best to treat the person in a supportive and friendly manner, as you will have to live with her or him for at least a year if tenure is not granted.

Note that in some high tech companies there is a decided move away from annual reviews. The process is simply too time-consuming and onerous for the benefits achieved. Instead, some of these groups are instituting more frequent, on the scene feedback that can actually change outcomes in the short as well as long term. Watch for this shift in the academy and related workplaces though it may not be instantaneous.

Evaluations, Student

In some institutions, the plain brown envelopes and number two pencils with ample erasers that once came out at the end of each semester for student feedback to professors have been replaced by official online forms. These formal evaluations are supplemented by ubiquitous, but notoriously unreliable, online rating sites. It's fair for students to grade professors, but this practice can play into a consumer attitude among students. Negative evaluations can make a professor feel undermined; repeated strongly negative evaluations can jeopardize chances for continued employment, particularly for adjuncts, or tenure and promotion. This may seem like a perverse incentive to teach easy material in conventional ways; most teachers resist the temptation. Still, student evaluations have their place.

If you are serious about improving your teaching, you will read all evaluations with care, and take them with a grain of salt. (Promotion and tenure committees do both.) While there are often one or two who will vent, the vast majority of students, especially in a well-formulated course, will wax poetic about how much they learned, how accessible you were, how much you helped them, and how they appreciated your efforts. What is problematic about the whole procedure is that the results are often so cut and dried, so starkly numerical that it is hard to communicate nuance (e.g., that the student who hated you also failed the course because he never came to class). There is also no way to detect, or account for, student expectations of professional behavior based on gender, sexual orientation, or racial stereotypes, but research indicates that students penalize nonmale and nonwhite faculty more easily for perceived lapses. Be aware of—and educate your colleagues about—how students may assess women's and minoritized faculty's teaching contributions in biased ways.

One strategy for making student evaluations more useful to your teaching and the success of a course is to conduct your own private evaluation well before the end of term. Candid student input partway through the term can allow for midcourse corrections or clarify unspoken misunderstandings or dissatisfactions. It can encourage students to participate more actively in the work of a course if they believe you actually care what they think before you turn in grades and the term is over.

Some schools post the results in informal ratings that students share when "shopping" for classes. Other schools guard the results lest your privacy be invaded and that one course you botched follow you for years. Overall, student evaluations are a useful tool for gauging whether you are reaching your audience, whether what you are teaching is being learned, and whether you are fulfilling your part of the bargain as a professor.

EXAMS, QUALIFYING/COMPREHENSIVES/GENERALS

Every graduate program has a slightly different route to completion, but exams of some sort are a common feature. They may be called qualifying exams, comprehensives, or generals. These exams are a way to ensure that students are well prepared in the field before moving on to write a dissertation.

It is important to work closely with your advisor in shaping the exams, if that option is given, and in preparing for them. This means developing the requisite book list and taking the courses, especially graduate seminars, which will best prepare you. Include works by women, persons of color, and other minoritized knowledge groups in your exam book list. This signals you are aware that knowledge comes from a variety of canons. Your advisor and other faculty who will read the exams may not be aware of some of the latest contributions by feminist/womanist/*mujerista* thinkers, but you can certainly advocate their inclusion. The exams can often be geared to orienting your research for the dissertation, thus speeding along your progress for the program as a whole.

The exams can be an ordeal, or they can be a useful exercise in gaining and demonstrating proficiency. Approach them like a job. Be systematic and thorough in your preparation. Consider creating summaries of books as you read them during your coursework. You might also use flashcards or digital recordings to prepare. There are numerous online tools to assist you in preparation such as www.Zotero.com, www.flashcardsdeluxe.com, and www.Dragonspeak.com. In general, know your program requirements, develop a study plan and perhaps an accountability partner, and prepare to do your best. Don't let the hype that sometimes develops around exams get to you. After all, you have been successful this far, so there is every reason to be confident that with adequate study you will do fine. If the experience becomes a burden, do not hesitate to get the counseling or other support you need to get through it.

Exams formats vary from four hours in a proctored room for each field to open-book 72-hour take home exams. (Obviously, expectations about length and polish will differ in each case.) A few programs allow students and advisors to select from several options. If this is the case, consider what plays to your strengths and the requirements, if relevant, of others in your household.

Faculty Club

If your institution has a faculty club, consider a membership, and/ or if it is automatic, consider using it. The club can be a convenient place to lunch with colleagues, conduct meetings, and hear interesting lectures. Some clubs even have overnight accommodations, a great choice for visiting lecturers or colleagues from other institutions.

While some of these places look like wood-paneled men's clubs, think about joining and using the club with your women colleagues. The atmosphere will be improved markedly by your presence; some of the pretense and old-school tie feel may diminish. On the other hand, if the faculty club is more than you can bear, retire to your favorite coffee/tea/chocolate shop, simply taking your business and your colleagues elsewhere. Someone might get the message and you will enjoy yourself more.

Faculty Handbook

Most institutions provide new employees with a book—or a weblink—that contains much of the relevant information related to institutional structure, benefits, promotion, leaves, and the like, though if you are an adjunct, there may be woefully little specific to your situation. Your faculty handbook should include details on accommodations for disabilities and religious practice as well as the institution's **Affirmative Action**, sexual/racial harassment, and/or nondiscrimination policies. Read it carefully to understand the lay of the land. It is a definitive source for information you will need to function effectively in your institution. The faculty handbook is considered in most institutions part of the legally binding contract of your employment, so know its contents well. However, be aware that there may be greater flexibility available to you than what is presented in the faculty handbook. Be attentive to human resources and administrative assistant personnel. There are invisible institutional practices, unspoken or informal aspects of an institution that are usually at least as important as, if not more so than, what is written down. But the law does not respect them in the same way as a written resource.

Some companies and nonprofits will have similar sets of guidelines, but except for very large corporations, government organizations, or religious bureaucracies, few employee handbooks are as thorough as those for colleges and universities.

Family (see also Children, Relationships)

Families come in an infinite variety of forms. Virtually everyone has one, whether it consists of parents, pets, a partner (or occasionally partners), children, a strong circle of friends, and/or extended relatives. Avoid making assumptions about family that privilege the mom, dad, and 2.2 children model to the detriment of the rest. Easier said than done, of course, when pensions, Social Security, and the like are all bound up in that one model. But this is another place where privilege dictates certain norms that can and should be changed.

Many of us have major responsibility for others whose lives are affected by our choices. Some colleagues support their siblings' or their spouse's children, so they need the same family leave and tuition benefits that would go to their own children. Others care for aging parents who may require as much time, attention, and medical care as young children do. Some are "sandwiched" between younger and older generations requiring care. All of these beings (some of our colleagues consider their pets as their closest kin) are part of the constellation of relationships that bring us love and well-being, as well as anxiety and exhaustion. Thus, paying equal attention to them is part of the twenty-first-century way of being in our field. Some institutional cultures have yet to catch up, but change is happening.

Fellowships, Graduate Student

Many institutions offer fellowships for graduate students. Consult your local financial aid office for details on other fellowships offered by various, sometimes quite obscure, groups. A web search will help, but there is no substitute for knowing someone who is on the committee or has an in with someone who is.

Fellowships are a fact of life for those considering or pursuing graduate studies in religion or, sometimes, theology. Given the mounting educational debt for graduate students in general and particularly for those graduating with degrees in the humanities, at some point, you will apply for fellowship monies to support your studies. This is especially true for some graduate students of color who often assume large financial burdens in order to achieve the social class mobility hoped for with a graduate degree. Fellowships make it possible for many students to remain in their graduate programs, but you must start looking early and often for funding. For some, understanding the terms of a fellowship begins immediately upon acceptance into graduate school, where the fellowship may be formulated into your acceptance. Others come not from schools themselves but from different organizations. For example, the Ford Foundation (http://sites.nationalacademies.org/PGA/FordFellowships/PGA_047960) and the Forum for Theological Exploration (http://fteleaders.org/fundfinder/c/women) offer predoctoral and dissertation fellowships for women students of color.

Graduate fellowships of either sort may be granted as a multiyear or an annual award. Study the language of your letter of acceptance with care, and be sure you understand its terms. Find out whether the fellowship is contingent (on grades, on teaching, on getting outside support to match). A fellowship might cover tuition and fees but offer no stipend to cover living expenses. Alternatively, a stipend might take the form of salary for a teaching or research appointment.

Most students will, at some point, need to garner outside fellowship support, especially during the dissertation writing stage. Generally, applications for such funding are due in the fall semester for the next academic year. You should discuss deadlines with your advisor well in advance, as it may be necessary to complete certain milestones (such as qualifying exams or prospectus approval) to be eligible for funding. (If you advise students, keep these matters in mind.) Financial aid offices and departments often publish lists and contact information for pertinent fellowships or have a searchable online database. **AAR** awards international **dissertation** research grants and publishes fellowships and grants announcements in its *In the Field* online publication. The Ford Foundation, Charlotte W. Newcombe Doctoral Dissertation Fellowship, Mellen/ACLS, and the American Association of University Women also sponsor dissertation fellowships. Ask about selected lists of available fellowships specific to your field, as reading through general fellowship and grant opportunities can be daunting.

The financial aid office or your department might even provide examples of successful proposals, which can be enormously helpful. Read fellowship announcements carefully, noting due dates, intended recipients, length of funding, and specified purpose of the fellowship monies (e.g., final-year dissertation writing, travel, or foreign language acquisition support). Give yourself plenty of lead-time. Applications take longer than you think. If your program does not make this information accessible, you might ask them to consider doing so.

Once you have chosen your target fellowships, applying involves several steps. First, you will have to provide several letters of recommendation. Busy faculty members require plenty of notice (a couple of months, with a reminder a month or so prior to the deadline). Be sure they have all the information they need to write your letter with relative ease, and be sure to follow up. Faculty cannot be expected to keep track of these due dates; do not be afraid to remind your recommenders of impending deadlines. Second, you will be called on to provide transcripts, various timelines, proposals, outlines, and synopses of your work. These take time and should be crafted with great care. Vet your work vigorously before sending it out. Schools and departments often lead workshops on fellowship opportunities and grant writing. You can also ply advanced students with coffee or a meal in exchange for their advice.

Finally, do not be afraid to cast your net widely. Competition is fierce, and your project may appeal to various funders. Capitalize on the interdisciplinary nature of a religious studies project. Go for it.

When you are awarded your fellowship, note that the Tax Reform Act of 1986 specifies that all grants and fellowships that exceed the cost of tuition, fees, books, and related classroom expenses are subject to U.S. income tax. Often, there are no initial withholdings on stipends, leaving you to take responsibility for reporting stipend amounts and making tax payments when appropriate. Check with a tax preparer if you have questions about this.

FELLOWSHIPS, PROFESSIONAL

As a professional, you will be eligible for fellowships of various sorts. There is a world of funds available for the enterprising professional who can write good proposals. For example, the National Endowment for the Humanities and the Guggenheim Foundation offer grants for relatively senior scholars with projects. The Women's Studies in Religion Program at Harvard Divinity School offers a one-year residency fellowship, as do many humanities centers at universities and colleges. Some require doctorates while others recognize "equivalent professional achievements." This is particularly useful for activists and community workers who lack advanced degrees but have hard-earned knowledge to share. There are numerous postdoctoral fellowship opportunities available for junior faculty fresh out of their degree programs. The **AAR** *In the Field* online publication lists some of these sources, as do university offices.

As with graduate fellowships, be sure to look broadly across disciplines. Some fellowships are specifically for women like the American Association of University Women American postdoctoral research leave fellowships. Postdoctoral and professional fellowships require at least as much work as graduate fellowship applications. Leave time to request letters of support, acquire permission to take a research leave, and complete the application well before the application deadline.

Some fellowships involve a faculty appointment and teaching. Some may require you to be in residence. Some provide research and travel monies along with your fellowship, sometimes even for dependents; others will take the place of your salary, while still others may match your income. However you are funded, be sure to be aware of the tax implications of your fellowship. Check with a tax professional for any questions.

If you have a sabbatical, which is often funded for one semester, consider applying for a fellowship that will allow you to extend the time to a year. Some schools encourage faculty to do so and provide grant-writing help to enable them to apply for fellowships. It is in the interest of the institution to help you, as it adds to its faculty's luster when they win prestigious awards. Remember that it may take multiple years and repeated applications to win an award, so keep trying, and begin applying well ahead of when you anticipate a sabbatical. If you are turned down, ask for feedback. You may discover you were close, and it is worth trying again. If you have not got a ghost of a chance, this is also useful to learn, so as to avoid wasting time and energy in repeated applications.

FEMINIST

Definitions of feminism abound, but the bumper sticker that says, "Feminism is the radical notion that women are people" remains a good summary. Feminism arose around the world out of the struggle for women's rights and women's survival. It is a globalized movement involving theoretical analysis and strategic commitments to securing the well being of women and dependent children in a world that has long privileged men. Feminism began as a gender-based concern. But due to the influence of womanism (see **Womanist**), *mujerismo* (see *Mujerista*), Asian American, and Native American women's work (and now Muslim women's "Muslima" approaches), feminism now signals a complex analysis of and effort to change racist, sexist, classist, imperialist, colonialist, heterosexist, and other structures of oppression that keep women, especially young, poor women of color, from surviving and thriving.

Early feminist work in religion in the United States can be traced to suffrage and abolition efforts in the 19th century that included analysis of how religions misunderstood and mistreated women. It began in the academy in the 1960s when the gendered nature of religion was exposed and the sexist assumptions of many religious traditions were challenged. In subsequent decades, feminist work has reshaped the field, as virtually every religious subspecialty has been subject to feminist analysis and reconstruction.

In some places and traditions, the incompatibility of religion and feminism has been assumed or argued, both from dominant views within (patriarchal) religious traditions and from secular feminists, some of whom have asserted that religion can only oppress women and women will only find liberation by leaving their traditions.

While the term "feminist" is contested and made more complex over time, the goal of equality and justice for all that feminism has heralded from the beginning remains to be reached.

FESTSCHRIFTEN

Festschriften are books written in honor of a colleague, often on the occasion of her/his sixty-fifth or seventieth, seventy-fifth or even eightieth birthday, or upon retirement. There are other ways to lift up the importance of a colleague's work—for example, with a conference, a special section of a journal, an art project, or the like. Some of these can have a broader reach than an academic volume. For some feminist scholars, this bridging of divides has been a priority in their life work. In a hybrid reimagining of the *Festschrift*, one pioneering theologian was recently honored by an e-book with a wide circle of contributors and types of contributions, including letters and poetry as well as essays. In keeping with the scholar's commitment to widening circles of knowledge, it was made freely available online for download.

The most common academic model is a collaborative book that includes an essay about the person and her/his work, or essays on themes related to or sparked by the colleague's endeavors. Although still not honored with *Festschriften* in the same proportions as men, there are more examples of prominent female senior scholars now than a few decades ago and consequently, more *Festschriften* dedicated to them.

It is a privilege to be invited to contribute to a *Festschrift*. The essay or other contribution need not seem like uncritical homage. Rather, it is an opportunity to acknowledge a person's contribution to the field in a polite and professional way, perhaps best by exhibiting one's own work as it has been influenced by hers/his. Usually one person offers an introductory biographical chapter leaving other writers free to name their own relationship with the honoree and then move on to contribute some new thinking in concert with her/his agenda.

Forerunners

This guide would not be possible if some phenomenal women had not paved the way. They include our personal ancestors, as well as our foresisters in the field of religious studies. For fear of leaving any out, we will not name them here. Let this entry serve as a reminder to thank them often and to do them proud. Know that you are rapidly becoming one for your students and theirs, so delight in our shared lineage.

Fundraising

Most graduate programs in religion do not offer courses in fundraising, but it might be a good idea if they did. Learning to raise money is a skill worth having. Many jobs in the nonprofit sector require it. Increasingly, even academics in the humanities are strongly encouraged to raise some of their own funding. A fellowship or a post-doctoral grant is a form of fundraising.

Just as there are corporate and cooperative ways of building a business, so too are their corporate and cooperative models of raising money. One good resource is the *Grassroots Fundraising Journal* that has a socially responsible and community-based approach (http://www.grassrootsfundraising.org/). Online fundraising options, including crowdsourcing, are slowly transforming the way artistic and activist projects seek funds. Scholarly projects may be next.

Wherever and however you seek funds, the bottom line is ask, ask, ask. Funders can always say no, and sometimes they will for very legitimate reasons. (Sometimes for illegitimate reasons too, including distaste for feminist projects.) But the main reason people do not get funding is because they do not ask, or they do not ask well. Beyond simply asking, there are many specialized workshops in how to write proposals and how to conform your project to the granter's guidelines. There are capital campaigns and direct mail appeals, annual gifts and annuity options. A knowledge of the basics will help you get and give intelligently. Our backgrounds condition us in many ways around money. It is worth spending some time figuring out how you relate to it, what your lack or abundance of money has done to shape your thinking about fundraising. It is not a job for everyone, but it is a reality, like budgeting and **debt**, that we ignore at our peril.

GLOBALIZATION

The field of religious studies, like everything else in the world, is increasingly globalized. This means we can be in close communication with colleagues around the planet; the Internet has made international collaboration a reality. But it also means that the United States plays its hegemonic role in our work as in other fields. After all, lots of international colleagues come to the **AAR/SBL Annual Meeting**, but how many people from the United States go abroad for similar learning experiences?

Women colleagues report that while there are obvious advantages to international networking, cultural differences are often obscured, resulting in a skewed sense of what is important. Our challenge is to utilize those aspects of globalization that link us—the Internet, air travel, and the like—and to resist and reject the dynamics that allow fewer and fewer people to make more and more decisions for everyone else. One example is the increasing pressure to do theological and religious studies work in English to guarantee a wide audience for publications. Apps like Google Translate help, but the reality is that journals and websites in languages other than English are the exception rather than the rule in our teaching and research. Globalization is perhaps our biggest challenge in the decades ahead, one that will measure how willing we are to move beyond hegemonies of many sorts.

GRADUATE SCHOOL

The road to a career in religious studies usually begins in graduate school, typically a doctoral program, but possibly also a theological degree from a seminary or another kind of master's degree. One would have to be hiding under a rock not to have heard the famous advice, given in large part because of the dismal prospects for solid faculty jobs for recent PhDs: just don't go. Yet there are very good reasons to pursue a master's degree or a doctorate so long as one does not harbor illusions that the degree will place you on a straight path to a stable, well-compensated teaching job.

If you elect to pursue graduate work in religious studies with an eye on other employment prospects as first or backup choices (see **Alt-ac**), think hard about the schools you apply to. Instincts, personal preferences, and research will serve you well in choosing a graduate setting in which to pursue your interests. Your instincts—about whether you can work closely with a faculty person, about the institutional culture, about communication and power dynamics between faculty and students, and even about the geographical setting, not to mention financial incentives—are a source of information that deserves respect and attention. Of course, this does not replace thorough research and asking smart questions.

Think carefully about and compare resources (libraries, cross-registration with other schools, disability services, formalized student support groups). Get a firm understanding about the financial support (stipends) offered to students, and whether that kind of money is guaranteed throughout your years of study, or whether you must continually compete for it, and exactly when it evaporates. Make a realistic budget. Think about institutional expectations and demands on grad students (teaching, tutoring). Think also about the intellectual tenor of the school and its departments, about available symposia, colloquia, and interdisciplinary programs. Compare the programmatic issues: How are the subfields in the department presented and shaped in terms not only of courses offered, but also in terms of course requirements and comprehensive exams? Despite the injustice of it, many academic benefits down the pike depend on the prestige of the institution at which one studied.

There is no substitute for visiting a place, which gives you both insight about institutional culture you will not get from the institution's brochures and the added benefit of allowing you to meet the people who will be deciding about your acceptance there, should you choose to apply. (It can also tell you vital information about accessibility. Are there elevators in the Religion Department? Ramps?)

A few elite institutions will pay for admitted doctoral students to visit in the spring, but this is rare.

One common piece of advice is to apply to a large number of schools, though this can be very costly in time and money. Some schools offer hardship waivers for application fees; investigate and assume that the department admissions committee will not know. A spot in a good program is a competitive enterprise, and time-consuming, but figure it is an investment in your future.

Take seriously the requirements of the application, even if you do not like the assignment (writing your life's ambition in a 300-word essay or taking the Graduate Record Examinations). Don't sabotage your future over bureaucratic necessity. Your ability to navigate hoops more or less gracefully will serve you well when you get into the graduate program of your choice. If you are not accepted, you can inquire (politely) as to why you were turned down and then try to remedy the matter and apply again. Often, though, it is simply a numbers game, with many solid applicants competing for too few places and even less financial aid. Top programs tend to only admit those students they can fund fully, at least at the doctoral level. It is rare for institutions to fund masters students beyond tuition assistance, the work-study and loan route, but there are cases.

Once accepted, the task turns to surviving, nay, thriving! Depending upon your program, subfield and your personal situation and style, graduate school can take a long time, meaning more than six years for a doctorate. Whether shorter or longer, it is exhausting. If you enter a doctoral program with a **dissertation** topic or research interest in mind, you might take less time than if you enter with only a vague idea of what you really want to write about. In any case, the balancing act between creative risk and disciplined focus will probably serve you best. In fact, thriving in graduate school in general requires an ability to balance: to balance relationships and work, teaching/working and studying, choices between traditional and more risky fields of study.

Everyone is different, and there is no single right way. Remember, your balancing act is more for the duration of a marathon than a sprint. Be patient with yourself. Being specific with your advisor about your needs and expectations will help. If you can, find and cultivate a mentor relationship or two. Creating networks of supportive colleagues, both in your cohort and outside, will give you sources of information and advice that will be invaluable. The **AAR** and **SBL** offer graduate student orientations at their annual meetings. Take advantage of them.

GRADUATE STUDENT COMMITTEE

Students make up nearly one third of the **AAR** membership, and they are fully integrated into all sectors of the AAR. There is a Student Director on the Board. The Graduate Student Committee (GSC) reports to the Student Director to assure input from a wide variety of opinions. The GSC is comprised of the regionally elected student directors and it guides the AAR in designing programmatic responses to the needs and concerns of student members, primarily graduate students, particularly regarding professional development. GSC sponsors a Student Lounge at every annual meeting; a business meeting that also serves as a member orientation; a Special Topics Forum; and student roundtables. GSC also often partners with the Wabash Center for Teaching and Learning (http://www.wabashcenter.wabash.edu/home/default.aspx) for a pre-meeting workshop.

Graduate students can serve through the AAR Ambassador Program. Ambassadors act as points of contact for the AAR in the home departments. Students can also get involved in AAR regional meetings (see **AAR Regions**), attending the GSC events at the Annual Meeting, reading the online Graduate Student Newsletter or "Speaking of Students" feature in *Religious Studies News*, and by staying connected through the AAR Students Facebook groups.

SBL has a Student Advisory Board (SAB) that is comprised of appointed students and a faculty liaison that work to coordinate student participation in SBL activities. During its Annual Meeting, SAB offers professional development sessions tailored to junior scholars. SBL students are encouraged to get involved by serving as on-campus representatives for SBL in their home departments and by attending the regional and Annual Meetings.

GRANTS

Foundations and other agencies offer a variety of grants for scholarly and other sorts of projects. If you work in a nonprofit organization, chances are good you are partly grant-funded. If you are looking to start an organization or project (see **Entrepreneurs**), you may seek a grant for seed money. The **AAR and SBL Annual Meetings** often feature a time for grant-making organizations to meet with grant seekers. A Web search is an important early step; if your institution has a grants officer, she/he can help you find out what is available in your field and review your grant application.

Like anything else, writing a grant proposal is a skill to hone; it can serve you well outside the academy. The Association of Theological Schools' website has a funding manual for faculty in theological education that aspiring grantees can follow to strengthen their grant applications (http://www.ats.edu/resources/faculty) (see **Resources**). Some organizations post examples of successful proposals on their websites.

The Lilly Endowment, the Louisville Institute, the Calvin Institute of Christian Worship, the Luce Foundation, and the Wabash Center for Teaching and Learning in Theology and Religion, and other agencies fund religious studies. Be forewarned that competition is keen for the relatively few offerings. Make use of the Internet to keep up on the latest prospects. A conversation with a program officer about your interest can be a helpful way to assess your chances and get on the radar screen of those who make decisions.

Even a small grant can make something big happen—like a travel grant to attend a conference can make the difference between going and not going. Summer research grants can catalyze research that will get funded with a more substantial fellowship. Large or small, just be sure you fulfill the terms of the grant, submit all required paperwork in a timely way, and let your imagination be the limit of what you wish to work on, as there may be funding available. For example, the SBL **Committee on the Status of Women in the Profession** also helps administer a travel award that enables women, racial and ethnic minorities, and members from developing countries, Asia, and Eastern Europe to attend the annual meeting, especially if they are presenting a paper.

Guest Lectures

Guest lectures take many forms. Some are ways that graduate students learn how to teach by conducting a class or presenting their work. But others, to which this entry refers, are occasions when colleagues are invited to share their knowledge with a new community.

Whether being invited to present a guest lecture or inviting someone to do so, the rules are about the same. The best analogy is to houseguests—as the one invited, you want to be a gracious guest; and as host, you want to provide everything that will make your guest feel as comfortable as possible.

That means that when an invitation is offered it must include the topic, time, place, expected audience, honorarium, travel and housing arrangements, and some insight into the local scene. When the invitation is accepted, the speaker needs to provide the lecture topic and/or title, materials for publicity (including **Curriculum vitae** and photo), Social Security number, mailing address, and anything else (short of shoe size) that may be required. Give attention to small details like your name as it appears on your driver's license so if the inviting group makes your travel plans they are correct. This can save untold headaches at the airport.

When the event takes place, the speaker should arrive promptly (best to plan to arrive early), be met and escorted to her room, offered food and drink as appropriate, and allowed a time to freshen up. She should then be escorted to the lecture locale (nothing worse than wandering aimlessly around a campus). Hosts need not hover, and guests need privacy, but common courtesy dictates that an outsider deserves a guide to get efficiently from place to place. She gives her brilliant presentation, takes questions, and conducts a discussion before bidding a gracious farewell. Often there is a reception or a meal involved, a chance for informal time with students and colleagues. If you are hosting, be sure to ask about dietary restrictions. The host then escorts her back to her quarters or makes sure she gets to her plane, train, or taxi on time. The guest submits her expenses; the host reimburses and sends the honorarium in a timely way along with a cordial note of thanks and copies of any follow-up press. The guest sends a gracious thank you note, and if asked, a copy of her lecture for publication if agreed upon ahead of time.

That was the textbook case. Most of the time it goes smoothly, but as lecture circuit veterans will tell you, disasters lurk. Advice: get everything in writing; keep correspondence to refer to; make sure you and the host/guest have physical contact (by phone or in person) with one another prior to the event. Nothing is more disappointing than for a speaker not to show up, or to show up late. Likewise, it is embarrassing to have to shake down institutions for honoraria owed months back and held up because the host forgot to submit the expenses. Planes/trains run late, so plan accordingly. A word to the wise: bring your own hair dryer and/or other essentials, rely on your smart phone alarm to keep you on time, and expect the unexpected as you go.

Guest lectures can be a wonderful way to diversify curricula and expose students to innovative thinkers in the field. If you are the lecturer, be careful which invitations you accept. How the arrangements are made will often mirror what the experience on site will be. If your host bungles the invitation, chances are good that you will have other glitches as well. If you are the host, know that you are asking someone to leave home and family to be with you and your colleagues. It takes some doing so plan ahead and smooth the way as best you can. Your students, the audience, will thank you.

One more thing—expect and give women the same honoraria that men receive. This is tough as such numbers are often kept private. You can ask around, though—departments and programs vary widely in what they offer, from a nominal $200 for a lunchtime speaker to $2,500 or even more for a prestigious annual lecture. Sometimes big-name institutions offer small honoraria and smaller institutions more generous ones. Fees are often, but not always, negotiable; when you as the guest agree to a visit, unless they offer you a very generous sum, feel free to negotiate the honorarium as you would a job offer, expecting that your time and talent is worth the same as a man's. Be specific and be insistent, while recognizing that some amounts are fixed. You are negotiating for yourself and for those who come after you. If you feel you are overpaid you can always donate to a nonprofit or give the money to a student. But if you finish the experience feeling as if you were shortchanged, no one benefits.

HARASSMENT

Harassment is typically thought of as sexual or racial, but it has a much wider scope. Other types of harassment may also involve gender and/or or racial bias. Harassment refers to nonverbal and verbal conduct or physical aggression, intimidation, or hostility that is persistent enough to limit a person's ability to fully function/benefit in an environment. There are incidents of cyber harassment; harassment of disabled persons; harassment regarding sexual orientation, national origin, and religious beliefs. Harassment may be particularly pernicious for women, who are especially targeted for verbal harassment and demeaning comments in both the physical and virtual world.

Micro-aggressions can often escalate to full harassment. Cyber bullying of academics is becoming more common. Women are threatened with violence, including rape, or publicly silenced through these means. Students sometimes display this aggression in our classrooms as well. Students often question authority in particularly problematic and combative ways that reflect their inability to constructively receive criticism without lashing back. While there have been several bills recommended to Congress (such as the Tyler Clementi Higher Education Anti-Harassment Act), most legal protections come under institutions' nondiscrimination policies. As with any type of harassing behavior, documentation is key. Seek legal advice and alert authorities if you feel you are in physical danger. Do not take chances.

HARASSMENT, RACIAL

Racial harassment is a serious matter. It happens in this field, as in others, with a frequency that is hard to measure since so many instances are covered up or otherwise treated lightly. Many institutions have implemented policies dealing with racial harassment, typically similar to their policies on sexual harassment (see **Harassment, sexual**). These policies may be incorporated into a generic nondiscrimination policy that includes racial harassment and discriminatory practices.

Women of color are often subjected to both types of harassment. The *AAR Career Guide for Racial and Ethnic Minorities in the Profession* offers concrete advice for responding to racial harassment, and it is found on the Status of Racial and Ethnic Minorities in the Profession Committee AAR webpage (https://www.aarweb. org/node/135). The AAR's 2008 nondiscrimination policy prohibits all forms of harassment and unethical discrimination. The SBL follows an Ethics Statement of Professional Conduct that seeks to foster a professional, nondiscriminatory environment for its members. See Appendix III for this model.

If you experience an incident of racial harassment, be sure to document instances with as much detail as you can recover. Confide in a friend for support. Avoid self-blame and self-doubt. Seek legal advice on the best remedies in your particular case. Know that racial harassment, however subtle or overt, is intolerable and illegal (see **Racism**). If you witness an act of racial harassment, speak up.

Harassment, Sexual

Women have been sexually harassed in the field of religious studies, as in most other fields, since we arrived on the scene. Hair-raising stories of women being propositioned at conferences, during job interviews, and on the job remain all too common, the result of unequal power dynamics between women and men in a sexist culture. Lawsuits have been filed, but for the most part these indignities are borne quietly by women for fear of sullying their reputations, a misplacement of blame. The real risk involved with reporting these incidents has led us to a culture of denial that privileges harassers. As harassment of any kind is dependent on the privilege granted because of race, gender, sexual orientation, ableism, nationalism, religion, etc. we must address these privileged positions as we seek justice for those who have been harmed by harassment.

Sexual harassment is a serious issue in many workplaces. Be sure to check that the institution where you work has a policy against such behaviors. Policies vary widely. Many institutions require some type of sexual harassment training that will alert you to resources and put potential perpetrators on notice. Be aware of institutional protections as well as policies that can impact your personal interactions. Some institutions have rules about dating (e.g., faculty and students or employee and direct supervisor). Grievance procedures differ, too, so the best advice is to be informed about your local options and err on the side of caution in professional relationships that have a personal component.

The **AAR** has a policy that applies to the Annual Meeting and to its own office. See **Appendices I and II** for the policy and the grievance procedures as a sample. We must hold our colleagues, students, and coworkers accountable for professional conduct. The Status of Women in the Profession Committee of AAR has published *Religious Studies News* articles on sexual harassment that are good resources for women in religion. Additionally, the American Association of University Women has had a long-standing interest in combatting sexual harassment and its website has much useful information. Finally, the SBL has an Ethics Statement on Professional Conduct that serves as a warning or code of ethics but has no governing authority. See **Appendix III** for this model.

If you feel you are being sexually harassed, document events, dates, time, place, witnesses, attire, and exact words spoken or gestures used. Note as many details as you can remember while the occurrence is fresh in your mind. Keep those notes at home, not in your office. They will be invaluable if/when you need to seek legal remedy (see **Sexism**).

HEALTH (SEE ALSO ILLNESS AND ACQUIRED DISABILITY, SELF-CARE)

Some of us are luckier by genetic and cultural heritage, as well as life experience, than others, but all of us can prioritize our physical, as our mental, health to rank above our jobs, and encourage the conditions for others to do likewise. This is easier said than done when the demands of making a living get in the way of having a good life, but diet, exercise, rest, and relaxation will maximize what nature and nurture have given us.

If your employer or institution offers health insurance, be sure yours is current. If you are not eligible, consider a high-deductible policy or investigate new insurance exchanges. Affordable health care is not as accessible as it should be, but being insured is important in case of major medical issues.

Even if you are generally healthy, keep your appointments for yearly check-ups. Do not forget your eye and dental health as the years go by. Have necessary tests for conditions that may run in your family or gene pool.

Physical and mental health are interrelated. Many factors pose a challenge to mental health, including stress, prejudice, economic problems, genetic predisposition, personal history, and physical problems. Do yourself and those who depend on you a favor by making self-care a priority. To prevent or try to remedy burnout, consider therapy, a leave of absence, a change in job, anything that will bring you back to mental health and keep you centered. But sometimes, what is wrong goes beyond needing self-care, and people who struggle with mental illness do not cause it by failing to take care of themselves. (Self-care is important; self-blame simply makes things worse.) Serious mental illness, including depression, bipolar disorder, or other conditions, can make getting out of bed seem insurmountable, let alone completing a major research project like a book. But mental health issues, just like physical health challenges, do not preclude people from having successful and productive careers assuming they have the right supports.

Professional help is available, and most insurance plans cover at least some mental health services; for the uninsured, local programs often make therapy available to those who cannot afford to pay. Seeking help for a chronic condition or a serious episode requires overcoming very real stigma about mental illness. We can all partner to erase the stigma and encourage one another to take good care of ourselves.

If you are seeking a job, there is no reason to share your health history with prospective employers, but be sure to consult the institution's human resources department and get to know and use your options.

When health adversities of whatever sort strike, decide how you want to manage them. If you are a student, it may be important to talk with your advisor. Before you do that, you may want to explore what policies are available for leaves and what resources the university has. If you are faculty or staff, let colleagues pitch in and help. Designate someone to let the word out, but only as much or as little information as you deem fit. Despite the importance of confidentiality, information may leak out beyond your control. Be especially careful about easily forwarded online discussions and online disclosures, since they can spread far beyond your intended audience on social media. You might want to have very sensitive conversations by phone.

Heterosexism (see also Coming Out)

The long-held normative assumption that a religious studies professional will be a man goes along with the notion that he will be heterosexual. Most of us using this guide are living proof that the first assumption is wrong; some of us disprove the second as lesbian, bisexual, and queer women make distinguished contributions to the field. Still, our field is rife with the outmoded assumptions of heterosexual normativity that simply need to be replaced. We are all responsible for resisting heterosexist assumptions.

Fortunately our professional ranks are replete with opportunities to move beyond heterosexism. There are **AAR/SBL** sessions on queer studies in religion, lesbian feminist issues, and the like. There is a mentoring lunch at the Annual Meeting for **LGBTIQ** students. There are caucuses, committees and receptions. But all of the supplementary options in the world do not substitute for an open and bias-free context in which to do our work. That remains to be constructed.

HIRING (SEE ALSO INTERVIEWING)

As women have achieved status in the profession of religious studies, more women are responsible for decisions about hiring inside and outside the academy, though this entry attends mostly to the former. Often the best advice in these situations is to try to remember how much tension the process of applying for jobs induced when you were on the other side of the table, and to make sure that you provide an environment for applicants that will reduce stress and bring out the best in them. We take academic hiring as the template here, but all that follows applies in the myriad settings where those trained in religion will work.

Make sure job advertisements clearly reflect the obligations of the position, whether administrative or faculty. If you are on a faculty search committee, be sure that the list of candidates for initial interviews, as well as the short list for campus visits, fairly represents the applicant pool. Diversity within a department is positive and requires bringing a range of candidates for closer consideration. To wind up with diverse faculty, you have to pay attention at every stage—the job ad, the construction of candidate lists, interviews, and the final deliberations. If you are hiring for adjunct or contract positions, try to keep considerations of fairness firmly in mind. You may not control how much your institution pays per course (if you do, be generous!) but you may have some flexibility in scheduling a course that will work with an adjunct's schedule.

For tenure-line faculty positions, you may want to convince your department to forgo all Annual Meeting short interviews and do video interviews online instead. Although these are not ideal, having to spend exorbitant sums to travel to a meeting for a twenty-minute interview puts a major economic stress on candidates. Many departments are unlikely to forgo in-person interviews entirely; offering a Skype option for candidates who are not planning to attend is a reasonable compromise. A mix of online and Annual Meeting interviews partially levels the playing field for those who cannot attend in person.

If you do this, remember that online interviewing can be awkward; make appropriate allowances.

If you are interviewing candidates at the Annual Meeting, make sure you get a sufficient number of people from your department to participate, or you will run yourself ragged and not make good decisions. When you invite people to campus, provide them with a combination of opportunities to show what they do well. Get the committee involved with providing transportation, company at meals, and escorts to show the candidate around campus. Informal settings are often the best way to get to know people, and to provide them with useful information about your campus and your city. Remember, the candidate is judging your school and department as much as you are judging her/him, so you do want to leave a positive impression.

When interviewing women candidates, do not automatically assume that they would like to teach courses related to women. (If you have no female candidates, wonder why!) Also, do not assume that male candidates will *not* want to teach about women and gender. If appropriate given candidate interests, involve the women's studies program on your campus in a social function or invite them to attend the **job talk**. The same advice applies to lesbian/bi/trans/queer candidates and candidates of color, although in these cases the candidate may well also want to meet with the **LGBTIQ**, black, Native American, Latina, or Asian caucus members to find out about how they will be received on campus. It is important to learn specifics about life for their particular group in your town, and to answer important questions like: Where do black faculty live? Is there an LBGTIQ community in the area? However, do not schedule such meetings without asking the candidate first. Make sure you understand the **Affirmative Action** guidelines on your campus.

The hiring process can be stressful for the people doing it as well as for the candidates, so make sure, if you are chairing the committee, that you are sensitive to your colleague's needs, as well as to your own self-care. As a committee member, feel free to speak up if a part of the process seems unjust or discourteous.

Sometimes an unsuccessful candidate will turn to you for feedback. This may involve confidential search committee information that cannot be shared. But sometimes a candidate will sabotage herself. If this is the case, give honest but kind feedback. She may be hurting herself unconsciously and unaware of how she comes across. It is tricky business to know how to say such things, but imagine if you were in her shoes what you could hear and what you could not hear.

HOUSING

It is generally advisable that new employees live close to their campus or workplace in order to become acquainted with the institutional culture. This is trickier for contingent faculty or others who may have to stitch together multiple jobs to make a living. Some institutions offer university housing or financial incentives to make purchasing a home in the area affordable. Still others will offer a chance to live rent-free as "resident faculty" in a student dormitory. Investigate your options, both financial and emotional, when choosing a locale.

Often women are stereotypically expected to "make a house a home" and the energy involved with this process should not be underestimated. Consider a pro/con list as you decide where you want to reside. Residing nearby allows you to get used to and manage your workload without the added problem of long commutes. It is helpful here to have a good understanding of your new institutional culture. In some institutions, faculty are routinely expected to host faculty/student gatherings at their homes. However, financial constraints (exorbitant rental/purchase prices in the surrounding areas), privacy and sexual issues such as running into staff/students frequently (especially for lesbian, bi, trans, queer, and/or single women), partner employment, the absence of religious, ethnic, and cultural communities, or research agendas may make long commutes the better choice (see **Commuting**). The campus can be a large fishbowl.

Those who opt to commute and choose to consolidate the workweek into several long and intense on-campus or in-office days may be faced with suspicion and resentment among colleagues who live closer to campus. Despite the negatives, living away from work may offer you more emotionally than your colleagues can understand. A "safe space" where you feel community is an intangible benefit that can negate the problems associated with living further from your colleagues. If you choose this route, it may be helpful to spend more active time with your colleagues when you are on site, that is, inviting them to coffee/lunch or stopping by their door for a focused conversation, etc. Choosing a residence at a certain distance from your place of employment can be seen as a lack of commitment to the institution, but women have lives and make choices that are multidimensional given the competing demands most women face from family and work.

ILLNESS AND ACQUIRED DISABILITY

There is an old Yiddish proverb that loosely translates, "if you want to make God laugh, make plans." While unexpected events sometimes bring joy, they often come in the form of misfortune: accidents or illnesses that come upon members of our family or us unexpectedly and change our lives. While planning may not be possible in these cases, and we may not want to think about the possibility of a major health upheaval, it is good to be aware of your institution's policies on disability, and to investigate the availability of private/employer-sponsored disability and long-term care insurance as well. It would be useful to be familiar with the organization's Equal Employment Opportunity Center and/or the Office of Disability Services so that you are aware of local resources. It is good to know what your options are, and being prepared in any way you can is a good idea.

That said, it is not possible to prepare for the changes that illness and acquired disability can bring to your life or the lives of those who are close to you. Of course we all have minor disabilities we need to cope with, from the need for eyeglasses to getting the flu, and the disability rights community will wisely remind us that each of us is only temporarily able-bodied. However, when you or someone you live with is diagnosed with a major illness or new condition, your life will change radically. People respond to these events differently, but most find that they benefit from making others aware of the change and getting support. You will be the best judge of how your chair, dean or other superior will respond to your needs, but they cannot respond unless you are clear about what you are asking for, whether it is an unpaid leave or extra teaching or work support. While departmental colleagues may also be helpful, you also need to make considered judgments about how much you would like to tell them. Moreover, whether or how much to inform your students is also a judgment call. It is a delicate balance between maintaining your privacy and making sure you get the support you need.

Some people find support groups helpful for thinking through dimensions of a particular illness. Dedicated websites about, for instance, breast cancer, heart bypass surgery, or lupus can also share how others have handled a situation similar to yours, but beware of becoming overwhelmed. Some people suggest that you get a friend or partner to filter information on websites, as it cannot only be overwhelming but often scary as well. Mobilizing a network of friends and colleagues is also crucial. From raising funds to providing meals, letting other people support you is a very important way to get through the critical phases of some of these difficult situations.

If you are the caretaker for someone with a serious illness or acquired disability, remember that you will need support too. Nurturing and caretaking is expected of women in our roles as partners and mothers. It is often, indeed, a satisfying experience. But it can and usually does become more than one can bear. The need for the caretaker to be taken care of, and to take care of herself, is often overlooked, and chairs, deans, colleagues, and bosses may not be as sympathetic about granting time (or cutting slack) as you require. Therefore, it is all the more important for the caretaker to find ways to take breaks and get support for herself as well. Mental health holidays, long weekends, and the like will help. So, too, will asking friends to assist with shopping and/or provide respite care so you can get away. All of this adds up to the reality that we live in communities, and we all need help.

IMMIGRATION

The situation for faculty and other workers coming from abroad has worsened dramatically since September 11, 2001. Unless asked specifically, one should not volunteer one's immigration status during a job interview. It is not illegal to discriminate against noncitizens, and, indeed, is increasingly encouraged by faux patriotic rhetoric. Note that the "Immigration Reform and Control Act of 1986" prohibits employment discrimination based on nationality if the person has authorization to work. Some colleges and universities are informally advising department chairs not to extend job offers to international applicants because of the ensuing immigration complications.

If you are not a U.S. citizen, once you receive a job offer and decide to accept, you need to be prepared for a harrowing experience of powerlessness and potential humiliation with the Immigration and Naturalization Service (http://www.uscis.gov), an experience that can only get worse now that the INS has been fused with the Department of Homeland Security.

No visa application should be undertaken without legal counsel by an immigration lawyer. Some institutions will have a retainer to process H-1B visas for international employees. In limited cases the institution absorbs the costs. In other cases the faculty member has to pay. Although large universities have well-established programs for international students and scholars, with staff familiar with current immigration regulations, you cannot be sure that your university or organization knows the ropes. If anything goes wrong in the process (and something often does), you are the one who will leave the country, not the staff person handling your immigration papers. Lawyers are expensive (and not always successful), but they work exclusively for you. Some law schools may offer sliding-scale immigration law clinics; the quality and scope of help offered vary widely.

Since immigration laws are in flux and in many ways being tightened, there is little specific guidance one can give other than the following (which, too, is subject to change and should not be taken for legal advice):

1. If your status changes, you should apply for change of visa status immediately (from a student (F-1) visa to a temporary worker visa (H1-B) to permanent residency (Green Card)). Note that your institution must file your petition for H1-B status. You cannot file it independently. There are strict deadlines, which, once missed, will force your institution to undergo another national search.

2. If you have secured a tenure-track position and begun the process of applying for permanent residency, you cannot leave your position until your green card is granted. This can take up to three years. If you switch jobs, you will have to start all over again.

3. If you are taking a faculty job, note that only a tenure-track position will give you a green card. If you have a visiting or temporary appointment, you are only eligible for a temporary worker's permit and you will need to continue searching for a permanent job. Rules for other types of employment differ.

4. Never leave the country while your paperwork is being processed by the INS. Reentry can be and has been denied on a whim, and you may get stuck outside the country. You should always leave copies of your immigration paperwork with the responsible staff

person at your institution in case of emergencies when you need your employer to intervene on your behalf.

5. Once you have received permanent resident status signified by your green card, you can apply for citizenship after a period of five years. Some people remain on green cards for the duration of their academic careers.

6. However, resident aliens are often not eligible for certain grants and scholarships and you may have to apply for a reentry permit when you go on sabbatical for more than twelve months. If you leave the country for your sabbatical, your citizenship clock (of five years) begins all over again.

Immigrant status can also become especially problematic for older women. They may not be eligible for certain health and welfare benefits, and they may pay higher inheritance taxes. All of these issues reflect the tenuous positions of migrants worldwide and the difficult impact of globalization on the freedom of movement of all people. Canadian and Mexican citizens who have an offer of a position that requires a BA or higher degree have the option of a temporary NAFTA (North American Free Trade Agreement) visa. These are offered only at the border at the discretion of the border immigration officers. These can be hard to get, but be prepared with your **CV**, job contract, diplomas and degrees, transcripts and citizenship papers. Even then there are no guarantees.

Check with the INS for updates on these matters, and, of course, consult an attorney for legal issues. Know that the laws change rapidly and sometimes unpredictably, so stay current and stay strong.

Some U.S. workers may wish to emigrate to work in another country. Visas and work permits will vary widely, so the same advice to consult a lawyer and expect certain complications applies.

Inclusive Language

Languages reflect cultural changes with regard to gender, race, disability, and other important social matters. Institutions increasingly expect that language used in official documents as well as in teaching and writing will reflect these changes, using "humankind" instead of "mankind" or "night" instead of "darkness." This is not a capitulation to "political correctness," but an evolution of language that serves to include rather than exclude, honor rather than dismiss. Simple changes (don't use "blind" when you mean "obtuse") avoid offense and help strengthen prose. For those of us in religious studies, gendered language about the divine is particularly fraught. It evokes strong feelings. Many people get around the issues it raises by alternating between masculine and feminine pronouns, or avoiding them altogether (e.g.,, Godself, God). The bottom line is to use language that expands options, not contracts them, that invites people to name themselves on their own terms.

INDEPENDENT SCHOLARS

People who do intellectual work outside of the established academy are sometimes referred to as independent scholars. Some become independent scholars for reasons of temperament, scholarly interest, employment choices, or lack thereof. All this means is that they do not have an academic institutional affiliation, though most of them work for a living somewhere, including in fields unrelated to their areas of scholarly expertise. They are not to be confused with Alternative Academic Careers (see **Alt-Ac**), though there is some overlap. Rather, independent scholars do their work without benefit of or limits from academic institutions.

There are advantages to such a choice: no dull faculty meetings, no boring teaching assignments, the ability to pursue one's own research interests. However, disadvantages accrue as well: often lack of library privileges, no institutional structure for benefits, economic challenges, and the need to work outside the field in order to fund one's work inside it. Some of those who are called independent scholars are really religious studies-trained colleagues who work in fields other than academia, so that term can cover a rather dubious assumption about our homogeneity.

Independent scholars are more than welcome as part of the **AAR/ SBL**, especially in women's circles where the matter of affiliation is decidedly secondary. The **AAR Annual Meeting** now has a gathering time for independent scholars. Still, we advise sensitivity and awareness all around so that the subtle agenda that we all be employed at recognizably respectable places not rear its ugly head. Some of the best work in the field is still done by people who are not tenured anywhere or employed by a university. The challenge is how to recognize it fully, fund it justly, and encourage even more people in a shrinking academic job market to try their hand at the creative possibilities that independent status confers.

Institutional Analysis

In order to survive and thrive in religious studies, it is crucial to analyze the institutions in which we do our work. Academic religious studies takes place in a variety of institutional settings: public institutions and private institutions, large research universities, smaller liberal arts colleges, colleges with religious affiliations, seminaries, community colleges, and independent centers and institutes. Many of us also work in a range of other organizations including publishing, nonprofits, and the like. This analysis focuses mainly on academic settings but the dynamics are instructive across the board.

Experiences in the academy will vary greatly depending on the type of institution(s) in which one does one's work and with which one interacts, as well as the type of position one holds: tenure-track, multiyear contract lecturer, or per course adjunct. Requirements for promotion and tenure, teaching loads, expectations about the level of involvement between faculty and students, and expectations about religious identity and practice all vary with the institution. The rewards or dangers of particular types of activity will also vary by institution. Spending a great deal of time outside the classroom with students may be absolutely necessary and highly rewarded at small liberal arts colleges, but it may not be valued at large research universities and it may seriously limit the time one spends on one's own research.

Academic institutions are also part of larger communities, and the relations between schools and the cities, towns, and/or neighborhoods in which they reside can often be tense and conflicted. In towns, colleges or large state universities may be the dominant institutions; in big cities, academic institutions are but one relatively small part of the cultural landscape. Because colleges and universities are class-based institutions, town-gown conflicts often revolve around economic and cultural issues.

In thinking about the institutions in which we work, we need to consider how they affect the communities around us. Efforts at community **activism** or ethnographic research will be received differently depending on the history of town–gown relations and the contemporary situation. Is the college, university, seminary, or center open to the community? Does it share resources or is it closed to the outside community while dominating or controlling surrounding land, employment, and resources?

Each institution has a culture and hence a politics of its own. In entering a new institution, whether as a student or worker, it is important to find out as much as possible about that particular institution. One can find important information by reading the institution's website, its handbooks and regulations, by asking questions about institutional history, and by attending to details ranging from daily interactions to the architecture of a campus. Accessibility, for example, says a lot about an institution's inclusion policies.

Higher education as a whole is also affected by broader American trends toward privatization and enclosure by the market of spaces and functions previously considered public.

As with other nonprofit institutions such as hospitals, universities are beginning to move toward profitmaking enterprises and market-based imperatives. In the past thirty years, there has been a massive increase in the administrative infrastructure of universities and a concomitant decrease in the role of democratic faculty governance. A president's role has moved increasingly toward an emphasis on fundraising, even at public universities and colleges. At the same time, the rise of **MOOCS** and other online teaching seems likely to shift a lot of education from the classroom proper to the Internet. This is a shaping factor in institutional life as well.

Institutions have more female students and more females with advanced degrees **teaching**. Does this mean more opportunities for women in religion or is this doomed to increase the number of female adjuncts, who now outnumber men 3:2? Does this mean more feminists **mentoring** for undergraduate students, more female faculty colleagues and administrators, or will this ultimately just mean more work for women and a devaluation of scholarship as female work? As our institutions prepare for 2040 when the United States is expected to have racial and ethnic minorities in numeric majority status, it will be useful to have thought through all sorts of diversity in institutional hierarchy.

The sections below provide a general outline of how institutions vary by type, but one also needs to learn about and develop skills for reading particular institutions.

Public Institutions

When one works for a state university, one faces directly the imperatives of the bureaucratic state. Because state legislatures ultimately control funding, the culture of the university may depend on the approach of the legislature. Is this a state that generally supports education, or is it a state that tends to be more suspicious of, or even to downplay, education? What is the role of the state legislature vis-a-vis the education system?

Many state institutions are research universities, which tend to be larger and have lighter teaching loads and heavier research responsibilities than liberal arts schools or community colleges. They are likely to reward publication and grant money, and are less likely to be primarily concerned with teaching. While the institution will assert its interest in good teaching, its criteria for tenure and promotion may base its evaluation 80 percent on research, 10 percent on teaching, and 10 percent on service. Junior faculty members at these institutions would be wise to put their time and effort into publishing and applying for grants and fellowships. Money and prestige are often the terms of reward. Less intimacy is expected between faculty members and undergraduates, although faculty members may be expected to spend large amounts of time with graduate students. Attend to how this labor is divided.

Still other public institutions function in different ways. Close interactions with students are expected. Your labor will include much more teaching and service than research, which may suit you (though few publications will pose a problem if you want to move to a more research-intensive institution later). In public teaching institutions, you may find that you are the "only" of your kind in the department as most public institutions hire faculty to be generalists (their specialty plus coverage of everything else). If you are the "only" female, person of color, or person interested in X, you may experience some **isolation** or lack of support in the department. Yet, you have the opportunity to create a niche for yourself and thrive in an environment that could be generally glad to have you there.

Large institutions may have various types of jobs in addition to tenure-track faculty positions. Research centers, for example, may offer employment opportunities, but these opportunities are often based on "soft money" (grant money that is raised from year to year and may disappear) and, hence, these jobs are less stable. Such institutions are relying increasingly on adjunct faculty labor, rather than on tenure-track jobs (see **Appointments, adjunct**). Adjunct jobs often involve intensive teaching loads, for lower pay, with less job security. Organization among adjunct faculty can be crucial to gaining reasonable working conditions in these positions.

Community colleges emphasize teaching. Students at such schools differ from those at flagship research universities. They may be employed full time, be of nontraditional age, and work on a degree part time. They may not have qualified for admission to a university and are preparing themselves for transfer. Some schools practice open admission and provide remedial training for those who need it. The students will be from the local community, whatever its makeup, and commute to campus. All these factors mean that, while the emphasis is on teaching at such institutions, the ability of students to focus on their education will vary considerably. In addition, a faculty member will confront a diverse student population, including some students who may have different age, class, and cultural backgrounds than the teacher.

Additionally, some schools are affiliated with certain minoritized communities such as historically black colleges and universities, tribal colleges, Hispanic-serving institutions, or all female colleges. These schools are perceived to favor members of their own communities in hiring, but in practice they typically are looking for the best candidates for the position regardless of their personal backgrounds. Remember to include these institutions in your job search and as a space to look for potential mentors, **allies**, and colleagues.

PRIVATE INSTITUTIONS

Private colleges and universities offer certain freedoms that are not found in public schools and can present a different set of constraints. While private institutions do not face the need to please state legislatures, they can experience intense pressure from their Boards of Trustees, which include alumni/ae of the institution and others from the public and private sector whose expertise may be sought. As the cost of higher education rises, however, boards are increasingly dominated by wealthy individuals and corporate representatives whose expectations are that the college or university should be run like a corporation. Smaller private institutions may be facing difficulties in fund raising and budget constraints, while larger private institutions, particularly elite research institutions, are increasingly circumscribed by an ethos of profit making. Just as the political culture of state institutions varies depending on the state in which they operate, so the political bent of private institutions also varies. Some have long histories as liberal institutions, while others tend toward the conservative.

Some private institutions are large research universities and some are smaller liberal arts colleges. Private universities, particularly elite research universities, may have even stricter demands for tenure than do state research universities, some requiring two books of junior scholars in the humanities fields. The vast majority of candidates for tenure are approved nationwide. However, the percentages can be much lower at elite research universities, some of which grant tenure only at the rank of full professor, which places someone just six to ten years out from a Ph.D. in competition for a tenured position with colleagues at other institutions who have been in the field much longer. If considering employment at a prestigious university, inquire about the expectations for receiving tenure along with statistics of how many junior faculty members who are hired in a given institution actually receive tenure. Some elite institutions are notorious for overworking junior faculty, who serve the institution well, only to reject them for tenure because they have not published enough or because of some intangible matter of fit. It is always satisfying to see those people who have been turned down for tenure go on to get MacArthur Awards and/or tenure in friendlier places. Many others, though, strive to protect junior faculty from unreasonable service demands, which may fall heavily on associate professors.

Most small colleges are private institutions. Teaching loads tend to be higher and sometimes research responsibilities are lighter, but check with each institution. Presence on campus and participation in a wide range of campus activities are highly valued. Small colleges also often ask faculty members to spend time with students outside of the classroom, not just in office hours, but also in social settings. New faculty members should attend to how their colleagues deal with such expectations and demands. Do these expectations vary by gender and race? Are women expected to be more open and available to students? Are people of color expected to mentor and sustain all the students of color? Speaking openly of these expectations, making them and the division of labor visible, can help departments to develop arrangements that are more equitable. Above all, keep your boundaries clear so you are not taken advantage of or left aside.

RELIGIOUSLY AFFILIATED COLLEGES AND SEMINARIES

Many institutions of higher education in the United States have religious affiliations. For some institutions, these affiliations are largely dormant. Although they may continue to affect the overall culture of an institution, they are not expressly applied. For other institutions, particularly for seminaries, these connections may be central to the life of the institution. In addition to academic goals, these institutions may have expectations, both stated and unstated, for students and faculty members to participate in the religious life of the community. Both students and faculty may also be rewarded for participating in religious activities in the broader community. It is important to be as clear as possible about these expectations when entering such an institution. For these institutions, questions of how to address religious diversity can be particularly difficult—whether diversity across religious traditions or diversity found within the particular religion or denomination of which the school is a part. In some more conservative establishments, the religious expectations are explicit and enforced. Buyers beware.

Religiously affiliated schools can make hiring decisions on factors other than quality. For example, a Catholic order can prefer one of its own members over a more qualified person who is not a member. And such schools can perpetuate the hegemony of the major world religions to the exclusion of smaller, less well-known traditions. This is part of the ongoing challenge of religious studies: to make the gold standard reflect the diversity of the field not the parochial interests of a few.

INDEPENDENT CENTERS OR INSTITUTES

Centers often offer freedoms that are not found in traditional academic institutions, but they can also be less institutionally stable since they are frequently funded by soft money. There is a trend for some large institutions to handle innovative issues and/or issues they want to marginalize (such as those involving women and racial/ethnic minorities) through centers. In some cases, the center moves to the center; in other cases the center is really on the margin and stays there. This can make the larger institution appear more inclusive and broader than it really is.

The process of setting up one's own center, or working at an already established independent center can require an entrepreneurial spirit and fund-raising capabilities (see **Entrepreneurs** and **Fundraising**). It can be done, both within large institutions and beyond them. It takes real vision, perseverance, and lots of sweat equity but can result in magnificent contributions to our field.

INSTITUTIONAL CULTURE/POLITICS (SEE ALSO INSTITUTIONAL ANALYSIS)

Each institution has its own culture. It includes such intangibles as clothes and lifestyle, willingness to debate, and even whether faculty are addressed by first name or title by students. It is subtle and nuanced; it also varies according to who you are in the institutional hierarchy. Women and people of color find that out right away and often the hard way.

Your best bet is to read everything you can but then find an ally (see **Allies**). Sit down and ask the hard questions until you feel you have a handle on how the unarticulated power dynamics of the institution work. Your own intuition will kick in, but having somebody to check your perceptions against, and doing it early, will save you a lot of aggravation. This kind of support for one another is an integral part of solidarity within institutions. Reaching out to new colleagues who might otherwise be marginalized is part of the "lift as you climb" process.

If you are in a position of institutional power, as we now have more women in administration, be mindful of ethical uses of institutional power. Radical audacious power sharing can be achieved and it starts with how we treat each other individually from the staff to upper administration. As you get a sense of the institutional culture and your role within it, be sure to discern true allies without presuming that those who seem "like you" will share your values and ideas for the culture of the institution.

INTELLECTUAL PROPERTY

Laws governing intellectual property are constantly shifting, particularly as online publication blurs previous boundaries. Enlightenment
notions of authorship and originality prevail in the academy. They
govern ideas about plagiarism, which is the appropriation of other
people's work. Outside the academy, people tend to be considerably
looser in their interpretations of what is a fair way to quote, paraphrase,
or otherwise use a text, and students may expect these same standards
to apply in the classroom. Whatever critiques you may have of the
assumptions undergirding intellectual property rules, be scrupulous
in your use and citation of other people's work. There are sad tales of
women's careers screeching to a halt when they have, however inadvertently, used their graduate students' work or otherwise appropriated
what was not rightfully theirs. (When in doubt, a capable lawyer is a
good investment.) Additionally, be sure your own work is copyrighted
or otherwise credited to you. Many women report seeing their ideas in
other people's work without permission or citation. Last, think about
what online distribution (outside of electronic journal publication)
might mean for your ability to publish later in more traditional venues, which remain the gold standard for academic evaluations. Some
publishers will refuse a journal article or book if a significant part of
its contents has been posted online. Like so many things having to do
with online access, these rules are in flux. If you are primarily interested in reaching a large audience, however, online venues can reach
far broader audiences. Just do not be surprised when people take your
ideas and run with them.

INTERDISCIPLINARITY

Religious studies is an interdisciplinary field defined by its object of
study: religion. The question of object and study are not easily separable. Recent historical and philosophical work has shown how the
idea of a trans-historical, cross-cultural phenomenon called "religion"
was created in part through the study of religion and how this process
was intertwined with European colonialism (see **Religious studies**).
Academic disciplines, on the other hand, are most often organized
around method of study (history, philosophy, sociology). As the concept literally implies, a discipline is knowledge created by controlling

and adjudicating the processes by which that knowledge is sought. Historians must meet standards of empirical evidence, sociologists must gather data through recognized quantitative and/or qualitative methods, and philosophers must submit to logic and argument.

Not surprisingly, feminists and other progressive scholars have often criticized these disciplinary practices, since the standards of each discipline were developed by the predominant practitioners—in the United States, white men of privilege—and they reflect the biases of these people. For example, historical standards of evidence have often focused on printed documentation and hence have necessarily produced knowledge primarily about those persons (usually powerful white men) who produced documents. Approaches such as oral history or material cultural studies that might overcome some of these biases have sometimes been resisted by those with the power and authority to protect the discipline, although they have flourished in the last few decades.

Disciplines can also be conservative insofar as they create separate, coherent areas of study. Because disciplines are used to police the boundaries of whom and what is studied, scholars who might ally to create new forms of study can be kept apart. After all, it took decades to develop women's studies. Disciplines also contribute to the simplification of complex phenomena and social problems, as only one method of study predominates in a given sphere. Thus, disciplines have been one of the necessary sites for struggles for justice in the academy.

In order to address some of these problems, new fields of study related to progressive social movements—women's studies; racial and ethnic studies; lesbian, gay, bisexual, transgender, intersex, and queer studies; and postcolonial studies—have most often developed as interdisciplinary fields. These fields brought together various disciplines to address complex phenomena such as the lives of women and/or people of color. However, interdisciplinarity is not simply the amalgamation of different disciplines. It can also pose questions that cannot be answered, and sometimes not even be asked, within the structure of the traditional disciplines.

Interdisciplinary programs are themselves open to question from the outside. At some universities, women's studies or African-American studies, for example, still face critics who argue they are not legitimate areas of inquiry. There are also internal critics and **allies** who debate the proper parameters of the field. The transitions in many programs from women's studies to "gender studies," or African-American studies to "ethnic studies" or "critical race studies" warrant analysis. On the one hand, they are a welcome acknowledgment that women are not the only "people of gender," and that white people have race. The burgeoning field of masculinity studies is important and much exciting work is being done there. On the other hand, there are risks that women will be excluded and ignored and that feminist work on which the field is based will be lost if the focus shifts purely to gender. Some institutions have opted for names like Women's, Gender, and Sexuality Studies in efforts to make the approach conform to the "biasfree" academic norm, effectively erasing the advocacy stance on which it was formed.

There is another risk. Universities and colleges are adaptive institutions, so administrations have sometimes taken up "interdisciplinarity" as a code word for cost-cutting and administrative consolidation. In these cases, rather than opening areas and possibilities for study, interdisciplinarity is used as a justification for closing them down. For example, religion and anthropology departments are sometimes merged, or even religion and film departments, for reasons that remain obscure other than funding cuts. In addition, defining a field in terms of an object of study is not necessarily progressive. Studying religion without serious questions about how religion is objectively formed means that we may extend European and Christian assumptions and dominance.

Just as disciplines separate areas and potential allies, so can fields of study. The separation between and among women's studies, racial and ethnic studies, **LGBTIQ** studies, and postcolonial studies has created serious problems for the study of the intersections of the differences named by these fields. It also undercuts possibilities for alliances across these fields, making the resulting transformative demands more easily managed by the university. Young scholars need to be aware of the policing power of the disciplines, even as they may want to seek out or even develop interdisciplinary programs and methods to pursue the types of projects they value. While pursuing interdisciplinary studies, whether in a traditional department or interdisciplinary program, students may want to protect themselves by also pursuing certification—whether through exams or dissertation chapters—that allows them to apply for positions in a single discipline. Remember that tenure is usually granted by a department, which must review a scholar's work, and that positions relate to curriculum, which may be divided by traditional fields. These combine to make it difficult to get interdisciplinary work evaluated adequately for tenure, though this is changing somewhat because of the presence of interdisciplinary programs. And it can make finding an academic position very difficult.

Upon getting a job, one needs to be clear about expectations and review processes within a department or program. Be clear from the start about the type of scholarship you hope to pursue and the materials that you will use. If interdisciplinary methods are new to your colleagues, help to educate them about the growing importance of this work in your field. Share your work with them as you progress. When it is time for review for tenure and promotion, discuss the importance of reviewers who will not object to interdisciplinary scholarship, and suggest senior scholars who can act as reviewers or provide advice on your field as you understand it.

Scholars who work in interdisciplinary ways often must attend a variety of professional meetings: Chicano Studies Association, the Association for Asian American Studies, National Women's Studies Association, etc. Many institutions fund attendance at one professional association meeting a year, but often only if the faculty member is on the program. To attend other meetings may require you to pay yourself, so, if you need to be active in several learned societies, try to negotiate support for such activity at the time you are offered a position. An institution may be willing to specify an amount for travel to meetings, rather than limit faculty to one meeting, but be sure the amount is adequate for more than one meeting. Taking a proactive stance (in a nonhostile manner) can make a world of difference in terms of keeping open spaces for interdisciplinary undertakings.

INTERNATIONAL COLLEAGUES

The number of international faculty in higher education is rising steadily in the United States though immigration and visa policies are in flux. Depending on the discipline (especially in the sciences), between one-fifth and one-third of professors are immigrants. Religious studies is no exception, and your department will in all likelihood have or eventually try to cultivate an international flavor.

Academe is generally a welcoming place for people from around the world; there is a broad consensus that international, multicultural, and multireligious perspectives enrich the learning environment for students and faculty. For many international scholars, U.S. institutions of higher education provide the economically, religiously, and politically safe environment needed to engage in research that would be impossible in their home countries.

Despite difficulties with the INS (see **Immigration, Racism**, and **Xenophobia**), most immigrants find the United States open and hospitable and develop strong ties to their colleagues and institutions. A genuinely warm welcome is the least U.S. residents can provide in gratitude for the presence of a diverse and international community.

International Study

In an increasingly globalized world, international study is often required for religious studies professionals. It often means equipping oneself with another language (something that notoriously monolingual U.S. residents need to do anyway). It involves travel, intercultural experience, and the reward of friends and colleagues beyond one's shores. It is a great antidote to **xenophobia** and can add a completely new dimension to one's work, regardless of how early or late in one's life it takes place. Fortunately, many colleges require international study so future colleagues should be well on their way to an international perspective by the time they begin graduate studies.

Of course, international study is expensive, often a factor for women. It need not last for long periods but must be long enough for solid exposure. Organizations and foundations offer grants for summer research, which can be used for international work. Universities and colleges sometimes have funds for just this purpose. Study can be combined with meetings and conferences abroad, and is best done in concert with international colleagues who handle logistics and form a natural community on-site. The point is to do as much international work as time, money, and interest allow. The world is only getting smaller. Consider going to international meetings as well. There is no reason why the route to the **AAR/SBL** should be largely one-way. U.S. colleagues need to carve out time and funding for conferences in other countries as well.

INTERNSHIPS

As you prepare for a career in religious studies, consider internships as a practical, enjoyable, and sometimes life-changing way to get acquainted with the players, organizations, and major themes in the field. Imagine an internship at a nonprofit organization that works on women's spirituality in Santiago, Chile, or a semester interning at a group that works on reproductive health in Washington, D.C. Consider moving outside of your usual circles in your internship choice. If you are Jewish, think about going to a Muslim agency; if you are Christian, search out a Buddhist option. The sky is the limit. It is often through internships that young people find career direction, and practical ways to move in it. The supervisor makes all the difference in the world, so research and choose as carefully as if you were taking a paid position.

There are downsides to internships too. The major one is that unpaid internships exclude those who cannot afford a summer or a semester without income. Thus, the rich get richer as students who can afford to give their time get a lot out of it—connections, recommendations, and a step up the ladder as they pursue professional goals. This may change if legal moves to push for all internships being paid come to fruition. Another downside is that some supervisors do not know how to manage interns. They either treat them like full-time employees in terms of expectations, ignore them as if they were long-term unwanted visitors, or see them merely as extra hands on deck without any thought to what the intern is getting out of the experience. All of this means that internships, while potentially life-changing, can also be problematic. As always, choose carefully and ask a lot of questions, especially of former interns. Most organizations are only too happy to provide the names and contact information of people who have interned with them before. If they are not willing to do so, let it be a signal that they may not have provided very happy experiences and look elsewhere.

INTERSECTIONALITY

Intersectionality is a recent term to describe what in earlier decades might have been called "the multiplication of oppressions." It describes the intricate ways in which racism and sexism, for instance, play against each other, or the implications of class for disability, or disability for class. Intersectional analysis requires complex acknowledgments and balancing acts: no piece of scholarship (or personal identity) can adequately comprehend all the factors involved. Intersectionality is aligned with, but distinct from, **interdisciplinarity**. For women, intersectionality is a crucial concept for understanding how to analyze experience and strategize to achieve justice.

INTERVIEWING

Virtually every job requires an interview. Many books have been written on the subject; consultants will prep you on what to wear and how to act. None of it guarantees you a job. Our advice is to treat the interview as the first day on the job. If you do not like it or the "fit" is not right, better to find out sooner rather than later. In the current competitive climate, it can feel as if the interviewers have all the power, especially in academia, with so many candidates and so few jobs. In fact, as the candidate you have plenty of decision-making power as well as control.

Our advice is simple: Be prepared and be yourself. If this sounds simplistic and you prefer to strategize each move, that may work in your case. For the most part, you can expect that the members of the search committee are looking for long-term colleagues with that vague quality called "fit." They want someone they would value as a member of their community and who shows promise of a distinguished career. You may or may not be that person. Definitions of "fit" can also be affected by people's racist, heterosexist, and sexist assumptions about what religious studies professionals should look, sound, and act like. However, you are yourself and that will have to be enough.

Many first interviews are by phone or Skype. You may want to practice with a friend to be sure that you sound/look the way you want to. A landline is best for a phone-in interview as it can be more reliable than a mobile. Likewise, be sure that your computer is powered up. Test your screen and microphone to avoid embarrassing technical glitches that may reflect negatively on your candidacy. After all, if you are applying for a job that includes an online component, you want to demonstrate that you can handle the hardware.

Preparation for the interview includes thorough knowledge of the institution involved, or at least enough to ask intelligent questions.

It also involves choosing those parts of your **CV** you wish to highlight, and a well-thought-out rationale for why you would be the ideal person for the job. You cannot anticipate every question, but some rehearsing with a friend or in front of the mirror does not hurt. You can decide what information is off limits and prepare responses accordingly. Remember, your marital status, age, sexual orientation, whether you have children, and so forth are not necessarily public information.

Candor is key in an interview. Most people can tell when someone is faking it. But the economic reality is that people need jobs, so in many instances one can only be as candid as finances allow. Would that it were otherwise.

In academic settings, you may be called to the campus for an interview, proof that you are a strong competitor for the job. You may be asked to present a lecture and/or conduct a class. You will meet with faculty, perhaps administrators, and students. A campus visit gives you a chance to see if this is a place in which you would like to live and work. Be aware that you are being observed throughout, not just at the formal interview. Before you go, be clear on who will pay what expenses and save your receipts for reimbursement. It is to be hoped that institutions will follow the advice for hosts we discuss under **Guest lectures**.

Interviews can be learning experiences. Mistakes made once need not be repeated, which is why interviewing for a position, even if you do not get it, can be valuable. You might even ask a colleague involved in the process what you might have done differently or what the successful candidate did. Most of the time you will find it just was not a "fit," not a very helpful response but proof that the whole process is quite capricious.

Interviewing at the **AAR/SBL Annual Meeting** is done under controlled conditions. Rules are in place to make the process safe (no interviewing in hotel rooms as in days of old, for example) and efficient. Employment listings and interviews at the Annual Meeting require membership to **AAR** or **SBL**. See their website for details.

Isolation, Cultural and Religious

Many women find that being "the only" anything (racial/ethnic/gender group member, lesbian, professor of Coptic and Ugaritic, etc.)

can be a very lonely experience in a large or small institution. Such isolation is increasingly common as religious studies programs shrink due to budget concerns. Look to the natural **allies** in women's studies or African American studies or wherever your interests lie. Seek a worship community or other faith-based group in your area if those ties are important to you. Join professional organizations to keep in touch with colleagues in the field. If you are a second or third generation of a claimed identity you may find mentoring and colleagues with those who have blazed the trail before you. If you are an introvert, start with small conversations in your new community about your research, or ask advice on how to get acclimated or simply go to a new side of town/campus and meet new people.

Once you get started locally, remember to keep a strong connection to friends beyond your institution if this is helpful. If you are a first-generation college student, your home communities may not be able to help you process your transition. In this case, look within your new environment for new types of community. Utilize Skype, FaceTime, email, and the phone to reach out to communities that sustain you. As resources allow, consider getting out of town or asking for additional professional development funds so that you can go to conferences or to communities that support you and your research. In all, take seriously that we are meant for community and you deserve yours as well, even if your job has taken you far afield. Acknowledge that your alienation is real and seek resources to help you adjust. Therapy can help if you find yourself experiencing depression or other mental health challenges because of your isolation. Often this can be paid for out of your medical insurance. If you are uninsured, there may be a local provider offering therapy and treatment on a sliding scale for those who cannot afford to pay the insurance rate.

Job Sharing

If you are considering a job sharing arrangement, you and the other person should apply together for the job. If you decide later in the process to share one position (referred to in academia as one full-time equivalent or FTE), there are several legal hurdles (**Affirmative Action**, nepotism rules) to navigate. In the negotiation process, make sure your salary is at the upper end of the salary spectrum; insist on separate offices, separate travel funds, and separate (double) pension benefits. Merit reviews and tenure reviews are usually separate. If the person with whom you are sharing the job is a life partner, it is wise to put stipulations in your contract regulating the dissolution of the arrangement in case of divorce or separation, or the failure of one partner to achieve tenure.

Job sharing arrangements have some obvious advantages: They secure partner employment at the same university or other institution, and help to avoid the academic commuter couple syndrome. They allow people to care for children and/or elderly family members without giving up academic ambitions. In addition, they relieve the pressures of teaching for people who have ambitious scholarship goals but find themselves in environments with heavy teaching loads.

There are also some disadvantages. Most institutions with job sharing arrangements evaluate each member separately. While the teaching load can be divided easily (and evaluated separately), service cannot. Those on half-lines are continually battling against expectations that they should be more present and more active than their half-line salaries warrant. Most institutions get more than one full FTE out of shared arrangements, but only pay for part of it, including the retirement and medical benefits. While job sharing arrangements can make for sane and happy family lives, life on one academic salary is rough, and the injustice of being overworked and underpaid can wear on one's conscience and bank account. Realistic advice is that given the current job market and the pressures on women to handle family commitments as well as professional work, a well-structured job-sharing situation can beat the alternatives. Some may be able to find better, more creative solutions, while for others, job-sharing *is* the creative solution.

Jobs, Changing

Even though the academic market is tight, there is always a certain amount of job changing that goes on. It is nothing like the frequency of changing jobs in the corporate world, and far from what it used to be in academia. It used to be that you could reasonably expect to change at least once, that is, from a first job out of graduate school to a second, tenure-track position; or, if you received tenure in the first one, you could almost plan on a switch to a place you might prefer. When moving after tenure, it is common to take a leave of absence from your first institution to determine if the new job is good for you. Such leaves must be negotiated with both institutions, so check with colleagues to find out what arrangements are customary in your setting.

In the current climate, all bets are off in terms of job changes. Many people are clinging desperately to the one they have, even if they do not like it, for fear of ending up without any position at all. It is hard to assess how this will play out in time, but two cautions are worth a mention. First, once you accept a job it is considered bad form to hop to another too soon, except under very special circumstances. After all, the search committee went to great lengths to fill the opening and does not want to have to do so all over again. Second—and this may seem contradictory—if the job is clearly not a fit once you have been at the institution for a year or more, it is perfectly acceptable to begin to put out feelers. If you are offered another job but might want to stay where you are under certain circumstances (better pay, more leave, different teaching responsibilities) you may be able to negotiate a counter-offer, where your institution matches or improves on what you have been offered elsewhere.

Many universities' salary policies are structured so that apart from expected "bumps" in salary with tenure and promotion, the only way to achieve a significant raise is to present the university with an outside offer, which it will then try to match, assuming it wants to keep you. Given how much time and how many resources go in to academic job searches, trying to get a raise this way is a very inefficient process. Women are also far less likely to play this "game" than men. It is also the case that looking elsewhere is tricky business as it can send a mixed signal to your current employer. However, if you are given an offer, your current employer may decide to match or better it as a way to keep you on board.

The key to this whole process is maintaining integrity, keeping people informed while at the same time looking out for your best interests. A lawyer may be helpful in sorting out contractual details that will affect your decision. In any case, the real winner in these cases is the person who acts honorably.

JOB SEARCH

It used to seem simple, even if it was not easy: when nearing the end of one's doctoral program, one would apply for jobs. There was an established timeline, a clear process (application materials, confer-ence interviews, short list, job offer), and a relatively decent shot at a positive outcome. Of course, not everyone got **tenure-track jobs**, but there were also one and two year visiting positions, and an array of adjunct jobs one could take while turning the **dissertation** into a book and awaiting the next annual hiring cycle.

A small consolation, but real: reality has diverged so far from this ideal that it need no longer feel like individual failure not to move from doctorate to tenure-track job; the problem is obviously much bigger than any individual scholar. Although some people will get those jobs, it is not possible for every good scholar to get one, or even every excellent scholar. The numbers of highly qualified people and open slots just do not match.

So, now what? Ideally, you will have thought about employment prospects before entering **graduate school**. If you choose to pursue a religion degree despite limited opportunities for faculty jobs, it is use-ful to keep a variety of career paths in mind as you proceed through coursework, exams, and research. If you have done so, then as you approach the end of your studies you may have **internship**, work, min-istry, or volunteer nonprofit or **activism** colleagues to call upon for guidance as you research employment, an established online audience for your blog, or a network of feminist activists on whom you can call. It is both fortunate and unfortunate that not all job searches—includ-ing in **publishing**, the nonprofit world, or religious bureaucracy—are bound to the same standard timeline as academic hires. In fact, you might discover just how Neanderthal some academic institutions are in contrast with the fast moving world of high tech, social media, politics and the like where your skills are coveted.

The important point to keep in mind is that preparation in reli-gious studies means that you have skills and experience that are highly respected in other fields. You know how to handle a text, you can analyze certain kinds of data, you have critical skills that may make you a good strategist, and you have a broad overview of the world and its various cultures. These are transferable skills to many jobs in pub-lishing, the nonprofit sector, government, and politics. Offer them as they allow you to cast your job net far wider than the little academic circles to which you have become accustomed as a student. People go to law school to become lawyers, not professors of law; people go to medical school to become doctors, not professors of medicine. The same can be true for those who study religion, that we can become practitioners—ministers, administrators in religious organizations, directors of programs, etc.—instead of limited our imaginations to **teaching** religion.

Adjunct teaching may work if you can afford it and/or have a partner whose income can subsidize your poorly paid activity. Women are overrepresented among the ranks of adjuncts, not only because of gender discrimination in hiring for tenure-track positions, but also because of social arrangements and assumptions about males being providers. Some women, with and without **children**, are able to teach for unjustly low wages because their spouses provide the lion's share of family support. This is not a criticism of people who make these choices, with or without the hope that the adjunct will move into a "regular" faculty job someday. It is merely an observation about one aspect of our broken system. Since one's decisions affect others, it is important to think of the implications for other people if you take a job at low pay. No one wins except the institution that shortchanges its faculty.

For those who are applying for teaching jobs: more and more institutions are now requiring a teaching portfolio as part of the essentials for job applications (and sometimes as part of the **tenure** dossier) as well. A portfolio may simply consist of your **syllabi** and teaching **evaluations**. Portfolios can also include peer reviews and self-reflective narratives about your teaching philosophy, or a narrative analysis of your experience in an individual course, as well as samples of student work you have graded, and websites or handouts you have created as instructional tools. Say something in your teaching statement about women and gender. Use your syllabi to show, for instance, the ways you integrate women and gender into the survey course in religious studies. This will set you apart from other candidates. Include a list of workshops or seminars on teaching in which you have participated. Keep an updated annotated bibliography of books that you have read to help you improve your teaching skills. Add copies of notes sent by grateful students or colleagues. In short, document your growth and development as a teacher.

If you are offered a position, *negotiate*. The **negotiation** process may involve offers and counter offers, that is, a package of wages and benefits made by one institution that will be matched or at least responded to in some way by another. Occasionally, someone will have two offers at once, but this is unusual especially in challenging economic times. It is more likely to occur when one is already in a position, and has an outside offer (see **job changing**). This is more typical in **administration** or the nonprofit world, but happens in faculty ranks as well. In any case, be aware that you are expected to negotiate, but that in some instances it can provoke backlash. Prudence is in order, and a keen assessment of the context to know whether there is room or not for asking for more than is being offered. Ask colleagues and mentors for (confidential) guidance here.

JOURNALS, READING AND WRITING

Journals are the print vehicles that convey solid scholarship in a field. You would be wise to get into the habit of perusing several journals in your subspecialty, as well as the *Journal of the American Academy of Religion* (*JAAR*). We are fortunate to have the *Journal of Feminist Studies in Religion* (*JFSR*), which specializes in feminist scholarship. Most journals have online versions, and universities typically provide subscription access through their libraries, both to specific journals and to larger journal databases such as JSTOR and Project Muse. Access to such resources can be difficult or costly for **independent scholars**; some institutions offer unpaid "research associate" status for which one can apply, granting library privileges. If you are a scholar without an affiliation, consider this if it will gain you access to materials you need. Remember this benefit when you look into emerita status (see **Emerita**).

Publishing an article in a refereed journal (like *JAAR* or *JFSR*) is helpful to one's academic career. It is not easy because the better journals turn down many articles for every one they publish. Do not be discouraged. Publishing is a matter of finding a fit between what you have written and a journal or other outlet that wants to publish it. Your rejected submission to one journal may be the lead article in another. Your piece that is too popular for a scholarly journal may be just right for the magazine of your religious community.

A few tips may help you get published. First, submit to only one juried publication at a time, paying close attention to their style sheet and citation method. Most editors and readers are unpaid, so their time is valuable. If they spend time reading and critiquing your piece, and then you decide not to let them publish it, everyone loses. Be sure you adhere to the publication's length, format, and content specifications. Lots of articles are eliminated before they are read for technical reasons. Second, journals are not like the Internet; they are slow-moving. When you submit an article, you can expect to wait several months before hearing whether it is accepted or not. If after a decent interval (perhaps three to four months) you have not heard anything, do not hesitate to inquire. It is not fair to you to hold your work any longer than that.

Third, always have a list of backup choices if your article is not accepted on first submission. The blow of rejection can be cushioned if you submit elsewhere, but do it right away. Even the best writers have their next place to submit lined up so as not to lose momentum. However, if there are small and manageable revisions suggested, do those first. Some journals can seem cavalier about how they handle manuscripts, accepting and rejecting seemingly at will. Others, especially feminist journals, can be rich sources of feedback as readers provide careful critiques.

If you get a revise and resubmit letter, please take it for what it is: the editors actually want you to revise and resubmit. This is not a rejection. As always, you must decide whether the revisions are something you can live with. Are they asking you to clarify your arguments? Take out your gender analysis? Add a comparative dimension? If the critique makes sense and you do it, chances are decent that you will get a fair and sympathetic second reading and perhaps a publication.

Be sure that whatever you submit is carefully put together and closely scrutinized by you and at least one other person for typos or other incidentals that may discourage readers from choosing it.

Finally, beware scam journals that charge fees to review, edit, or publish your article. Reputable scholarly journals never charge authors. A publication in a for-profit journal will not help build your credentials and will also keep you from publishing the material elsewhere.

Leaves of Absence (see also Benefits, Leaves)

A leave of absence can be granted or taken for a variety of reasons. Health-related issues are common. However, a leave can also be used as a placeholder, a way to save your space in an institution while you are trying out another one. Some faculty take leaves of several years to work in government service or in NGOs related to their field. Each institution has limits on such leaves, so investigate this before you commit. Unpaid leaves can also be taken when one has won a **fellowship** at a time other than a regularly scheduled sabbatical, or just as a refresher after a windfall.

Depending on the type of leave, you may be able to take benefits with you on leave, especially if a fellowship will pay your award to your institution, which allows you to stay on their payroll. If you win a fellowship, check to see if this is possible. In all cases, it is important for women especially to calculate the full cost of a leave, for example, lost benefits, lost Social Security credits, and the like. While it may seem a good idea in the short run, be sure it also makes long-term sense, or you risk lower benefits down the road. Consider self-care in all of this, and follow your opportunities.

LECTURE CIRCUIT (SEE GUEST LECTURES)

Some of us find ourselves on the lecture circuit after an especially popular book or because we work on issues of wide interest, or just because we happen to be smart, articulate speakers who can offer an audience a lot of food for thought in an accessible way. One can think of this prospect as **guest lectures** writ large, so all the wisdom found under that heading applies here and then some.

Lecturing can be a great way to reach people who are not in the classroom. It can also be a way to take the temperature of the public, to learn what issues and approaches are most helpful. On the downside, the travel and changes involved in any such undertaking (ask anyone who has done a book tour) are strenuous, so be prepared.

When saying **yes and no** to invitations, the size of the audience is less important than the connection between speaker and listeners. A handful of people who really want to hear what you have to say can be far more rewarding than a hall full of restless undergraduates who are there under duress. Be sure to talk with trusted colleagues about lecture fees. They range widely, and women are forever being asked to give their skills away for little or nothing. Don't do it! The choices you make set precedents for other speakers. Even if you can afford to take a low fee, think about the fact that you have just lowered the fee for the next woman who cannot afford to give her time away.

One last word of advice—enjoy it! Caveats and cautions to the contrary, this kind of travel and access is the stuff of privilege. It allows you to learn a lot in a short time about places, people, and ideas you might otherwise never encounter. Treat the whole thing as a gift you are responsible to use wisely for the common good.

LGBTIQ (SEE TRANSGENDER)

Sexual orientation and gender identity are important facets of human experience. There is no single word to describe the myriad ways people organize their sexual activities and gender identities except to say human. So the amalgam of letters "LGBTIQ" has come to stand for some of the possibilities: lesbian, gay, bisexual, transgender, intersex, and queer or, sometimes, questioning. Other letters will undoubtedly emerge. The key thing is that people are invited to name their own experiences on their own terms and expect to be respected. The variety and fluidity of human sexuality and identity is seemingly endless.

The terms themselves may be usefully ambiguous as well. Women who identify as lesbians may have sex with other women, or they may organize their lives around other women. They may have sex with people across a range of genders, only with themselves, or not at all. In our society, for example, asexuality counts as queer. Gay men may organize their lives around resistance to dominant gender norms or they may focus on men in ways that extend misogyny. Bisexual women or men may organize their lives around partners of different genders or one partner in lifelong commitment. Intersex people live with complicated contradictions, mostly socially constructed in a binary culture. Transgender people may inhabit a variety of gender positions that do or do not match their assigned "biological" sex. They may reinterpret gender by what they wear, how they carry themselves, or through hormonal or surgical intervention. Identifying as queer generally means resisting dominant norms of gender and sexuality. Such resistance can be lived out in many ways. Heterosexual people may identify as queer, while lesbian, gay, and bisexual or transgender people may not necessarily choose to do so. This is one of the most fraught and at the same time most dynamic dimensions of contemporary human experience. Use of the various terms can also differ across the age spectrum.

When taking up institutional authority or projects of social change, keep in mind and make openings for the multitude of ways in which people live their lives. Abundant new religious resources on the topic help to clarify issues and promote justice. But there is no substitute for honest, direct communication even if the bottom line is confusion or lack of information. No one is served by gossip or innuendo, and everyone benefits from clear communication, especially on delicate topics like gender identity and sexual orientation. The trick is to decide who needs to know what in a professional setting about one's personal life. At the same time, because justice on the sexual front is still a distant hope for most people, there is a certain amount of sharing as a lesbian or as a trans person that one may choose to do as part of the process of social change. Again, the hard part is deciding where and with whom to share, and what to do when others share for you. Care and respect go a long way in this complicated and changing environment.

LGBTIQ Committee

The Status of Lesbian, Gay, Bisexual, Transgender, Intersex, & Queer Persons in the Profession is part of the **AAR** structure. It develops programs to enhance the status of **LGBTIQ** persons. Specifically, the committee is charged with recommending policies and best practices to ensure the full access and academic freedom of LGBTIQ persons in the Academy.

The committee sponsors special topics forums and hosts an informal luncheon and reception during the Annual Meetings for further networking. The LGBTIQ Committee also publicizes job descriptions, calls for papers/proposals, and shares conference information pertinent to LGBTIQ studies in religion. It answers issues of special concern to LTBTIQ scholars of religion through its "Ask the Diva" column which is sometimes featured in the online publication *Religious Studies News* (https://www.aarweb.org/about/ask-the-diva-questions-and-answers).

Finally, the committee participates in the formal **mentoring** program sponsored by the four committees of the AAR. If you are interested in the work of the committee, consider nominating yourself or someone else to serve.

Media Relations

The media are crucial to public discourse, to open, free, and vigorous debate. Therefore, our relations with the media go two ways; they call us when they need an explanation or an expert opinion, and we call them when we need publicity for some event our institution is sponsoring that will benefit the public. The **AAR** and **SBL** now offer connections to their members with the media on selected topics through a project called *Religion Source* (see **Resources**).

A local religion or education writer may call us for our opinion on a piece of pending legislation or on some current event. A national outlet may want a theological, ethical, or historical explanation of something. A columnist or commentator might want to know how sacred texts inform a current event. (The answer may sometimes be: they don't.) You may feel the need to interject your views into the public conversation by submitting an Op-ed piece for the local news. It is at this moment that our function as teacher and scholar reaches beyond the classroom, beyond our particular institutions, beyond the academy.

Many media people still think that scholars of religion look like their childhood religious leaders, so they are not likely to call women, people of color, and/or those who are not ordained without prompting. This attitude is changing, albeit slowly and with help. Some women scholars of religion have appeared on national television programs and websites, so women's insights are gradually becoming part of the public discourse. Nevertheless, it is still quite unusual to see more than one woman featured with a group of men, especially when it comes to major news events like the death of a pope, clergy sexual abuse, or the funeral of a queen. Then male experts are trotted out in legions as if women know nothing about the topics. Educating the press about religious variety could be a fulltime job.

The key to good media work is clarity. It takes time to learn how to be concise. Most of us are trained to pay attention to nuance and detail, argument and counter argument. Sound bites are just that: ten to fifteen seconds in which we must convey very complicated thoughts in glitzy, memorable, and, most of all, short ways. Practice!

Media training is important if you plan to do a lot of this. You will learn what to wear (solid colors, little jewelry, avoid white and black), how to posture (be offensive without offending), when to respond and when to let gratuitous remarks go by, what to do if the microphone goes dead (smile and pray), and above all, how to STAY ON MESSAGE. The latter is especially hard for us, as we have learned so well to elaborate on everything, to nuance our arguments to a fare-thee-well. Good practice for media work is Thanksgiving dinner with your extended family. How they hear things you say, how they respond to you, will give you a good clue about your audience out there in television land.

Sometimes we call the media: for example, when our institution brings a world-renowned scholar to our community or sponsors an annual lecture series. Public relations departments of our institutions do this best. If none exists, develop a list of media contacts and issue an advisory to each several weeks beforehand. Then a release goes out just before the event, inviting media representatives to attend (gratis of course). Local newspaper and radio/television stations are obvious outlets. Social media rules. Think also of free weekly papers, of local cable stations, and lists on the Internet as ways to get the word out.

The more we as women can develop our skills in media relations, the faster we will change the mistaken impression that all experts on religion are men. A good first step is to see and greet media folks as **allies**, not as aliens, to welcome their questions, however banal and gum-chewing they may seem, and consider the effort invested in media work to be well expended. It is time that such work is counted as "service" to an institution, a contribution that is not yet recognized in most places.

A few caveats: Some institutions have strict protocols and pathways for the creation of a media "presence" or who can speak for them. Be sure you know your institution's rules before you speak on its behalf or in ways that could raise questions about your ability to do so. For "headline" events or not, media operate on their own timetable. Responding to a developing story will often require you to stop what you are doing and respond to a reporter's query RIGHT THEN. This may be worth it if the *New York Times* is asking, but not your local news affiliate. Most colleagues who have worked with the media have both positive and negative experiences. For every successful interview there is the nightmare sound bite that strips all context from your remarks. But sometimes if you are able to devote time to a decent conversation with a journalist you can actually change the way an article is going to be framed. Keep in mind that most religion writers, for example, know relatively little about religion. Some nuance, especially if given on background, can help to shape/spin a story. Just keep in mind that it is time-consuming to educate the media and they do not pay tuition. Nonetheless, to see a story carry a perspective you have shared, indeed a quote from you, can be very satisfying and culture changing.

Mentoring (see also Advisor/Advisee Relationships)

A good mentor may make or break your academic career. Mentors give feedback on one's intellectual work. They soothe bruised egos after a publisher has rejected one's scholarship. Mentors encourage you to "revise and resubmit" a rejected article. They put underhanded, mean comments of senior and junior colleagues into context. Mentors point out the small print in the faculty handbook and give tips for preparing one's tenure file. Mentors cut to the chase of campus politics and help you find **allies**, avoid enemies, and create a network of colleagues beyond the institution. Mentors give inside information about comparative salary structures and benefits packages and help you negotiate or renegotiate your contract. Mentors prevent you from going crazy by pointing out the inconsistencies, contradictions, and double binds of academic life.

White men have always mentored white men, and some women have benefited from male mentors. More often, however, women and people of color have been forced to succeed without the assistance of mentors. As a result, we have not learned to ask for mentoring or to offer mentoring, something that hurts us all in the long run. It is beneficial for minority groups to see and connect with others in similar situations, as graduate students, faculty, administrators, and in alternative academic careers. Given that the numbers of junior scholars is many times that of senior scholars, there are not enough such mentors to cover the needs of those entering the field. So finding a good mentor may require some creative searching. Someone may be a good mentor for some aspects of your career but not all aspects. Even a tenured professor can use a mentor's advice on progressing to the next stage of her career, entering a new subfield, changing institutional cultures, etc.

Mentors, unlike advisers, do not need to be at the same institution as you. A mentor in another institution can offer **sponsoring** and a different type of mentoring style than what is normative at your institution. Peers can mentor each other, a particularly untapped resource for graduate students. Of course, students who have "been there and done that" can help you avoid pitfalls and lead to paths of mutual success.

Additionally, formal **mentoring** programs exist. The **AAR** has piloted a mentoring program sponsored by the four committees of the AAR: Status of Women in the Profession (see **SWP**), Status of Racial and Ethnic Minorities in the Profession (see **REM**), Status of Gay, Bisexual, Transgender, Intersex, and Queer Persons in the Profession (see **LGBTIQ Committee**), and the Status of People with Disabilities in the Profession (see **PWD**). This program pairs doctoral students and nontenured faculty with senior mentors in the field. For women of color, there are additional resources like the United Methodist Women of Color program; the Pacific, Asian, and North American Asian Women in Theology and Ministry; or the Womanist Approaches to Religion and Society list serve. Other mentoring programs and organizations have sustained histories of mentoring like the Hispanic Theological Initiative; the Forum for Theological Exploration; the Asian Theological Summer Institute; and the Human Rights Campaign Foundation LGBT Mentorship Summer Institute for Religious and Theological Study. (These lists are not meant to be comprehensive.) Most of these programs have applications and deadlines, so plan ahead and be prepared to apply again as you will have differing mentoring needs as you emerge in the field of religion.

Keep in mind that mentoring is reciprocal. While the balance of power makes clear who leads and who follows in this dance, the mentor derives a good deal, too, from the relationship with the graduate student or junior faculty member, both intellectually and emotionally. If you have a good mentor, consider yourself lucky. If you are a good mentor, thanks!

MICRO-AGGRESSIONS

Micro-aggressions refer to subtle verbal/nonverbal behavior that communicates hostile or negative slights to marginalized groups. While the term was originally coined in the 1970s to discuss racist ideology and misconceptions, now the term is used more inclusively. Micro-aggressions may be reflected in assumptions about intelligence, skills, or identity. They may be done consciously or unconsciously and can be delivered by any group. They are most recognizable between those with greater areas of power and privilege. Some examples include:

being referred to as "hotties," being expected to clean up after events, having important events scheduled during a cultural/religious holiday, having to deny/downplay one's romantic relationship, being considered staff not faculty, being complimented on speaking "good" English, having persons raise their voices when you are blind, or having to explain what you are doing in a certain area of town/campus. These and many other small gestures are often intertwined with **sexism, heterosexism, racism, and ableism** and are experienced as everyday inequities that frustrate and demean our collective lives. We must remain vigilant and use education to end micro-aggressions by speaking out against these infractions against our collective worth.

Midcareer Issues

There is an expression called the "post-tenure blues." Some women get it and some women do not. It is related to a set of questions about midcareer changes, promotion, or advancement not necessarily related to **tenure**. Some women, once having attained tenure or having been tenured for a number of years, wonder, "What next?" "Is this all there is?" We may ask ourselves, "How do I keep my career alive?" "How do I teach the same required courses when the repetition becomes boring?" "Do I want to stay at the same institution?" "What new directions in research and teaching or community activism might I make?"

Of course, the onset of doubts varies from woman to woman. Sometimes it is concurrent with midlife questions, but oftentimes it is not. Age is not necessarily a factor. Many of us reevaluate our careers and regroup. Issues of growth, and whether or not we can continue growing where we are, become a part of the reevaluation and regrouping. Priorities shift and our careers with them. It is all quite normal. The key is to find people and resources that encourage such shifts.

To even speak of the post-tenure blues invites the reminder that having a tenure track job at all, let alone tenure, is a luxury few are granted. One key is to remember that tenured women can devote some of their newfound security to helping transform the system. Those with tenure can take unpopular stances: speaking up in faculty meetings about hiring more people of color, lobbying for adjunct **unions**, insisting in the face of colleagues' intransigence that queer scholarship counts. That's not to say that junior faculty cannot or should not do these things, merely that tenured faculty are uniquely positioned—some would say obligated—to do so.

Women at the associate professor level should also think about promotion. Compared to men with similar qualifications, women tend to wait longer to seek promotion, and are more easily derailed by service requests. Whatever else, as one emerita professor noted, "Continue to be productive in print."

This productivity may take you in a new direction. Just because a woman begins with one career track does not mean she has to stick with it for life. That is true whether you are moving into religious studies after a career in another field, or whether you have been in religious studies for a number of years and want to change your research/**teaching** focus. Second career students in the field of religion are common. They are also some of the more interesting people because they bring whole new disciplines into the mix. For example, one woman with an expertise in graphic design is bringing that skill set to thinking about religious imagery and symbolism.

Many of us find our minds and hearts moving in a new direction and decide to leave a career in another field to pursue a career in religious studies. Some of us found ourselves placed in a subspecialty in religious studies that we never felt was quite the right fit, but we took it when the job we were looking for or the politics of the moment made it the best choice. Some women simply outgrow an earlier interest in one area and/or their research leads them to a different emphasis. You may outgrow your department and find that there is a different department in your university you prefer. Alternatively, you may outgrow your institution and find that you want an institutional change.

Keep records of the changes you make in your syllabi and research. Develop relationships with the colleagues who work in the area you find yourself shifting toward. Those of us who have made this shift have learned the importance of carrying along others with us as our research and teaching interests change. Presenting papers at professional meetings in your new area is a helpful way to reintroduce yourself. Becoming acquainted with and joining working groups in the field you are moving into facilitate recognition of your work in the area. It helps in the interview process to bring others up-to-date on your work, and even to talk about the process of changing research and teaching emphases. It is a sign of **professional development**, often a prelude to a new, more productive time in one's career.

MOOCs

Massive Open Online Courses are a new phenomenon on the educational horizon. They are economical and efficient ways to teach large numbers of students at the same time. They can democratize knowledge, making elite institutions accessible to the public at large for nominal fees. Some prestigious universities are offering them with professors crafting input that can be easily uploaded and digested at a student's own pace. They are part of a spectrum of online or mixed offerings, some of which are available only to students enrolled at particular institutions.

How much these MOOCs will reshape the higher educational landscape is still not clear, and it is wise to be wary of potential commercialization and homogenization of knowledge. But online teaching more generally is an increasingly popular way to teach basic subjects even in some graduate programs. Women need to hone their technical skills to be competitive on the teaching side where organization and presentation are crucial. If this is the future of undergraduate education, for example, then women need to get on board despite whatever reservations we may have about method. Otherwise, our dearly achieved content will be eclipsed by less differentiated material simply on the basis of access to technology.

Money Management (see Debt)

Money is usually an unspoken topic in religious studies. It carries so much freight with regard to class background, self-worth, discrimination, and mystery that it ought to be in every graduate school curriculum. The reality is that we come from different economic backgrounds and our lives differ because of it. A little frankness will go a long way toward justice.

There are many books for women on how to manage your money and many financial planners who will be glad (for a fee) to help you make investment choices and plan for retirement. Consider someone who takes a flat fee for her services rather than someone who makes a commission on products and therefore has an incentive to sell you certain things rather than others. Educate yourself. Few of us in the humanities are savvy about the finer points of the stock market, the difference between bonds and equities, the advantages of a Roth IRA, or the importance of 529 accounts for children's college education, but we can understand better than we do. Long gone are the days when women were not expected to understand finances or support themselves or their families.

Graduate school is a major expense, usually a debt-producing one. It is also an uneven playing field in that it is easier to manage for those who come from families that could save for their education than for those who are, for example, the first in their family to go on to higher education, often without benefit of any such savings. Someone who graduates from college without debt has different options than those who are saddled with tens of thousands of dollars of loans to repay. These differences have a long-term impact: for example, who can do an unpaid **internship** and who cannot afford it, who can study abroad and who cannot, who can take the best job offer and who must work in underserved communities to defray some of her indebtedness, or even take a private sector job in which she is uninterested in order to pay back loans. These inequities require structural changes to correct them. But they also require honest conversation so that we can help one another and smooth the way for those who follow.

There are simple things we can do that will get us started on the path of sound fiscal management over the life of a career. Begin with your graduate institution's financial aid offices and insist that you get the maximum in grant, work-study, and other outright (as opposed to loan) forms of assistance. Then negotiate student loans as best you can. Once on the job market, a realistic picture of salaries is key to ensuring that we are being paid commensurate with our brethren and indeed with other women who may be savvier than we in negotiating. Differentials persist, between male and female adjuncts as well as among regular faculty. Those in tenure-track and tenured positions should check on salary differences at midcareer. For a variety of reasons, women tend to spend a longer time at the associate level. Check to make sure you and your female colleagues are not experiencing salary compression while male colleagues have jumped ahead. Sometimes the women's faculty caucus at your institution can be helpful in addressing these issues, and if there is no caucus, it might be helpful to form one.

For some women, the first job is also the first time they have disposable income, so the job of managing money becomes even more important. If you have student loans, how much of your paycheck is really discretionary? What if you want to buy a house instead of renting an apartment? What if the old car just isn't reliable anymore? An accurate budget adhered to strictly and a moratorium on new debts are an essential combination for financial health. However, circumstances—such as an elderly parent needing care, a health crisis, or moving expenses—may make it impossible to implement. Some people find that by consolidating student loans they are able to decrease monthly payments. Check with an accountant to get your best option, and save, save, save.

If your organization or institution allows you to contribute to a retirement or pension fund, maximize allowed contributions. Take advantage of tax laws that favor income saved over income spent. Consult a financial advisor about how to invest any excess income you may have, learning how much risk you can tolerate and when to choose the safest course. Check with your tax person (get someone who knows as much about taxes as you do about exegesis) about how best to document and hopefully write off business expenses. Some costs related to research, for example, can be expensed against grant income. Don't take our word for it, but consult an expert who can save you some money, even after paying fees. If you fear it will be too expensive, ask about local resources for low-income people. Sometimes retired professionals make themselves available to give advice at local libraries near tax time. Other professionals reserve a portion of their time for sliding-scale clients. Again, they should know their field the way you know yours, so shop around to find a consultant who fits your bill.

All of this is conversation some men have on the golf course and/or in the locker room. We need to start it with one another, always with an eye toward sharing the resources among us so that no one is left out while others have abundance. It can help to "buddy up" on this, sharing your financial picture with a trusted friend who can help you to stay the course you set for your own financial success.

While you are at it, think about drawing up a simple will, choosing a health care proxy as well as someone who has access to your healthcare information (Health Insurance Portability and Accountability Act), someone to hold your Power of Attorney, and a guardian for any **children** for whom you are responsible. Lawyers can be costly but worth the investment, and Legal Aid may be able to help you if you cannot afford to pay. Moreover, some institutions offer seminars and other kinds of help on these matters through their human resources departments. Some of these things can be done easily with online forms. The most important thing is to have these life-planning measures in place so that your heirs have no worries and you can live peacefully.

MUJERISTA

Commitment to women's well-being from the perspective of Hispanic/Latina women is called *mujerista*, a term favored by some colleagues in religious studies. It is similar to, but distinct from, *feminista* in that it is understood not in relation to feminist work (see **Feminist**), which is often perceived as Anglo efforts to achieve women's rights, but rather akin to **womanist** or African American women's efforts to survive in a racist patriarchal culture. *Mujeristas* hear and articulate some of many Latina voices on their own terms. They create a framework for social justice based on their experiences. *Mujerista* work involves the whole community, and is done in concert with other women and men who seek the well being of women, the community, and the earth.

NEGOTIATIONS (SEE ALSO **CONTRACTS;** **LEAVES OF ABSENCE**)

Negotiating is a fact of life and conventional wisdom suggests that women tend to be bad at it. Why? Because women tend not to negotiate. We fail to ask for more money when we get initial job offers and we take no for an answer far more easily than men. We often assume that if we are deserving, someone will notice and simply give us what we deserve. Unfortunately, this is not the case. Women also sometimes fail to negotiate because we intuit, correctly, that we may face resistance and hostility to a greater degree than men.

All job offers result in some form of negotiation until both the institution and the prospective employee are clear about and can agree on conditions for employment. Most women in Western settings have been socialized not to talk about money. We have a lot to learn from our sisters elsewhere who go to the marketplace and bargain with vendors, and especially from those who are vendors themselves.

Most professional contracts do not have extensive flexibility especially in a soft economy. Nevertheless, there is always room to negotiate, especially *before* any contract is signed. Once you do sign, your power all but evaporates. So think carefully about the basics—working conditions, teaching/research/academic load, office, health benefits, retirement plan, disability insurance, sabbatical possibilities, tenure options, professional development, childcare, and the like. It does not hurt to share your contract with an employment lawyer, who might notice a loophole you have missed.

Do not forget to look at the seemingly smaller stuff that can make/break your experience. What about a computer? Will you have secretarial support? Are there teaching, research, and/or work study assistants available to you? How large will your classes be? How long must you teach that introductory survey course until you get to try your hand at a graduate seminar? Will you teach online as well as in the classroom? If you are in the nonprofit or professional sector, will you have support staff, **vacation** time, etc.?

Only after you have ascertained the answers to these and other questions relevant to your kind of employment, and discussed the offer with a trusted friend or colleague, should you consider accepting it. For academic appointments, it is customary to respond to written offers within two weeks. Some institutions will pressure you to do so more quickly, but do not be rushed into a rash decision. Of course, if you are not planning to take the position, it is only courteous to say so quickly so as not to delay the search, allowing the committee to move on to its next candidate.

Negotiating an offer is a serious process that institutions understand. The key is to be honest with everyone along the way. It may turn out that you reject the offer because in the negotiating, you realize that dealing with this institution reminds you of your first husband during the divorce or an unpleasant relationship you once had. Better to cut your losses, insofar as you can afford to, and find a job in an organization where you feel respected. Remember that you are in your most powerful position *before* you sign, so be sure you will feel comfortable afterward. Barring unforeseen catastrophe, even in a recession there will be other jobs to consider, other avenues to explore for your considerable talents. Once you are on campus for an interview, it is clear that you have the credentials for the job. What is at stake is the "fit." You can only control half of that, so relax and enjoy the experience.

Negotiating does not end when an employment contract is signed. If you are invited to give talks, serve as an expert witness, or contribute to an online forum, you may (or may not) be offered an honorarium. These are often negotiable, but women often don't ask. One woman outside the academy gets it in writing that she will be paid the same as any men invited to the same event. Some women ask to be paid for blogging contributions. Remember that in asking for something, or for more, or for parity, you are not asking only for yourself but also for the women who come after you. Still, be aware that since women are not *expected* to negotiate, any effort can result in sexist stereotyping and potential backlash, making the process all the more important for you and future colleagues.

NETWORKING

Networking is a trendy way of saying keep your eyes and ears open and reach out to your sisters in the field. It is not some magic solution to getting that dream job or a foolproof way to avoid discrimination. It is necessary for survival because we live and work in communities, despite the many pressures to divide us. Finding "our people" and coming to count on them for support and critique is essential to survival. So is making yourself available for others to count on.

In religious studies, networking opportunities begin in the home institution, where links with others in the department or section are important. Social media is a great boon to networking. Likewise, a good discussion group or email list can put you in regular touch with people in your field.

The Womanist Approaches to Religion and Society Group at the **AAR Annual Meeting** is a good example of a network. African American women share their work, share the word on the street, and share their wisdom. They meet the day before the AAR Annual Meeting, and have on occasion included a community outreach component in their gathering. The **Women's Caucus** in Religious Studies is another good place to go. Its sessions connected with the Annual Meeting are rich opportunities to meet other women, hear from some of the seasoned members, and profit from their experiences. The Status of Women in the Profession Committee (see **SWP**) organizes a lunchtime session for networking. Both **AAR** and **SBL** have various receptions, breakfasts, and other meetings to encourage networking, for example, for **independent scholars**.

Graduate students, gay/lesbian/bisexual and transgender people, and **international colleagues** all need and have created their own networks. Ask around and find yours. If it is not readily apparent, gather two or three colleagues and start one. Expect that your professors and mentors will invite you into their networks. If they don't, look for faculty who will. Otherwise, the common needs of colleagues, and the specific needs of groups that are marginalized, will go unmet. So much still gets done informally, at lunches and among old friends, that it is imperative that networks enlarge to include ever more people. Do not dismiss your own networks, either. Social media is a new means of finding and connecting to networks. You can make connections between people that you know, enriching both of their connections.

ORDINATION

Ordination is the process of becoming a member of the clergy. Not all religions have formal clergy or agree exactly what it means to be a member of the clergy. Of those religions with formal clerical ranks, not all ordain women; Christian denominations vary widely here. Wiccan, Goddess, and Pagan groups have a variety of formal and informal ordination processes for priestesses and priests and many of these groups have more priestesses than priests.

Divinity school or seminary is a typical precursor to ordination for most Christian and many Jewish groups; alternative seminaries and religious schools are increasingly accessible to other religions. Many, though certainly not all, people who pursue Master of Divinity (M.Div.) degrees go on to be ordained. People who pursue religious studies without planning for ordination often seek a Master of Theological Studies (MTS) or a Master of Arts in Religion (MAR) degree. Theological schools provide a range of preparatory courses for ministry as a career, including preaching and pastoral counseling. Women make up only about a fourth of faculty at theological schools, though, so there are fewer role models for female students who are increasing in numbers in the schools.

Not everyone who goes to divinity school seeks ordination; not everyone who gets ordained gets a posting in a congregation. But ordination can have important benefits for those who want to work in a variety of nonprofit settings or for official religious organizations. The M. Div. is also sometimes a precursor to doctoral work in academic religious studies. It can also lead to a practice oriented degree like a Doctorate in Ministry.

Where ordination is available within a religious tradition but not (yet) accessible to women—for instance, among Catholics—female theologians and scholars may be disadvantaged in relation to their ordained male counterparts. Some denominational schools give preference in hiring to members of their own denomination; this may be doubly true for those who are ordained. In some hybrid positions, ordination is a plus or even a requirement, for example, in the case of a campus minister or chaplain who may also teach.

Some religious groups do not have formal ordination, but may still discriminate against women in leadership roles. For instance, Muslim community leaders in the United States come from a variety of backgrounds, including formal religious training of various sorts in other nations, academic religious studies training, and online and other study in the United States. Muslim women are increasingly pursuing religious training and taking prominent posts in community and national organizations, as well as ascending academic ranks. Few lead congregations of any size, however.

Ordination is only one type of religious authority. For example, chaplaincy is a route to ministry that may or may not include ordination. Chaplains have religious and pastoral training but are not necessarily ordained. They serve in hospitals, prisons, the military, and on university campuses. Female chaplains from traditions without formal ordination may still be barred from certain chaplaincy jobs and there are debates over which groups may have chaplaincy representation. Things are changing: Wiccans are now beginning to be allowed to serve as chaplains in the military, for example.

Questions about gender and religious authority are vital for all women in the field of religious studies to investigate, but they are felt particularly acutely by observant and/or believing women whose **vocation** calls them to exercise formal or informal authority within their communities and congregations. This is an area where the landscape is being transformed, albeit not quickly enough.

Postcolonialism

Postcolonial discourse is an emerging area of study investigating oppositional thinking that began at the first breath of European colonial conquest of the world. It is similar to postmodern thought in that it seeks to deconstruct master narratives and challenge binary oppositions. Many institutions understand that the world is growing ever smaller and try to prepare students for this new reality. Therefore, they work to bring in people from other countries and cultures to create a global community. This means that some of our teachers, our students, and our peers will come from countries that have a colonial history.

Not all colonialisms are created equal. The United States, once a colony, is now arguably the most powerful country on the earth, exporting its own hegemonic cultural and economic influence. Postcolonial work requires careful listening and a willingness to see and accept the authenticity of the Others within the definitions formulated by the Others themselves. Like **racism**, **sexism**, and all forms of oppression, colonialism's legacy presents a challenge for everyone in the field, not simply for those most directly affected by it. Religions are classic tools of colonialism, so understanding and deconstructing them is essential to getting beyond hegemonic norms. Doing so is not disrespectful; rather, it is embracing the historical reality and trying to change it for future generations.

Poster Sessions

Poster sessions are common in many fields, especially the sciences and medicine, though less common in the humanities. The **AAR** used to have them but discontinued them. Still, you might have an opportunity in another setting. They are a chance to display current research and engage in conversation with colleagues who may be involved in similar projects.

One applies for a poster session just as one does for presenting a paper. The difference is that instead of presenting to an audience, one presents, via a poster board, to individuals who stop to talk during a designated period during the meeting. A sharp, well-written, and well-mounted display on a 4′ x 8′ board is the medium. Words, pictures, graphics, and other means to convey research and results are made available to interested passersby. Though very different from presenting an academic paper, poster sessions are especially useful for generating interest in new research and connecting with people who have similar interests.

Power, White and Male

When we think of religious studies in historical terms, the image of a white male bastion of power springs readily to mind. Some would argue that the picture has not changed much: that most religious groups are still headed by men, that predominantly white religious organizations have far more money and political clout than those run by women and/or people of color, that most tenured professors are still white men. True, perhaps, but to leave the story at this point is to ignore the enormous strides many women and people of color have made and the valuable solidarity engaged in by many white men who understand their common stake in the increasing diversity in our field. People with power, like tenured professors with job security, pensions, health care, and the like have a lot of power to share. Getting used to sharing it is another matter entirely.

Nonetheless, power is power. It is the ability to make choices, to deem relevant or irrelevant certain aspects of who we are, to render important or trivial ideas and projects, to fund or defund efforts, to invite or disinvite, in short, to shape the reality in which we do our work. This guide is an investment in consigning this entry to the dust bin, and replacing it with "Power, shared and equal," which we hope will describe our field in future editions.

Note in the second edition: Unfortunately, this entry remains too real to delete. In fact, some women, especially some white women, have more power than they did on first writing. But the dominant demographic and power holders remain white men in religion, even while women are doing increasing amounts of the ordinary administrative work in the field. Some are cleaning up disasters wrought under some white men's leadership, for example in seminaries and theological schools where neglect of infrastructure and abuses of power have resulted in serious problems. Nonetheless, we remain hopeful that we will be able to eliminate this entry in a future guide of this sort.

That said, we also recognize that white women in power in many instances are replicating behaviors of white men. Reports of grievances being filed for appalling behavior on the part of women in leadership prove that the problem is far from solved simply adding women. Moreover, many colleagues, especially colleagues of color, report that they are accustomed to dealing with white women as academic leaders and have found some men to be very useful **allies**. While numbers have changed, fundamental power structures have not. Shifting that power equation so that no one has such unfettered power over another is where future efforts need to be focused.

Presenting a Paper

One of the defining experiences of a career in religious studies is the first attempt to present an academic paper at a conference, notably at the AAR/SBL Annual Meeting or a regional meeting. First comes the business of getting a proposal accepted (**Appendix VI**). This is done by submitting a proposal to the blind review process of a program unit of the AAR or SBL (see **AAR Annual Meeting** and **SBL Annual Meeting**). Once a proposal is accepted, whether for a panel presentation or for a paper, the hard work begins of writing something that will: (1) fit the time allowed, (2) keep a specialized as well as general audience awake, and (3) showcase your expertise to the max.

Everyone is nervous the first time. Practice helps to calm the jitters. So does wearing something you feel good in. Have a friend time you so that you finish in the allotted period. On presenting a paper, see **Appendix V** "Be Brief, Be Witty, Be Seated," along with guidelines for "Making Your Presentation Disability Friendly" (**Appendix IV**).

When all is said and done and your first paper is over, congratulate yourself on scaling one of the field's heights and look forward to your next one. You may decide how much you like this part of the work. Some people are naturals at it. If you present and afterwards detest the experience, take it as a hint that maybe this part of the work is not for you. There is simply no need to structure your life on the basis of something you really do not enjoy. If you enjoy presenting papers and especially if you do not, if you aim at formal academic employment and promotion, it is particularly important that you publish the results of your scholarship. This enhances your own reputation and makes your contributions to the advancement of knowledge.

Privilege

Whatever your age, gender, race, socioeconomic class, sexual orientation, gender identity, religion, physical ability, or ethnicity, you know something about privilege, having it or not. While many of us experience oppression based on unjust social structures, most of us also benefit from privilege from our status as part of the educated elite and especially those in the academic world.

We often tend to notice the ways in which we are disadvantaged and ignore the power we have. Therefore, it is also important to recognize that there are situations where, for example, whiteness gives white women a decided if unspoken edge over African American, Asian, Latino, and Native American men and women, or when Christian hegemony brings Christian women closer to the centers of power than their unaffiliated or Wiccan, Muslim, Jewish, Hindu, or Buddhist sisters or brothers. Rather than simply feeling discomfort about that privilege, we can use it well by recognizing it and taking concrete steps to change the power equation. This means structural changes and a preferential option for those who are marginalized. It requires deliberate steps by those who have privilege to share it by giving up positions, encouraging younger colleagues and colleagues of color. It means making our work accessible in every way from meeting in rooms that accommodate everyone to having our written materials recorded for those who are blind.

It will take generations to undo the harmful effects of **racism, class, colonialism, ableism**, and the rest. But sharing is essential if we claim to embody the values that the very religions we study uphold. Besides, common decency permits no less.

Professional Associations

The **AAR** and the **SBL** are only two of many professional associations related to our work in religion. Find out the name(s) of one or several that meets your needs, and join. Their newsletters and **journals**, occasional meetings and online discussion groups are great sources of information and **networking**. If you are a faculty member, your home department may consider activity in one of these groups part of your service requirement (see **Service**).

A major innovation is the creation of racial and ethnic minorities' professional organizations. For example, there is the Society of Race, Ethnicity, and Religion, which publishes the *Journal of Race, Ethnicity, and Religion*. The Wabash Center for Teaching and Learning in Theology and Religion also hosts colloquia and workshops for various communities and these serve as useful professional associations as well. Any list here would be partial; instead, search online and ask colleagues about possibilities for your networking and career advancement. Many organizations have opportunities for you to serve and get more involved.

If you teach in an institution of higher education, you may want to consider joining the American Association of University Professors (AAUP). Their bulletin, *Academe* (http://www.aaup.org/reports-and-publications/academe), addresses many national issues of interest to women in education (see **Resources**).

PROFESSIONAL DEVELOPMENT

Professional development is the umbrella term for all that you do to keep growing and producing in the field of religious studies. It means expanding your skill base so that you become increasingly attractive as a colleague or employee in a rapidly changing field. It includes teaching effectiveness, especially the development of computer skills to bring your teaching in line with contemporary modes. Effectiveness of communication is something we can all use help on, whether oral or written. Branching out into a new subspecialty or developing administrative skills are all routes to professional development, as are learning to write grant proposals, develop websites, or organize conferences.

In academia, this is the rubric under which the pre-tenure and tenure evaluations are carried out, as well as most other evaluations in cognate fields (see **Evaluations, annual**). You are expected to publish regularly, whether books, journal articles, and/or reviews. If you know this is your weak suit, start early to get help from colleagues or from private sources (there are writing coaches now) so you will not be caught without a paper trail when you need one.

Professional development is a good hedge against unemployment. Many skills transfer from one field to another. Professional development can also be a vehicle for learning what is out there job and skill wise that you might not have noticed before.

Public speaking of various kinds is an important skill. For scholars, presenting papers at professional meetings (see **Presenting a paper**) is considered part of your professional development. Being a respondent requires synthesizing others' presentations and giving useful feedback. Acting as a presider is less important, but worth a mention to show your willingness to serve. Speaking on panels, presenting guest lectures, getting grants, and doing **media** relations can all be part of your professional development. It is important lest you risk stagnating at the just slightly postgraduate school stage, a natural location one year out, but a problem if five years later you are still there.

Summer seminars and grant acquisitions can be part of your professional development. New research projects, especially collaborative ones that involve people from different departments in your own institutions or work by colleagues from a number of institutions, are considered a big plus. These activities break the monotony of routine teaching and inform your teaching with new and exciting content.

If you are in the nonprofit sector, government, or private industry, professional development is an integral part of your work. The landscape is changing so quickly that most of us struggle to keep up. But our options are limited lest we risk growing stale in the job or missing major opportunities because we are ill equipped to deal with them. Bottom line: keep growing. Continuing education is the most reliable way to do it.

PROFESSIONAL ETHICS

Professional ethics refers to the many moral issues we face in the regular course of our work. It includes matters of personal conduct, institutional responsibility, confidentiality, as well as the many aspects of our subspecialties, for example, decisions relevant to research protocols or handling of sources. Plagiarism is a particular challenge, especially with Web-based research increasing exponentially the opportunities to use work without proper attribution. For women, and especially women of color, the trickiest aspects can be matters of others' personal conduct (see **Relationships**), where differences of perception, lapses in judgment, and cultural prejudices can result in serious problems, many of which are highly resistant to solutions. **Racism, sexism,** and other forms of oppression make sorting out the threads of an ethical problem very challenging.

One suggestion here is to rely on those **allies** within your institution and the networks beyond (see **Networking**) to help alert you to expectations that may be unwritten. This is a reminder to all of us to convene such conversations regularly so as to maintain high professional standards within our field without condemning people unfairly who make honest mistakes because they were uninformed or because other people are prejudiced.

One thoroughly avoidable problem is lying, fudging, or otherwise inflating one's CV (see **Curriculum vitae**) or resume. Not only is it unethical to doctor one's professional history, sooner or later, one will be found out, which invariably leads to disaster. Simply put, don't do it.

PROMOTION

In academia, faculty and, to a lesser extent, administrative ranks are strictly defined and moving between them can be a major undertaking. As long as there is a pecking order, there will be a top rank. In academia, the graduate student assistant is on the bottom, followed by lecturers, who are usually adjuncts, and perhaps term-limited contract faculty. In **tenure-track jobs**, one becomes assistant, then gains the rank of associate (typically when tenure is granted), and then, perhaps, full professor. Some schools provide endowed chairs or the rank of "university professor" for those they consider the most distinguished full professors. It remains to be proved whether such rankings (which usually carry not only increased salary and benefits but also other privileges as one ascends the scale) are the ideal approach. For now, it is what we all face.

Less formal structures for the same dynamic are found in the many other institutions in which we work. Outside of academia there are myriad opportunities for professional growth and far less limited paths. Nonetheless, there are usually informal ways in which hierarchy is maintained despite some concerted efforts to socialize responsibilities and make work places more horizontal.

Promotion can be as capricious as **tenure**, as subject to the whims of colleagues and committees, administrations and budgets. In an ideal world, promotion would be based on the achievement of certain well-specified criteria, the accomplishment of a certain degree of **professional development** commensurate with rank. Promotion to associate can carry with it tenure; sometimes it does not. Sometimes long-term service will be enough to garner a full professorship, often not. Women are often reluctant to apply for promotion at the same rates that men do; institutions should be aware of such disparities and try to remedy them. There is little rhyme or reason in this system beyond what each institution determines. Preparing for promotion reviews (see **Evaluations, annual**) is essential. Keeping good records (see **Files**) and balancing your work according to the formula prescribed by your institution (see **Service** and **Institutional analysis**) makes the task much easier.

Know that promotions are like grades, subject to the prudential judgment of the ones making it, often with little recourse. Do not be afraid to appeal a blatantly unfair call. While it may not get you the promotion, it will at least force those who made the decision to be forthright about why. Such a process can help you prepare for the next time, and/or reveal such entrenched biases that the only promotion you want is out the door. Take into account that what you do has an impact on others so exposing the injustice, calling out the duplicity, or heralding the wonderful process are all important things to do.

Public Scholarship

All scholarship is public, but some is more popular and some is more specialized. The general tendency in academia has been to prioritize work geared to a small audience of fellow scholars and to underestimate and sometimes even demean scholarship aimed at a broader audience. These boundaries are shifting rapidly. Changes in the **publishing** marketplace make it unrealistic to expect every **dissertation** to appear as a specialized scholarly monograph, though so-called crossover **books** are difficult to publish as a newly minted scholar. However, online communication has changed how we share ideas. Social media make it possible for millions of people to read something at the push of a button. Television and web-based communication can bring the most erudite specialists into our midst along with the most pedestrian of comics. All of this requires careful discernment to know what is valuable and what is not, but the general fact that we can share knowledge way beyond what was possible even a decade ago is exciting. Women in religious studies are among those most successfully engaging in public scholarship.

Implications for publishing are equally amazing. While it used to be that writing a book was the best way to get ideas out, today a short blog can do the trick. People can respond in real time to new thoughts, helping scholars to share their ideas in concert with the needs and insights of a wide public. In some cases, scholars have successfully used blogs or more popular books to communicate their big insights, while also publishing in specialized journals for their scholarly colleagues. Others have found a popular blog or online presence has led to (rather than followed from) a book contract.

It remains tricky how to convey one's publications and media appearances on a CV (**Curriculum Vitae**). How will they will be evaluated (sometimes seen with disdain or jealousy) by peers? How to teach younger colleagues to bring the same rigor we expect in religious studies to every communication? There is plenty of work to do to bring standards into line with contemporary practices.

Publishing (see also Books; Journals)

Ours is a field that expects scholars to publish, whether books, journal articles, online materials, or in popular outlets. Women have made huge strides in this arena in the last twenty years, producing some of the best-selling and most widely translated materials in the field. Publishing remains a business deal, a way to get the word out while also generating a profit for increasingly fewer companies that are interested in our work. It has been a men's game, so women need to share with one another how it is done and to insist that publishers consider and promote women's work. The book displays at conferences, especially the **AAR** and **SBL Annual Meetings**, are good places to meet publishing representatives, and begin to develop relationships that will provide a face to go with your written work.

There are things to keep in mind about publishing as a business. First, it changes all the time. Editors change presses and companies are sold, merge, or close, so stay abreast of developments. Second, the press is interested in selling books; while academic presses will invest in obscure scholarly projects, they support themselves with books that sell. Hence, they are especially interested in "cross-over" books that are intellectually smart but can appeal to a wide, educated audience beyond a scholar's specialization. These are sometimes also called "high-end trade" books. Third, good writing is important. Graduate work militates against good writing and pushes toward academic-speak that simply does not work with a wide audience. Scholarly work is the backbone of graduate education, but it is not the heart of good writing. Content needs to be articulated in ways that an educated person who is not necessarily a specialist in the field can understand. Have an objective critic assess your work and give you honest feedback. You may need to unlearn some of what you learned in **graduate school** to communicate with a broad audience.

If you need writing help, consider taking a course in nonfiction writing or hire an editor to help you if you can afford it. Few presses provide adequate editing as editors are required to handle too many projects to do close work with authors. Do not count on the publisher to provide all the editing help you might need. Many successful authors would not think of publishing without a good personal editor, which, in days of old, might have been the professor's wife, who did it for free. As professional writers say, "There is no good writing, only good **editing**."

Your odds of finding a publisher are higher with presses that publish material similar to yours. Since you are the expert, you are the person who knows what the best books in your field are. Go to those publishers first. If yours is grouped with other books, they know they have an audience and can sell your book. The trick is selling your work to the publisher as different enough from the pack to elicit that audience's attention but similar enough that people know where to look for it.

Once you have a good idea for a book, or want to transform your dissertation into something that more than a few loyal friends will read, you need a cover letter, an outline and/or table of contents, and a sample chapter to send to a publisher. You will want to include some indication of the audience you intend to reach, other books that are published that compete with yours, and why your approach is unique and different. You can send this material to several publishers at once to get a sense of the market. But when one invites you to submit the full manuscript, or if you have one ready and decide to go that route instead of the more abbreviated one, be sure to send the full manuscript to only one publisher at a time. Check with other authors who have recently worked with that publisher about their experience. Some presses are much more heavy-handed about editorial control, which may be fine if this is your first project and you do not yet trust your own editorial skills. However, be careful about the press you choose and how much control you have. Things like cover and title are usually in the publisher's bailiwick. The book display at the AAR/SBL Annual Meetings is a good place to meet publishers and talk face-to-face about your projects.

Negotiating a contract, especially for a first book, is standard. Like all contracts, however, read it carefully before you sign. If you do not understand something, clarify before you sign. You might have a lawyer look it over. There are no get-rich-quick schemes in academic publishing. Just be sure who has the copyright, whether you are agreeing to right of first refusal for your next book, and whether you have input into the basics, such as cover, price, title, whether it will come out initially in paperback or hardcover, and whether they will publish an electronic edition (increasingly common).

Try to adhere to your agreed-upon deadline, but realize that few deaths will result if you are a little late. Better not to drive yourself mad, though extending the deadline is usually a one-time thing. Then just write it. Be sure to allow time for reading proofs, chasing down lost footnotes, and marketing. Fill out the author questionnaire carefully to be sure that people and publications you respect get review copies. Then enjoy the fruits of your labor. All writing can make a contribution.

When it comes time for tenure review, however, books are the most important thing, followed by peer-reviewed journal articles, and then anthology chapters, and finally book reviews (see **Reviews, book**). Consider setting yourself a yearly goal and then refuse politely other offers to write until/unless the projects fit into your timeline. You will find that if you are a successful writer, you will be asked frequently to contribute to anthologies, encyclopedias, and journals. It is hard to say yes to all such requests and still stay on track with other work. Consider turning all professional papers into articles, and/or collecting some of them for a volume. Other article ideas may be ultimately unfit for full scholarly treatment but exciting as provocative blog posts.

If you have good relationships with editors, you should introduce them to people whose projects you admire. Feel free to complain when they publish scholarship that is not up to snuff. If they are doing a good job with a series that involves feminist thought, point that out. If their author list is exclusively Christian and white, point that out too.

PWD, Status of People with Disabilities in the Profession Committee

The Status of People with Disabilities in the Profession Committee is part of the **AAR** structure. It works to ensure the full access of people with disabilities within the Academy. It develops programs and policies to advance their status within the profession. PWD encourages joint intellectual work among program units, sponsors special topics forums, and is responsible for providing accessibility information for the Annual Meetings. The Committee provides best practices for promoting the full inclusion of members with disabilities and participates in the formal **mentoring** program sponsored by the four committees of the AAR. If you are interested in the work of the committee, consider nominating yourself or someone else to serve.

Racism

Post–civil rights movements, racism has shifted from its ugly, overt manifestations to something less obvious and more sinister. It is important to recognize and name racism when it is directed against us, or when we ourselves, unwittingly or wittingly, participate in it, but it may be more difficult to detect or define. Racism is both systematic and subtle discrimination against and judgment of an individual based on identity with a particular racial group. It always has both an individual and an institutional manifestation.

How does racism look inside the academy? Racism is experienced in different ways. Sometimes it manifests itself as colleagues', administrations', and students' attempts to overlook race or to focus too much on it, colleagues treating one as if she/he were invisible or as if the only reason she/he is there is because of **Affirmative Action**. Invisibility can be a problem on and off campus. **Micro-Aggressions** are common and often go unanswered.

People who recognize you on campus may not say hello off campus. Racism happens in committee meetings and faculty meetings. For instance, a person of a minority group making a point may be met with silence while a person of a dominant racial group making the same point is affirmed. This happens for reasons of **sexism** as well. Women of color may need conversations and **professional development** for preaching and teaching in predominately white institutions since those institutions may be clear about one type of discrimination but clueless about another. For women of color, dynamics of racism, sexism, classism, and heterosexism are interlocking manifestations of oppression (see **Intersectionality**). They must be dismantled collectively.

Many students have never before had a teacher who is a woman of color and do not always respond easily to such a person in a position of authority. Some of us find that our colleagues make assumptions about what we are and are not prepared to teach. Our current curricula are often "white-washed" in ways that deny the contributions of persons of color just as for generations curricula have excluded women's knowledge. The goal is to do more than include one week on racial/ethnic minorities, but to fully integrate and appreciate the value of diverse perspectives. Because of this lack of attention to communities of color's scholarship, white colleagues do not always evaluate accurately the work of students and professors of color. Professors of color are sometimes labeled "harsh" when they require very rigorous standards. There are jokes and questions about **Affirmative Action**, the assumption being that affirmative action means the school has not hired the best. The problem is complex and resistant to change.

Because racism can be so subtle these days, (see **Micro-Aggressions)** it is difficult to know when one is contributing, however unwittingly, to a racist atmosphere. Thus, it is helpful if people of all racial/ethnic groups are open to dialogue about ways in which racism manifests itself and ways to eliminate it. Understanding the ways in which religious studies and religious traditions have been constructed racially helps to change them. It is important not to be defensive immediately if someone suggests that your words, deeds, or attitudes are racist. In confronting the racism of others, it is also important to acknowledge at the outset that they may not be aware of it. At the same time, when one is confronted with the complaint of having engaged in a racist exchange, it is important to be open to dialogue. If institutions are to reflect and plan for the value of diversity, we must be willing to engage in conversations on race, and we must not remain silent when faced with micro-aggressions or subtle acts of racial bias. Racial harassment policies are beginning to be defined and can be a good source of protection and/or redress.

REFERENCES AND RECOMMENDATIONS

Academic and professional recommendations and references are not precisely the same but have important things in common. For staff, it used to be pro forma that if you did a good job your supervisor would happily provide a letter of reference or serve as a phone reference when you looked elsewhere. If you did not perform very well, she/he might politely decline or write something quite tepid. Our increasingly litigious culture has changed this, especially in jobs beyond academia.

Now it can be hard to get a recommendation because employers fear legal suits regardless of the quality of your work. Know your organization's culture in this regard and plan accordingly.

For students and faculty the academic world still treats the letter of recommendation as part of the package, though it is not clear how long it will be before this changes. **Admissions** decisions are increasingly contested, and some people are understandably loath to get involved. Nonetheless, for now a letter of recommendation is still required for many academic moves, beginning with undergraduate admission, **graduate school**, and most teaching jobs, as well as **grants** and **fellowship** applications. One puzzles to imagine what will take its place but litigation is a powerful incentive not to commit much in writing.

If you are a student asking for letters of recommendation, be sure that your advisor and/or others who will perform this task for you know you well enough to write intelligently and to distinguish you from the many other students of their acquaintance. It is best to provide your recommenders with an up-to-date CV (see **Curriculum vitae**) and copies of the position descriptions. The same advice applies if you are a scholar asking a colleague to recommend you for a fellowship or a new position. Electronic submission for recommendations is standard at most places, and many have moved to dossier services, but if an application requires hard copies, provide addressed, stamped envelopes. Decide whether you want to waive your right to see the letters, as most schools will give you that option.

Do not assume that the recommender's fame is a substitute for a good letter. Be certain that your recommenders can write good letters under the deadline constraints. A well-written, nuanced letter from a midrange colleague or scholar can be much more effective than a hastily dashed-off paragraph from a senior scholar too busy to take the necessary care. If you are uncertain about confidential letters in your placement file, you may be able to ask your advisor or someone else on the faculty whom you trust to look them over. They cannot tell you the content of the letters, but they can recommend that you remove one or more and find other recommenders.

If you are the one writing recommendation letters, be honest but strategic. The frank fact is that writing a letter that does not convey much enthusiasm for a student is worse than telling the student to find someone else to write it. Readers on committees spot such letters right away. Likewise, be sure that you do not use some formula that could apply in general terms to many students. Be quite detailed about the individual involved. Otherwise, committees that read your letters often will discount them eventually. Never have a student write the letter and you sign it. Some well-known professors who are asked frequently to write letters have turned to this model, to the chagrin of their students, who accept it in lieu of a better offer. It helps no one and compromises the integrity of letters of reference, as well as the individual using such shortcuts.

We need to preserve the integrity of this system, neither inflating our students to get them into graduate school nor writing bogus letters for students we hardly know just because they think our official stationery will look good. Only then can we rely on one another for the kind of candid assessment that other employers seek all the time lest they hire someone who is not right for the job. Professionals reading such letters become adept at spotting vague, hyperbolic praise and appreciate those that come with thoughtful, specific, honest assessments.

What about whether and for whom to write letters? Some students assume that women will be pushovers. We often feel bad for students who approach us at the last minute, despite the fact that they have had plenty of time. One question to ask yourself when a student approaches you with a request that seems unreasonable: Would he or she approach Male Colleague X with this request? Feel free to set a policy: you only write for students that you have taught in two courses or one seminar; you require one month's notice; you don't write for undergraduates when you are on leave; or whatever works for you to feel comfortable in the process. Adjunct faculty disagree about whether to write letters for students: some see it as an important service and a barometer of their connections with students, while others see it as an unreasonable demand on their time, given that they are only being paid for classroom teaching. There is no right answer, since both are true.

RELATIONSHIPS

No magic wand here, just a quick word about the fact that all of us have relationships with our work colleagues. The question is how to live them out with integrity while being women in religious studies, given the sexist, racist, heterosexist, and colonialist assumptions that reign. For example, how does a single, heterosexual woman date someone in her immediate circle without having her personal life influence her first-year performance review? Or, how does a woman of color on a small campus develop her social life without having that fishbowl feeling? Can a lesbian woman have a commitment ceremony without fearing the loss of her job at a conservative school?

There are no easy answers, and many women have spent their professional lives trying to make it easier for others. Our campus environments are heteronormative and couple normative, so being in a primary relationship and just what type of relationship you choose may be more than just campus gossip.

Remember some basics. First, your right to privacy is guaranteed by the U.S. Constitution, so do not feel any need to share your personal life in an interview, a faculty meeting, or anywhere else where you do not feel safe, comfortable, and/or motivated. Second, intimate relationships with peers are subject to careful negotiation and discretion. Dating someone in your department may be more complicated than it is worth. However, it is not illegal or immoral, but subject to extreme caution. Third, relationships with students or those you supervise are deeply discouraged if not forbidden. They are simply too front-loaded with power dynamics that are difficult to change. If they occur, be sure they are public so that scandal is not a factor (also, making a relationship public may be a good way to discourage it if it is inappropriate) and that the conditions of power (for example, if you are the professor) change. That is a hard one, but it guards against inappropriate favoritism, and/or recriminations if the relationship ends. No one can grade or evaluate a person fairly with whom s/he is in an intimate relationship. Again, it is much better to avoid such boundary-crossing relationships; there are other fish in the sea (see **Professional ethics**). If the relationship is worth pursuing, it is worth delaying until the student is no longer under one's supervision. Enjoying cordial professional relationships, indeed, developing lifelong friendships with colleagues is one of the perks of this business. Enjoy them carefully.

Religious Belief and Observance

One need not believe in God, G_d, G*d, Godde, Goddess, or the Divine to work as a scholar of religion; some prominent figures in the field are atheists or agnostics. But in some specialties and some institutions, **Christian hegemony** means that some women have paid a high price for their public agnosticism, atheism, and/or belief in Goddesses. There is a subtle pecking order here, too, with Christianity on top, then Judaism, followed by Hinduism, Buddhism, Islam, and on to the many other traditions, with pagan and Wiccan folk toward the bottom. This is a regrettable phenomenon, one rendered ridiculous by the growth of religious pluralism of an increasingly globalized world. On the other hand, observant members of various faiths have had questions raised about their ability to do "objective" scholarship. The reality is that quality work in religious studies is done by believers and nonbelievers, practitioners and nonpractitioners from a variety of traditions.

Religious studies departments and seminaries/schools of theology are quite different environments in this respect, and cultures within each will vary. Some departments have quite a few religiously observant faculty members and others do not. In some places, it is understood that a given faculty member will get class substitutes during the Jewish high holidays, another will abstain from coffee and cookies when the faculty meeting is held during Ramadan, and one Mormon colleague won't drink coffee at all. The place of religious expression in our work will vary depending on the setting (see **Institutional analysis**). It is always inappropriate to expect that everyone believes as you do or to engage in public prayer as if that were the case. It is always appropriate to expect reasonable and respectful accommodations for your religious practice (or nonpractice). As the world becomes increasingly diverse religiously, we can reasonably expect academic institutions to become more welcoming too. Our efforts need to be trained on moving that process forward so that our field leads rather than follows.

RELIGIOUS STUDIES

Religion is a topic that everyone thinks they know something about. Beware of mentioning your field of study on airplanes! This may be a product both of the view that religion has to do with personal experience and the difficulty that many people have with thinking about its social dimensions. Rather than considering religion in terms of the social relations that produce both religious practices and religion as a category of study, many assume that religion is the most ancient of all human endeavors, that "from time immemorial man [sic] has been religious." The category of "religion" and the discipline of "religious studies," however, are the product of a specific historical process: to wit, colonialism. The concept of religion as a category was developed at the moment of cultural contact produced by European exploration and colonialism. This category could then be deployed in various ways in service of the colonial project. At different historical moments, indigenous practices were seen as the same as/different from/incommensurate with the emergent European idea of religion.

Thus, in thinking about the field of religious studies today, it is necessary to situate the field in this historical context and to consider the social effects produced by taking up "religion" as an object of study. For example, if the course that serves as an introduction to religion is taught as an introduction to and comparison of canonical scriptures, then the teaching of religion becomes inscribed in the colonial project of establishing and reifying canons of writing. Another example would be the phenomenological approach, in which human experiences and or behaviors are divided into categories such as myth, ritual, the holy, sacred, and profane, cosmology, ethics, and practice. This approach establishes a unified notion of the human that serves as the fundamental basis for comparison. These types of comparisons are often implicated in hierarchies in which some persons or cultures are put down for alleged failure to measure up to the standard of the fully human.

Religious studies is most often taken to be the overarching name for an interdisciplinary field of study that incorporates fieldwork, textual and literary studies, historical inquiries, and ethical and theological writing. Unlike fields such as English or history, there is no single disciplinary method that defines the field of religious studies. In fact, the study of religion is taken up in various institutional settings and transgresses academic boundaries. Depending on the institutional setting, scholarship, training, and teaching in religious studies might be formulated as "religion," as "theology or thealogy," as "the history of religions," as "professional training," as "philosophy," as "humanities," as "ethics and values," as "comparative religions"—all to different conceptual, ideological, and social effects. Religion is an interdisciplinary field of study that is also transnational. Transnational studies, like religious studies, can produce varying effects. Transnational studies have been taken up as both the cutting edge of progressive efforts to de-center European studies and as the institutionalization of neoliberal globalization that reinscribes the United States and Europe as the centers of world affairs.

Religious studies were not a central part of much university life in the United States until the 1960s, when the Supreme Court made a distinction between "teaching religion" (for example, propagating the Christian faith) and "teaching about religion." This decision allowed state-funded educational institutions to take up the study of religion, but the 1960s was also a time when many intellectuals lived in the expectation of the triumph of secularization. Women's studies in religion began at this time. Changes in geopolitics, however, particularly the Iranian Revolution in 1979 and the rise of the Christian Right in the United States, moved religious studies more to the center of academic life.

These shifts were accompanied by the emergence in the academy of multiculturalism. Multiculturalism indexes, if it does not always recognize, the importance of religion as a multivalent subject. At the beginning of the twenty-first century, religion has become a popular topic of study. The study of religion is taken up in different types of departments—anthropology, area studies, literature, history—in fact, virtually any department in the humanities and social sciences, and perhaps even the physical sciences as the religion/science dialogue deepens. This development of religion as an object of study across the university testifies to the importance of religious studies as a field, but it can also erode the contours of the conversations that constitute the field. People who are trained in religious studies must converse with colleagues across the disciplines in order to make work that has been done in the academic study of religion visible. Women have been leaders in this effort and continue to demonstrate through creative scholarship how it can be done more effectively.

One lurking problem is **Christian hegemony** in the study of religion in the West. Guard against replicating it in conversations. It is all too easy to apply Christian categories to many other traditions that do not necessarily fit the pattern.

REM, Status of Racial and Ethnic Minorities in the Profession Committee

The Status of Racial and Ethnic Minorities in the Profession Committee is part of the **AAR** structure. It recommends policies and practices to ensure the full access and academic freedom of persons from racial/ethnic minority groups within the Academy. It develops programs to enhance their status in the profession. REM encourages joint intellectual work among the various race and ethnicity-focused program units, sponsors Special Topics Forums and workshops, and holds a reception at the Annual Meeting to encourage **networking** and deepen relationships. REM has also published the *AAR Career Guide for Racial and Ethnic Minorities in the Profession* (https://www.aarweb.org/node/135). If you are interested in the work of the committee, consider nominating yourself or someone else to serve.

RETIREMENT

It seems remarkable that so many women are now facing retirement in our field. This is not because women do not retire, but because a generation ago there were so few who reached that stage that it was hardly the subject of discussion. Now retirement plans and options, **emerita** status, and *Festschriften* are regular concerns for women, as they should be. Just as women are still often discriminated against in **hiring**, **promotion**, and **tenure**, there are problems with retirement as well.

The major stumbling block is income differential, a result of unequal pay (sometimes resulting from hiring discrimination, including women's disproportionate inclusion in adjunct ranks, or slower promotion), numerous leaves for family and personal reasons that fall disproportionately on women, and lack of proper financial planning (see **Money management**). This is especially true for women of color and lesbian, bi, trans, queer women whose lack of access to white male money makes a significant, compounded difference over time. All of these require correction long before retirement time.

The year before retirement is the time to be sure all loose ends are tied up. Check to see that medical and other benefits are in order, and use any that will expire with the contract. It is the time to negotiate any post-employment benefits, such as an office, library privileges, or secretarial help. It is also the time to get one's own materials in order so that the move from an office can also be, if desired, a time to deposit things in an **archive**. Then enjoy the celebrations. Mark the next academic year's beginning with a good **vacation**. After that is a fine time to begin the next career (one colleague has since become a wonderful painter, for example), take up that long-ignored manuscript again, and otherwise continue to contribute to the field from a position of wisdom.

We have seen cases where progressive women have been eased out of their jobs prematurely. Tactics include legal wrangling or veiled offers to elevate them to nonteaching status for their own good— really ways to get them out the door. Beware such tactics, negotiate early and often, and use your lawyer wisely if problems occur.

Reviews, Book (see also Publishing)

Book reviews are a common way to analyze and communicate the content and analysis of a recently published volume. Writing them is part of the expectation of our field, a form of publication that "counts" in one's tally for **tenure**. At research universities, reviews are typically counted as **service**. Book reviews are often done for scholarly **journals**, but there are also online forums in which your review will be accessible to a larger audience. If you think a scholarly book should be more widely known, you can use your networks to recommend it by writing a review or blog post that situates the particular scholarly argument within its broader context and explains why those interested in particular contemporary topics ought to consult it. You can also review books at online booksellers.

Several rules of thumb apply here. For journal reviews, only request and review books you are confident you can handle objectively. Choose books that you deem important, not simply ones that come your way from publishers. Do not use the occasion to promote your own work. Summarize the contents, provide your opinion of its importance, and sign off. Reserve strong negative judgments for books that may be dangerous or misleading; in other cases offer careful critical comments with appreciation for what you do like. Without attention to such ground rules, reviewing can become an ugly and competitive business. There was a case of a feminist reviewing another feminist's work that led readers to conclude, "She wants her job." It was not pretty.

This is not to suggest that one ought to suspend critical judgment. To the contrary. The job of a reviewer is not to sell books, but to orient readers as to which ones are worth reading for them. Common courtesy and fair play go a long way toward encouraging all of us to do our best work.

When your book is reviewed, do not take comments too seriously, whether the review is good, bad, or indifferent. It is easy to feel flattered by a spate of good reviews. It is even easier to be deflated and depressed by one line in one review that strikes you as unfair or gratuitous. In any case, reviews are opinions, to which all are entitled, right or wrong as they may be!

SABBATICALS—SEE LEAVES, BENEFITS

The historical concept of a sabbatical is agricultural in nature. The land and people need rest periodically. For regular faculty, it is customary that after (usually) six years of work in an institution, you may be eligible for such a wonderful time. It can be part of one's employment contract (see **Benefits**; **Negotiation**) and is intended as an opportunity for rest and refreshment, a chance to write and retool. Sabbatical time clocks vary by institution. Additional leaves and shorter times between sabbaticals can occasionally be negotiated at the time of a job offer (or counter-offer). In practice, the sabbatical (it can be a semester or a year) is typically used to write a book, or engage in some research project related to teaching. Many people like to get away physically as well as emotionally from their institution. Consider a house swap or a stint abroad. Others stay on-site but hidden away from the usual committee, classroom, and advising demands. The biggest temptation, and women are often put upon in this regard, is to do "just a little" work, attend "just one or two" meetings, serve on "just this last" dissertation defense committee. Don't do it! You will regret it. Enjoy your sabbatical; you earned it, and you will not get another one for six more years.

SBL

The Society of Biblical Literature (www.sbl-site.org) is **AAR**'s companion organization for annual meetings. But its specific focus is, as the name implies, to "advance the critical investigation of the Bible from a variety of disciplines." Scholars in the SBL engage biblical studies in a number of areas, including—but not limited to—literary, historical, sociological, ideological, and textual studies. The SBL plays a role in developing technology, research, **publishing**, and communication for members, and offers a large number of electronic resources. One of its most important functions is to coordinate the **SBL Annual Meeting**. Of particular interest to women in religion are the following sections: Feminist Hermeneutics of the Bible; Gender, Sexuality, and the Bible; Recovering Female Interpreters of the Bible; and Women in the Biblical World. As with the AAR, SBL members can get involved with organizational governance as well as scholarly exchange.

SBL Annual Meeting

The SBL Annual Meeting shares time and space with the AAR Annual Meeting (see **AAR Annual Meeting).** It provides an opportunity for SBL members to share their research through scholarly presentations and seminars, to identify new publications in their field of interest through the joint book/software exhibit, and to build networks of colleagues and **allies**. The SBL Annual Meeting format is like that of the **AAR**—lectures, workshops, and panels, plus receptions and other social events. Job interviews are handled through the jointly-managed Employment Center (www.aarsbl.org).

SBL International Meeting

To promote the exchange of ideas in an international forum, the SBL has a meeting outside of North America in such places as Europe and Asia. All are invited to attend and to give papers. Be prepared for presentations in European languages with and without translation. This is a good opportunity to meet international biblical scholars and to broaden your cultural horizons. The meeting is usually held between the end of June and the middle of August. Program units of particular interest to women include issues related to biblical women, feminist interpretations, and gender criticism.

SBL Regional

The **Society of Biblical Literature Annual Meeting**, like the **AAR Annual Meeting**, can be a little overwhelming for a newcomer. The eleven Regional meetings, held in the Central States, Eastern Great Lakes, Mid Atlantic, New England/E Canada, Rocky

Mountains—Great Plains, Southwestern, Upper Midwest, Pacific, Pacific Northwest, Midwest, and Southeastern regions, are sometimes less threatening and more accessible. Any **SBL** member may attend any of the regional meetings. They are a good place to make your first presentation and to develop **allies** outside of your institutions. The regional meetings offer a Regional Scholars Program that mentors junior scholars and offers practical assistance in securing a place for their work at the SBL Annual Meeting. Some regional meetings are held jointly with AAR regional meetings (see **AAR Regions**), but not all of them.

Self-Care (see also Health, Work/Life Balance)

Women are socialized to put others first. We tend to counsel gentleness and self-care for others, while neglecting ourselves. Yet self-care is vital for all women, whether graduate student or professor **emerita**, nonprofit executive or classroom teacher. This means paying strict attention to physical health, emotional well-being, and spirituality, or, as one colleague put it, "Paying ourselves first."

Privilege is a major factor in work/life balance. Sure, all of us can learn how to say no, put exercise first, eat healthily, get plenty of rest, and set up date nights. But race, class, sexual orientation/identity, age, ethnicity, etc. play pivotal roles in our options and whether we can exercise them. This does not mean that only privileged women can live balanced lives. Many do not. But colleagues who are loaded with **debt**, supporting parents as well as **children**, dealing with complex **commuting** arrangements, facing health challenges, and the like simply do not have the same luxury to decide whether they will start their day at the health club or end it with a massage. Taking care of oneself becomes one more item on an already too long to-do list. For many colleagues survival is the goal. Still, taking care is important.

One doctor's best advice for a healthy life was to choose one's parents! You cannot do much about your genes (yet), but you can make conscious choices about food and drink. Exercise is as much about time as energy. Just carving out that hour for a swim and sauna (many local YMCAs offer membership fees on an income-based sliding scale and some offer free child-care for members during workouts), or that half-hour brisk walk can be the difference between high energy and low, between tranquility and stress. And rest is the opposite of what most of us do most of the time. It takes a concerted effort to get your required hours at night and to take sustained time for **vacation**. The point is that there is no formula that works for everyone, just broad categories that you fill in according to your choices and possibilities.

Other choices are not purely individual but can originate from our suggestions. How about serving herbal tea instead of caffeine at meetings? Why not make a date to walk and discuss a book, or conduct some committee business outside? (Be sure to consider accessibility for colleagues with disabilities.) What about canceling that extra session and sharing the information later by email so everyone can take a nap? Good health is collective as well as individual business.

Academic work is largely self-generated, beyond the demands of the institution. Most of us entered the field because we had personal research interests, and staying alive in our careers depends on this self-generated activity. However, work can take over and consume too much time. Be sure to take time off regularly. Don't work all summer. Give yourself leisure time. If you find yourself on weekends giving guest lectures, finishing reports, grading exams, or leading retreats, find a way to take a day off midweek. Don't fall into the trap of working seven days a week all semester long. This is easy to do if you have a steady paycheck and money in the bank, harder when you have student loans and children's braces to pay for. But weighing how much we really need versus how much some of us have, the case for sharing more, and the recognition that even the earth rests for better production, are things to consider.

Mental health issues are stigmatized in our society. Part of our educational work is to undo that, showing that just as high blood pressure or diabetes can run in families, so too can depression, bipolar disorder, and other psychiatric problems. No one signs up for them; they are simply part of the genetic givens with which we work. But everyone can become educated about signs and symptoms, needs and treatments across the medical spectrum.

Emotional well-being is important. The conditions for it include safe and just working conditions, freedom from discrimination, and supportive colleagues. If any of those are missing, do not be surprised if you are on edge, stressed out, and heading toward burnout. Make a change if you can! If you are responsible for those conditions for others, monitor your situation and change it unless you want to be responsible for the downfall of your colleagues. Again, finances all too often dictate people's options, but trading off time for money can sometimes be the better choice, if you can afford it.

Spirituality is a common word in our business, but ironically, one many of us pay more lip service to than actually practice. Choices vary widely, but cultivating some spiritual practice, whether meditation, prayer, chanting, drumming, yoga, whatever chimes your bells, can be a good antidote to the stresses of professional life. Your practice may be sports—individual or team—or music, whether listening or playing. It may be theater or cooking, handicrafts or gardening. Whatever it is, make time for it, and help others make time for theirs, too, by taking self-care as seriously as you take professional development.

SENSITIVITY, RELIGIOUS

Growing religious pluralism in the field increases the need for sensitivity to various religious beliefs and practices. But beyond sensitivity comes active advocacy for a wider religious studies arena that decenters the **Christian hegemony** of the past and reconstellates the field with a wide variety of traditions, practices, texts, and practitioners to learn about and enjoy. There is no substitute for knowledge here. However, as one is acquiring it, there are many opportunities to break with the convention of the larger culture and acknowledge and/or celebrate other religious expressions. For example, Pagan, Wiccan, and Goddess colleagues are religious; practices, feast days, and customs that are important to them deserve to be recognized. Tribal and horticultural religions are just as valid and important as book-based ones.

On a practical level, Jews, Hindus, Buddhists, and Muslims do not appreciate being asked how their "Christmas vacations" were. Respect for various traditions may mean canceling classes on holidays that do not appear on most calendars and respecting dietary and ritual practices. Let's look at one example. More sensitivity is needed regarding Muslim colleagues, whose numbers are increasing rapidly in the field. Issues related to ritual prayers, food, the fasting month of Ramadan, and dress show how important it is to know something about other religions to be a respectful colleague.

Many Muslims are serious about making their obligatory prayers five times a day. Non-Muslims who are planning meetings, workshops, and conferences should be generally aware of the times of prayer and allow breaks of ten to fifteen minutes so those praying at the scheduled times can do so without missing meetings. Regarding dietary matters, most Muslims refrain from eating pork or anything cooked with pork and some eat only ritually slaughtered ("halal") meat. Therefore, planners for events where food will be served should make sure that neither pork nor pork products are served to Muslim participants and that there are alternatives. It is always safe to serve vegetarian meals. Vegetarian Hindus and religious Jews will appreciate this consideration as well. Observant Muslims avoid alcohol; nonalcoholic beverage alternatives should be served with meals or snacks.

During the lunar month of Ramadan, which slowly rotates through the Western calendar year, many Muslims observe the dawn to sundown fast, during which they refrain from all food and drink, including water. At sundown, when the fast is broken, provisions should be made for those who are fasting to leave the meeting or conference for a light meal and a prayer. The holiday called Eid al-Fitr occurs at the end of the month of Ramadan. Muslims celebrate Eid with prayers at a mosque (or, sometimes, a public park or hotel ballroom if the local mosque space is inadequate), feasting, and exchanging gifts. To be aware of this holiday in the life of a Muslim is important. Many will want to take this day off from work. In addition, if possible it is good not to schedule meetings or other events on the Eid. Muslim colleagues appreciate being greeted with "Eid Mubarak" or "Blessed Eid." Similarly, the other major Muslim holiday, Eid al-Adha, comes immediately after the pilgrimage. This Eid is an even larger celebration for Muslims, and most Muslims will want to be off on the day of the Eid, and perhaps spend one to three days with their families.

If Muslim women in the group cover their hair or wear other "Islamic clothing," it is inappropriate to comment on their dress or to ask them why they wear it, or even to bring the subject up unless the women raise the issue themselves. Many Muslim women do not cover their hair; it is equally inappropriate to ask why not. This sensitive personal and political matter requires care. Other faiths have equally important customs. We need to recognize the importance of understanding and respecting the range of beliefs and practices among us. This is part of religious studies as well as a part of good citizenship to live respectfully in a democratic, nondenominational culture in which having no religious practice/affiliation is a respected option.

SERVICE

Service is an amorphous category used to describe the many ways faculty members contribute to their institutions beyond the classroom and research/writing. This may include your function as the chair or member of a committee, your leadership in your department, your willingness to be the faculty sponsor for a student club, or your choice to live in a residence hall in a supervisory capacity. It may also include your work outside the institution in **professional associations**. It can even encompass your role as a religious professional, if that is related to your primary responsibilities as a teacher. Some institutions count some types of writing, such as scholarly book reviews, encyclopedia articles, and articles or books for general audiences, as "service" rather than "research" publications. Ask about norms at your institution to be sure that you are doing all that is expected.

The caution here is twofold: First, document all of your service. It will be useful for those pre-tenure annual reviews (see **Evaluations, annual**; **Tenure**). It is easy to spend a lot of time on a committee or a project and then forget about it completely when you are filling out the forms. Second, be sure to balance your service with your scholarship according to your institution's formula (see **Institutional analysis**). Because many women are used to doing three things at once, they tend to get overextended, interested in what is urgent, and run out of time for what is at least equally important but seemingly less pressing, namely, scholarship. Women of color, lesbians, and women with disabilities are particularly pressed into specialized service needs from serving on minority emphasis committees, to being expected to advise/mentor all students of "their" constituency, to serving on a committee so that it has "fair" representation. This is seldom fair to the workload of the minority group member. If you find yourself with extra institutional expectations, negotiate for a trade-off of other tasks. It is important to do your share, but you are not required to do more than your share. Don't be beasts of burdens for departments that ultimately rank service as a lesser value than scholarship or **teaching**, or for departments that need to hire more people to carry the load.

Service is important but those lucky enough to be on the tenure track must be aware that the tenure clock waits for no one; before you know it, you may have given generously of yourself with little to show in other areas in which you will be evaluated. There is nothing wrong with such generosity, per se. In fact, some of the very best professors find themselves in this situation, given urgent needs. However, it is not conducive to **promotion** and **tenure**, so be clear about your choices.

Sometimes our various communal homes require service from us that we are happy to provide whether that is talking with someone who has just come out, helping someone deal with a racial predicament, or acting as a public scholar for a community that has sustained us. Often these acts of service have no place in our tenure portfolio but they are moments that connect us in deep and true ways. While we cannot forget the ticking of the tenure clock, we also cannot be bound by it. It is our time to give and we should be able to make compromises to assist communities we really care about (see **Yes and no**).

Ultimately, it is up to you to be savvy in your service commitments. Serve where you place value and where your service is valued. Service is the role to which most women were socialized, and it is about time we got to shape it and choose it, not labor under unfair expectations related to gender.

Sexism

Some may suggest that a guide for women in religious studies is itself sexist. But sexism is not about focusing on women or men; instead, it is a form of discrimination, like **racism**, aimed at women because of their sex/gender. Of course, postmodern deconstructions of sex/gender render it difficult to say with certainty just which persons are women. It is increasingly easy to see where and how discrimination takes place, and transgender people are very often the objects of discrimination. But the larger point is that no one ought to be treated negatively because of their gender identity or sexual orientation.

The history of religious studies as a field is replete with examples of sexist behavior, including the relatively late entrance of women into the field, the continued prohibition on the full participation of women in many religious traditions (see **Ordination**), and the persistent recalcitrance on the part of some institutions to grant women full status as faculty. Lack of respect for parenting plays a role, of course. However, this guide is proof that efforts are underway to change all of that. The continued need for a guide at all is also proof that precious little progress has been made in comparison to what is needed. Men can learn from women's experience, new a custom as that may seem to some!

STAFF

Staff members are the backbone of any institution, including colleges and universities. They include support workers such as administrative assistants who basically run projects and departments. Also included are student personnel workers and those who provide services such as printing, janitorial services, information technology, food service, and the like in large institutions. Many of them are women, some underpaid and underappreciated but among the finest **allies** one will ever find. If we have made any advances as women in the field, surely it is because many secretaries and administrative assistants have run interference, tipped us off to institutional culture, and gone out of their way to give our work priority. Justice and good sense dictate that gains for women in the field begin with staffing. We can support those gains by supporting **unions** and living-wage efforts as well as by simply being conscientious about working conditions and personal interactions for all members of the team.

If one has become an administrator, supervision of staff comes with the job. This means regular performance **evaluations**, encouragement of professional staff, and creating a humane work environment. Many administrators find personnel issues among the most difficult and headache-inducing aspects of institutional leadership. It pays to know one's human relations staff and work closely with them. If working with many kinds of people is not your forte, then **administration** may not be for you. Many staff members long outlast their bosses, carry the institution's history, and are its heart and soul. They deserve respect and fair pay.

SPONSORING

A sponsor uses her professional networks, connections, or position to get a junior person connections or opportunities that she would not otherwise have. Some of these roles overlap with **mentoring**— facilitating introductions, for instance—but others involve suggesting the junior colleague's name as someone to give a lecture, write a book chapter, or present at a conference, for example. In some ways, this is just an extension of what good advisors do for their students and what we all should do in general terms for our colleagues. We all have our networks (see **Networking**) and are limited by whom we know. If you are well known as a scholar of religion, you probably get invitations that you cannot accept, but you can pass along the names of qualified junior people to invite instead. If you are white, make sure that people of color are among those you sponsor. (If you do not know junior colleagues of color, ask yourself why and then act to change the situation.) Acting as a sponsor for someone newer to the field to you can be a good way to increase the range of opportunities open to that person while giving you the chance to say "no" to invitations that would leave you overcommitted. (See **Yes and No**).

SWP, Committee on the Status of Women in the Profession

The Committee on the Status of Women in the Profession (https://www.aarweb.org/node/118) is a standing committee of the **AAR**. It concerns itself with the range of issues facing women. Its current project is a **work/life balance** guide that will examine issues women face achieving an integrated life. The Committee drafted the original AAR Sexual Harassment policy (**Appendix I**) and its grievance policy (**Appendix II**). Its chair serves on the Sexual Harassment Grievance Committee.

SWP has also been working on issues related to **mentoring**, using a variety of venues for this project, including the launch of an AAR-wide mentoring program and a lunch session at the Annual Meeting that is co-sponsored with Status of Racial and Ethnic Minorities (**REM**) in the Profession, where senior women scholars meet with students to provide ideas and advice. The Committee publishes a "Not for Women Only" feature in the online publication of *Religious Studies News*. It offers a question and answer format advice column, "Ask Academic Abby," (https://www.aarweb.org/publications/ask-academic-abby-january-2013). It has contributed graciously to the revision and republication of this *Guide*, originally published by the Committee in 1992 and reworked with its help in 2004.

SWP makes targeted efforts to coordinate with the **Women's Caucus** and program units of the AAR that focus on women in religion. It also collaborates with its partner committee in **SBL** through contacts and sessions at the **Annual Meeting**. It has advertised and monitored childcare at the Annual Meeting and is involved in assessing its success. SWP has devoted its Special Topics Forums at the Annual Meeting in recent years to increasing the visibility of feminist scholars in religion in discussions of issues of religion and public policy. The Committee also functions as a "watchdog" on gender issues related to initiatives of the AAR. Your input to SWP is welcome.

Syllabi

Designing your syllabi can be a terrific way to combat the multiple forms of oppression as well as to engage in **activism**. Your choice of texts and your **teaching** style make a difference. This is the time to check to be sure that there are articles and **books** by women and scholars of color on your reading lists. There are no courses on how to prepare syllabi in religious studies. The art must be developed by looking at models from courses you have taken (bad examples show you what not to do!) and/or work your colleagues are willing to share. The Wabash Center for Teaching and Learning in Theology and Religion (see **Resources**) maintains a database of syllabi. Remember, syllabi are like other academic materials. They belong to their authors. If they are published, they can be used like any other source, that is, with proper annotation.

A syllabus should make clear classroom policies about basic matters like office hours, grading, assignments, and expectations about student use of **inclusive language**. It should direct students with disabilities to your institution's policy for accommodations. It can also point students to other resources for their study of religion, including blogs (see **Resources**) or organizations. A useful syllabus outlines the general contours of a course but leaves enough flexibility for the course to flow with both student and faculty input throughout the semester.

Teaching

Teaching has historically been the most common work of those who train at the doctoral level in religious studies, though full-time teaching at one institution is increasingly difficult to find as a "first job" or otherwise. Teaching may be in a small or large institution, whether at the high school, undergraduate or graduate level. Many of the issues are the same: developing courses, deciding on grading, balancing the workload, and "growing" as a teacher. Teaching is a discipline and an art form all its own, beyond the actual content of the subject at hand.

You have a variety of role models as teachers. Your own style will come in time, but at the outset, it is intimidating to think about imparting information, much less knowledge, to groups of people who may or may not want it. Your best bet is to teach from your strengths—in terms of content and approach—insofar as your institution will permit. In fact, most first-year instructors must teach what needs to be taught regardless of their area of expertise. Depending on the institution and your type of appointment, you may not get much leeway in choosing your courses or even the readings you assign. Nevertheless, try to negotiate in order to teach at least one course in your main area of expertise. If you do not, you may falsely conclude that you do not care for teaching as much as you thought, when in fact what you do not like is teaching what someone else thinks students need to know.

The first year can be difficult as one learns both the ropes of an institution and a lot about oneself as a teacher. Most common mistakes include putting too much material on the syllabus or taking on too much work on top of the required course load, something to which women are especially prone given our socialization. People of color are often pressured as well by institutions anxious to show their newfound diversity (see **Tokenism, Service**). Taking on too much is an easy mistake to make because we all want to make a good first impression and show ourselves to be team players. But it will inevitably backfire as the constraints of time and energy make learning the difference between "yes" and "no" (see **Yes and no**) vital. Burnout is epidemic among first-year teachers, enthusiasm notwithstanding.

Realize that course development takes time. You may begin with a general concept, some bibliography and ideas, but by the second or third time through you will find that the course will take shape in ways you never imagined at the outset. Rely on colleagues to review your work and make suggestions. Student evaluations will help, too (see **Evaluations, student**). The Wabash Center (see **Resources**) maintains a database of **syllabi** that you might consider for ways to make your course more innovative.

Grading is a vexed problem that goes along with teaching. There are many good ways to provide useful feedback to students—commentaries on their written work, individual meetings, and evaluation of group and/or individual projects. However, when it comes to assigning a letter or numerical grade, comparing students with one another and/or against a norm, the fun stops, and the work begins. A few institutions have dispensed with this ritual entirely, relying instead on Pass/Fail or a similar option. At the other extreme are institutions that expect their professors to correct for the recent grade inflation by grading on a curve. There is no easy solution, especially since students tend to see grades as reward or punishment rather than as evaluative tools.

Women faculty especially are sometimes put upon by students, sometimes even by administrators (for example, when an athlete's eligibility is in question), to "adjust" grading, to put it delicately. Resist this with all your might. Despite the vagaries of grading, your integrity and power are at stake. Consult your chairperson, dean, and/or ombudsperson for advice on how to handle these difficult matters. But know that you have the final word when it comes to your course.

Be aware that we are now teaching in a consumer-driven classroom where students expect certain outcomes for their tuition dollar. As a result, students can be more confrontational when corrected or when their expected outcome is not achieved. This may be expressed through negative teaching evaluations (see **Evaluations, student**) or through direct threats of violence or retaliation. In our feminist classrooms where we seek to create egalitarian communities, what is your expected level of decorum and respect from students who are not your equals in knowledge (but may feel that they are) but are at the very least co-learners? How does feminist emphasis on egalitarianism confront students' tendencies to devalue female authority? These are issues worth discussing with peers as you develop your own classroom environment.

Another serious concern for all teachers is how many and what sorts of courses they can or must offer. Check this carefully in your contract, as workloads vary from institution to institution. See if you are expected to teach in a January session or in the summer; if you can choose in which semester you will carry a heavier load; and if you get a reduction for your administrative, committee, and/or research work. Bargain hard. Everyone else does (see **Contracts**; **Negotiations**).

Still another concern for those who teach is how to keep from getting stale, how to keep learning when the time demands of teaching are so enormous. This is not an easy matter, but attending the Annual Meeting of the AAR and SBL (see **AAR Annual Meeting**, or **SBL Annual Meeting**) or other professional meetings is a good start. So, too, is attending a summer seminar in your field, such as the offerings in bioethics or on teaching itself. Consider attending internal or external teaching workshops sponsored by your institution or places like the Wabash Center. This is especially important if you are moving into online teaching and need some new skills.

Many institutions are offering online or hybrid classes, a natural outgrowth of increased availability of technology. Such classes vary in format and may include online video and/or audio lectures, online discussion sessions, and the like. Proficiency in teaching technologies can range from the ability to load and download documents into Blackboard, Desire2Learn, Moodle, Angel, etc., to utilizing clicker student response systems in class, to blogging, using YouTube, or tweeting as a classroom tool, to instructing an entire course virtually. Increasingly, institutions of higher education are going paperless requiring students and faculty to use paperless systems to register for classes, submit work, do evaluations, and transmit grades. This is especially true of institutions participating in the Massive Open Online Courses (see **MOOCs**). Familiarity with a variety of online systems can give you an edge on the job market that highly values online learning. It can also save you untold amounts of time in the teaching.

Still another means of refreshment built into the system of teaching is a leave (see **Benefits, leaves**) and/or a sabbatical (see **Sabbaticals**), which are part of many academic contracts. In other lines of work, such as usually lower-paid nonprofit positions or in ministry, it is even more important to negotiate such benefits because burnout is a constant worry and a forty hour week is a thing of the past.

Teaching may be your lifetime work, or it may be something you do for a few years and then decide it is for someone else. Whatever the results, consider it one of the privileged forms of labor because of its value opening minds up to new possibilities.

Teaching, Assistantship /Research Assistantship

Graduate students are often called on as a condition of their funding to serve as part-time teaching or research assistants.

A job as a teaching assistant (sometimes called a teaching fellow, tutor, or class assistant) is an interesting position. While some professors approach it as a practicum, an opportunity for you to learn and exercise your pedagogical style, others use you to get their own work done. Your power is provisional and contingent. The expectations vary from course to course; the subject matter may be more or less familiar making your job that much harder. The grading you do must accord with not only your own sensibility, but even more so with what the professor wants. You may only run discussion sections or you may be expected to lecture several times.

Learn whether the department or the institution or both have stated guidelines about this role. Become familiar with your rights and responsibilities, and the length of duty. Your job will be infinitely easier if you can work cooperatively and communicate clearly with the professor with whom you are working and other teaching fellows, if any, assigned to the same course. Before the course begins, schedule an appointment to discuss and clarify expectations. If you run into trouble, learn whom you can ask for assistance (the chair of the department, the dean, and your advisor). This may be your only "formal" training as a teacher before you are unleashed in front of a class on your own, so take advantage of it.

Working as a research assistant may involve only mundane tasks like photocopying or hunting down library resources. But it might also involve doing a literature review, informational interviews, or other more complex tasks that help build your own research skills. Learning with a seasoned researcher can be a huge help as you take on your own projects.

Both teaching and research opportunities are great preparation for an academic career. But be honest if you do not like the work. Take it as a hint about your future and pursue something else. If you do like it, consider it a prelude to a satisfying career.

Tenure

Tenure is that much-disputed and seemingly endangered custom of granting lifelong employment to those members of a faculty or organization who meet the requirements of that institution. The tenure system is intended to protect **academic freedom**. It can guarantee creative people a place to work without fear of firing, but it can also keep the proverbial deadwood in place for years on end. Tenure continues to be considered the "logical" outcome of a traditional academic career, from secondary and undergraduate levels through the doctorate, to the first job and then tenure, though the hiring crisis and the increasing use of adjuncts means it applies to fewer jobs than it once did. While it is a plum of sorts, be clear that there are many other satisfying and equally useful ways to do your work than in lockstep system that excludes more than it includes.

There are pros and cons to a tenure system. For now it is entrenched in higher education—though it applies to a far smaller proportion of faculty than it used to. The security it provides is not absolute, however. Since one of the few ways to dismiss tenured faculty is to dissolve a department or program, some institutions under severe financial constraints may do so. Those with marginalized fields of knowledge are "streamlined" out, leaving those who do "traditional" scholarship untouched at the core of the curriculum.

Of women who teach, relatively few are fully tenured faculty members. The process involves an exhausting compilation of one's work, letters of reference from outside reviewers, recommendations from one's department, assessment by one's peers, student evaluations, and usually a decision by a Promotion and Tenure Committee that is then presented to the institution's highest board or committee, or perhaps to the president, for final action. Bias against women can creep into the process at any stage; however, the increased number of female associate and full professors means that more women are likely involved in the process of reviewing female candidates' tenure files. The same is true for people of color. And in both instances the presence of women and people of color is no guarantee that people like them will get a leg up. But at least there is a larger pool of people to consult for advice.

Preparing for tenure is very much like preparing for an annual review (see **Evaluations, annual**), but cumulative. Be sure to file all relevant papers—records of classes taught, lectures given, service to the institution, outside service, publications, and the like. copies of your annual reports will help. **Networking** within your institution will help you gauge realistically where you stand. Networking beyond your institution will give you a good list of people who could write to vouch for your work, although institutions prefer that outside reviews come from people in your field who know your work but with whom you are not acquainted or, at the very least, who can provide an "arms-length" evaluation. Letters of support can come from anyone. Some universities and colleges are careful to solicit letters of support from programs and departments with which professors have worked, even if they are not the tenure-granting department. This is vital for candidates whose work is interdisciplinary, as in **women's studies.**

Despite the painstaking preparation, deserving candidates are sometimes denied tenure. For example, some elite universities are known for turning down some of the very best scholars (who often go on to greater glory and/or tenured positions in other institutions). One question is whether it is better to try for tenure and be turned down, or to accept the handwriting on the wall if it is clear you will not get it. Another question is how quickly you need to look for another job if you will not try for tenure. Still another question is how to appeal negative tenure decisions. All of these issues vary according to institutions as well as individual dispositions. They require your best consultation with trusted colleagues, and a good employment lawyer. Remember that tenure is not the be-all and end-all of your career. Many of our best and brightest will have several careers; perhaps none of them will be tenured jobs.

Once you have tenure, you may discover that it is not a panacea (see **Midcareer issues**). Nonetheless, it will give you some leverage when you look for another job, as well as peace of mind where you are. Congratulations, and use your tenured position to make change!

Tenure Track Jobs

Tenure track jobs are not quite as rare as unicorns, but they constitute a small and decreasing percentage of academic jobs, including in religion. They do exist, and are understandably coveted by many, but most graduates of doctoral programs will not get them.

These are the basics: Once upon a time, most academic appointments were tenure-track, with standard time-frames (typically six or seven years) and promotion scales attached: untenured assistant professor, tenured associate professor, tenured full professor. This is no longer the case. Many academic jobs are contingent, from term to term, and pay by the course; others are short term, one year or two year appointments with titles like "lecturer" or even "visiting assistant professor," but without expectation of continued employment, adequate benefits, or promotion. These are the economically driven realities of contemporary higher education that incoming graduate students and outgoing graduating students need to acknowledge. Happily, there are many other ways to put your degree in religious studies to use.

If you are lucky enough to get a tenure track job—and note that while merit plays a role, so do privilege, prejudice, and sheer chance—be sure to read the **faculty handbook** and familiarize yourself with the expectations and culture of the institution. For example, research universities will differ significantly from community colleges in what they expect of their faculty. There is plenty of advice for female academics (see **Bibliography** and **Resources**) that applies to religious studies in general as well.

TOKENISM (SEE ALSO RACISM; SEXISM)

Tokenism exists in all the places where **racism**, **sexism**, and other forms of discrimination lurk. It is the practice, however unconscious, of choosing (read: using) people to create the appearance of diversity when indeed power structures have not changed one whit. For example, hiring one person of color in an academic department of twenty is tokenism.

Women, especially women of color, know a lot about it. We are becoming increasingly savvy about how to use it to our advantage, for example, setting boundaries for our colleagues who seek a minority presence for "photo opportunities only." We may insist that no one woman/person of color/person with disabilities/**LGBTIQ** person/person of faith will be expected to advise only students of that same background, or demand that our subspecialty be integrated into the curriculum rather than the subject of an annual invited lecture. Religious studies remain fraught with tokenism on many levels, a vestige of liberalism that we are in the process of eradicating. You can help.

TRANSGENDER (SEE **LGBTIQ**)

Increasing numbers of people are finding that the gender assigned to them at birth and the gender in which they feel most comfortable differ. Options, including cross-dressing and reassignment (what used to be called "sex change operation" and is sometimes now called "gender affirmation surgery"), exist to lessen this dissonance, and increasing numbers of people are choosing them. Others identify as gender-queer and do not consider themselves male or female. The important thing is to let people define themselves and respect the definition they choose.

Some people will transition from living as a man to living as a woman, or from living as a woman to living as a man. Transition, as the name implies, is a process that takes time. It can be very expensive, especially if health insurance does not cover the hormones and surgeries that some people choose. It is life transforming in ways nontrans people can only imagine. Usually it results in a person's vibrant new enthusiasm for life in a new form, a kind of renaissance that unleashes creativity and energy. But the road can be rocky and the obstacles enormous.

There is much to learn and still more to teach to bring religions into line with the people who practice them. Those of us who research and teach can further knowledge among our colleagues and students about the range of ways cultures and religious traditions have understood sex and gender. Some traditions recognize a third gender; others have sophisticated legal mechanisms for dealing with intersex individuals. Appreciating these diverse ways of approaching sex/gender systems helps remove the illusion of inevitability for contemporary Western arrangements.

The gift of trans people to the world is our common understanding of the range of ways there are to be human, and the importance of letting each and every person decide for her or himself, with community support. We are far from this ideal, but with supportive colleagues, we can move in the right direction on this basic human right.

Travel Tips

Travel can be a perk of **privilege**, but it is also a fact of life if one is involved in education. Work-related travel is slightly more complicated than getting from here to there, especially for those with disabilities. It involves cost, choices, convenience, safety, and the unexpected. Whether for a job interview, a professional meeting, a guest lectureship (see **Guest lectures)**, research, or just plain **vacation**, getting there is half the fun for women on the road. It can also be dangerous, inconvenient, or completely baffling for people who do not do it regularly. These tips are an effort to alleviate some of that, especially for women for whom so much of the rigors of travel are made even more so.

Travelers have many choices—plane, train, car, bus, bike, and walking. Be sure to factor all of the time involved before you decide. For example, flying can take more time than taking the train when you figure in the airport waiting time and ground transportation. Bus or subway will usually be cheaper than a cab and can sometimes be faster. Your time is worth money when it comes to travel. Consider it when you decide on the cheaper ticket with a stop versus the nonstop that costs a bit more. Likewise, think seriously if you really want to drive a long distance or whether your time is better spent working on a plane or train. Consider the real possibility of traffic problems or car trouble. The anxiety may not be worth trade-off of having a car where you are going.

If you are travelling as a guest—to a job interview, for a lecture, etc.—the first point to ascertain is who pays for the travel. Be clear with the host institution or your own department as to which of them is paying. Check the rules governing travel. Stick to those rules. Few institutions pay for first class so book coach unless told otherwise. Keep all receipts for reimbursement or do not expect to see your money again. Institutions have accountants and accountability. If you are invited to use the institution's travel agency, jump at the chance. It will save you hours on the Internet and will probably mean that you will not have to expend your money to be reimbursed. More likely, you will have to buy the ticket yourself. If it is a financial hardship for you to pay for the ticket and wait for what can be an eternity for a department to reimburse you, do not be afraid to say so and get your money up-front. Or ask the host to make the arrangements and send you the ticket. They invited you, after all.

Safety is a major issue especially for women who travel alone. Would that it were otherwise, but always leave your destination phone number with a friend, family member, or with someone in your office. Get in the habit of calling someone when you arrive so at least one person knows where you are at all times. Your cell phone is a lifeline. Use it. Choose hotel floors with care, balancing the risk of high floors against the possibility of ground floor problems. Your room number should be confidential. Be sure your room key does not have the number written on it, in case you lose it. Ask for another room if the room clerk inadvertently broadcasts it in the lobby!

There is no preparation for the unexpected, but it will happen. Common sense dictates avoiding the last flight of the night, which studies show is cancelled more often than an earlier one. Know your options for earlier flights. Sometimes business finishes early and you can get home what will seem like a whole day early even if it is just a matter of hours. Tuck away some cash for a rainy day on the road when the ATM is out of commission. A GPS is invaluable for moving around, even for walking around an unfamiliar campus. Your smart phone will be your best friend. Travel as lightly as possible; a roll-on suitcase that fits in the overhead bin is essential. You can usually buy what you need en route but most of us are reluctant to ditch extra clothes as easily en route. Enjoy your travels. Most of the glamour is gone, but packing your swimsuit and/or workout clothes, walking shoes, and raingear will take away excuses for not exercising and provide alternatives to being cooped up in a hotel room for days at a time.

Travel can be hard on the body and challenging if you live with a disability, since accessibility is not always guaranteed. Unfamiliar water and foods can cause stomach problems. Air conditioning can render your skin dry as a bone. But the tradeoff is usually worth it—a new view of the world and new people with whom to share it. Travel is the stuff of privilege, so use it wisely.

UNDERGRADUATES

So you've decided to major in religion. Terrific. A thousand welcomes! Studying religion affords you the opportunity to range broadly, to read comparatively, to engage in interdisciplinary work, or to focus on a specific interest. Further, a major or minor in religion stands you in good stead in learning how to think alongside social scientists and those in the humanities. Contrary to public opinion, there are many things one can "do" with a major in religion, though in fact it needs no such justification. Going to seminary or **graduate school**, or choosing a religious **vocation** of some sort, are only a few options. Increasingly, journalists, social workers, doctors, ethicists, politicians, and those in the business and economic sector recognize the validity of attending to religion as an element of human activity and influence.

The usual advice applies: make sure your advisor is available to help you and to read your work, especially if you write a senior thesis. Do not neglect the **interdisciplinary** resources available to help you in your studies, not least of which may be **women's studies**. Enjoy your major and give it your own stamp. We all stand to benefit.

UNIONS

Teaching faculties at many public institutions, and increasingly at some private schools, are developing unions, which have been available to staff for much longer. They can be very useful for dealing with workplace issues from benefits to grievances, so much so that if your institution does not have one, be sure you know how such issues are handled. Unions help create equity and fight for better health and other benefits. Increasingly, graduate students and contingent faculty are organizing themselves into unions too. While their particularities differ in some ways from what clerical or autoworkers face, many issues remain the same. Organize, organize, organize.

Contingent or adjunct faculty may find unions helpful to achieve benefits and standardize work loads and/or pay. Negotiating for rights can be difficult for individual adjuncts; strength in numbers helps. If there is no union or some kind of collectivized group speaking for the needs of your fellow employees, consider starting a campaign.

Equity, benefits, workload, and the ability to negotiate the terms of employment have often been denied to graduate students, or been seriously neglected. The issues touch on many aspects of graduate student life, from partner benefits to expectations of teaching loads to stipends. Some institutions have argued that what graduate students do when they serve as teachers, preceptors, **research assistants**, **teaching assistants**, and graders is not work, per se, but pedagogical practice or "good experience." Institutions have argued that unionization threatens the "unique" relationship of student/teacher or mentor/mentee. Such rhetoric can disguise abuses and lead to more of them. Note that student athletes are being thought of as employees in some universities, opening them to the possibility of unionization. All of these are efforts to share the resources and revenues of higher education with the workers who produce them.

Issues of unionization differ from campus to campus and state to state: some so-called "right to work" states limit union effectiveness. It behooves you to learn about the place, or lack, of unions in the wider context of institutional practice and culture in the institution that you are planning to join as student, faculty, or staff. It also behooves all of us to organize.

Vacation

Time for rest and renewal is a right, not a privilege, though you would never know it by the average time U.S. workers get off. Indeed, the United States has one of the stingiest vacation deals in the world. Contrast our measly two weeks (if that) with the six weeks or more that many Europeans (until recently) expect in their workplace. In academia, the summer can seem like vacation time when in fact it is the only time to prepare courses, do academic writing, and get caught up on correspondence. In cognate fields like the nonprofit sector or publishing, a summer off is unheard of, so this is a serious issue that needs concerted effort to improve for everyone. Of course, paid vacation time of any length would be a luxury to those who are unemployed or work part-time for low hourly wages.

For women, the only advice is to take vacation time when you can get it, as often as you can, and without guilt. Did you ever meet a woman who felt she had had too much vacation? Try being the first, as you will be a pioneer in an area where we need to help one another do self-care! Once again, however, class issues come to the fore with many women having to work extra hard in the summer to earn money to supplement their often meager salaries and/or pay off their debts. Take all the time off you can afford. You won't get it back and it may lengthen your life to enjoy what you do have.

There are many creative vacation options, including house swaps. One smart group of women in our field rents a house on Martha's Vineyard every summer for several fun-filled weeks together. One feminist religious nonprofit organization always, but always, closes for the month of August. Such routinized approaches to vacation assure that we look forward to, take, and enjoy them.

Vocation

A vocation is slightly different from a job or a career. A vocation is a calling. It is a belief, a kind of knowing that you are doing that which virtually no one else but you in the whole of creation could or should be doing right now, and if you do not do it, it will not get done.

Calling work in religion a vocation is no excuse to accept less pay and longer hours. Beware the spiritualization of such concepts, at the same time that you choose to honor them. Embrace your vocation with gusto and enjoy!

Webpage, Personal

Most institutions are now putting information about faculty on the school's website. Some encourage each faculty member to have a personal webpage that students can use to access information about the teacher and her/his courses. Think very seriously about constructing a page, but decide whether you want your university to host this page or whether you want to have it on an independent server. There are advantages and disadvantages to each option.

Your professional page can be the front line of your digital reputation. Realize, though, that personal information, including things you post to social media, is also publically accessible, at least to some degree. Think about your use of popular social media, and err on the side of caution when it comes to sharing what are in fact private, not simply personal (as opposed to professional), matters. You want to have a polished profile. What happens when you search for yourself online? What narrative are you telling about who you are as a scholar?

Some may invest in a professional web designer, but for most a standard free program like WordPress can create a user friendly website that serves the needs of their students and the masses. Consider what photos you make available, what information you share about yourself, what other websites you link your webpage to. Incidents of cyber bullying are increasing for women so be prudent.

You may be using a personal webpage as a classroom aid such as posting a syllabus before class actually starts, listing further reading for the class topic, providing access to links to Web pages that are relevant to the class topic, posting instructions for assignments, and/ or making personal information about yourself available (such as a **Curriculum vitae)** or a list of classes taught)

Your personal webpage is just one arm of your media persona. Many academics have pages on www.academia.edu or www.LinkedIn.com, though the latter is more likely to be useful for people in **administration** or nonprofit work. They may also use blogs or social media for networking or to interact with their students, for example, Twitter or Facebook. It bears repeating: be careful with what information you share in social media.

Personal blogs can be **public scholarship** or they can be merely what was on your mind at the time. In an effort to reach a larger audience do not lose sight of your professional ethics and why you are publicizing the information. A blog can attract readers to your other writings, including articles or books. Generous use of links to other people's work is a wonderful way to expand and extend the conversation.

There are advantages and disadvantages to maintaining an active web presence. Advantages include the fact that students like to have this information available to them. You can have information in one easily accessible site and this may even reduce some use of paper. Students do not always have to contact you directly to get certain questions answered. Former students can check in to see what you are suggesting now as good reading material. Disadvantages include the fact that there is a time commitment involved in constructing and maintaining a personal webpage. Students who get used to using the webpage expect to have the information up earlier than you may be able to get to it. Anything you post is available to the general public unless you are able to have restricted access with password protection. Like many elements of technology, online presence is a mixed blessing but it is here to stay.

Be careful about intellectual property concerns and, as always, consult a legal expert on matters in question.

WOMANIST

African American women concerned with the well-being of women and the whole community, using their experiences and insights to create theoretical as well as practical strategies for change, call their work "womanist." The term originated in the writings of Alice Walker, who described "womanish" practices as those that aided the survival of black women and their families. Womanism is rooted in the everyday experiences of women of color and is deeply invested in their spirituality. In religious studies, womanist work has contributed mightily to women's efforts to bring about equality and justice. Within the **AAR**, there is a program unit devoted to womanist theory, the Womanist Approaches to Religion and Society Group. It sponsors a pre-meeting

In-Gathering for **networking** and scholarship. There is also a womanist list serve for African American Women in Religious Studies and an international womanist consultation for African and African Diasporan Women in Religion and Theology.

WOMEN'S CAUCUS

The Women's Caucus in Religious Studies began more than forty years ago. A group of enterprising women, graduate students as well as young faculty, realized that in order to survive the sea of men in suits that was the **AAR/SBL Annual Meetings** in those days, they would have to bond. They did so with enormous success, meeting yearly to bring constant critical attention to the needs and contributions of women in the field. They raised the need for childcare at the Annual Meeting and pushed behind the scenes for the election of the first women presidents in each society. The Caucus was the forerunner to the current program units that focus on women, of which there are now several.

The Caucus sponsors several sessions during the Annual Meetings. These are great opportunities to learn the ins and outs of the field, to focus on topics like violence against women, getting a dissertation published, and finding a mentor. The Caucus works with the Committee on the Status of Women in the Profession (**SWP**) to provide supportive spaces for women during the Annual Meetings. Leadership is voluntary and rotates. Feel free to get involved. The Caucus needs you and you need the Caucus.

WOMEN'S STUDIES (SEE ALSO INTERDISCIPLINARITY)

Women's studies emerged as a field to be reckoned with in the last decades of the twentieth century. Many centers, departments, and certificate programs were established. Although still young and changing as a field, it has already contented with intense backlash, both from opponents who dismiss its area of investigation as "political correctness" and from progressive allies who argue that its focus on "women" is passé.

In some places, women's studies has morphed into gender studies or gender and sexuality studies. In plenty of cases, this is a well-thought out move to expand from a focus on women's experiences, needs, and lives to gender in all its forms, including trans persons who may be left out of both women's studies and masculinity studies. In some instances, however, the shift away from women's studies can result from or unintentionally result in backing away from an explicit commitment to women's well being. It is a difficult balancing act, and institutions have pursued a variety of trajectories. Within the **AAR** and **SBL**, a number of program units approach issues of women, gender, and sexuality with overlapping approaches, sometimes complementary and sometimes competing. In each case, women's studies acts as a border field, and lends itself readily to interdisciplinary learning. Women's studies courses treat issues from a perspective that is implicitly or explicitly feminist, multicultural, and respectful of difference.

In religious studies, feminist, womanist, *mujerista*, Asian, Native American, "Muslima" and other explicitly women-centered forms of analysis and discourse constitute rich and powerful examples of women's studies. However, in many institutions those gains are eroding. Those who teach and study religion will find many areas of shared interest. Getting involved in women's studies will allow for hybridization, team teaching, and creative approaches to standard material.

A common question from doctoral students is whether they should risk working in women's studies. Or, should they do a "straight" dissertation and then concern themselves with women's issues later? For any given individual, this is a hard call; for the field as a whole, it is vital that this work continue and that junior scholars, who bring fresh questions and new insights, be among those undertaking it.

The situation is somewhat better than it was even a decade ago, and women's studies or gender studies has become part of the mainstream at many institutions. Quite a few jobs call for people working in or—more often—able to teach courses on women and gender. Although patriarchal pressures continue, if we are to have another generation of scholars and activists trained in women's studies in religion, it is imperative that our best and brightest do their work where it matters most. That will require a good bit of work from all of us.

WORK/LIFE BALANCE

Balance is a central quality-of-life issue for all academics, but it is an especially urgent problem for women because we are still expected to carry the major burden of care work in our society. Many challenges

prevent women at all stages of their careers from achieving a satis-
factory balance between earning a living and fulfilling other commitments and responsibilities. These challenges include the need to
care for self, children, elders, and extended family members, as well
as (sometimes) partners; and burdensome institutional expectations.
Women of color often face added difficulties as they are called on
not only to do extra committee work and "represent" their institutions in the larger world, but also to mentor students of color who
may have few role models. Women living with disabilities and chronic
health conditions regularly face extra challenges. Poorly paid and professionally insecure adjuncts, of which sixty percent are women, also
confront special problems.

Many women struggle with work/life issues in isolation and attempt
to find personal solutions to what are in reality structural problems.
One reader noted that this *Guide*, intended to provide helpful advice,
can seem to suggest an endless list of ways for women to cope with
unfair conditions, adding to women's burdens. While that is the last
thing the writers intend, we acknowledge that without changes in the
material conditions, the risk of putting additional burdens on women
is real.

The Status of Women in the Profession Committee (**SWP**) of the
American Academy of Religion has responded to these concerns in
a number of ways. SWP has sponsored Special Topic Forums on the
issue, and publishes a "Not for Women Only" feature in the online
Religious Studies News. SWP's planned online survival manual on
work/life balance will offer stories, strategies, policies, and critical
reflections that individuals face as they navigate their careers and their
own self-care. Check it out.

Beyond practical solutions, some people have also begun to question the model of "balance." Does the idea of balance mean turning
into functional cogs in corporatized machinery? Does it mean finding
ways to live with deep-rooted oppressive structures? These questions
are impossible to answer but important to ask. Each of our answers is
likely to be different, and our answers are likely to change over time.
But having the conversation guarantees a sharing of wisdom, and low-
ers the likelihood that we will all be seduced into impossible balancing
acts that no one should have to attempt. And the conversation may
well lead to lower tolerance for injustice and higher resolve to make
real changes.

Xenophobia

The United States of America understands itself as a country of immigrants and is generally open to newcomers. However, it is also racist toward immigrants of color, people from developing countries, and Muslims (or anybody who "looks Muslim," such as Sikhs), especially post-September 11. This is particularly troubling if your university or institution is located somewhere that white, Christian norms rule unbroken.

You will need the active support of your colleagues on campus to navigate potentially hostile environments of the town and county in which you are located. Make sure to ask about safe neighborhoods, Ku Klux Klan and white supremacist militia activities in the area, whether to list your telephone number, whether to get a post office box, and if you need an alarm system where you live. Your social life may depend almost entirely on contacts with your colleagues. You may have to weather a very lonely and isolating period (see **Isolation, cultural and religious**) until you find your people.

Xenophobia may also color your interactions on campus with colleagues, staff, and students. Cultural, religious, colonialist, and racial stereotypes may influence how people perceive you. Such biases can easily find their way into student teaching evaluations, merit reviews, and fuzzy evaluation categories like "collegiality" and "fit" for which people perceived to be outside the norm inevitably come up short. Try to become aware of these stereotypes and learn to anticipate and manipulate them in your favor. If you are part of the majority culture in this regard, take it as a personal responsibility to undo these pernicious stereotypes. It is a challenge for which the onus is really on those who occupy the privileged place (see **Privilege**), and the sooner xenophobia can be eradicated, the better.

Yes and No

There is always more to do than time will allow. Figuring out when to say yes and when to say no to invitations or expectations is a crucial skill. Our priorities will differ. In some cases, the deciding factor will be money (teaching summer courses provides important income; writing an encyclopedia article gives a reasonable honorarium) while in other cases, different factors dominate: an invitation to lecture at a place you have always wanted to visit (enthusiastic yes), the invitation to edit a special issue of a journal where you know some of the contributors, meaning you know that it will be tough to corral their contributions (reluctant no).

We need to help each other say "no" to the myriad invitations we receive that may distract us from our dissertations, books, recreation, or study. Sometimes a woman's no is necessary for others to step up and say yes. Here, as elsewhere, the problem can be structural rather than individual. The question is how much transformative work do we do versus how much simply making do with the existing system.

We need to be equally helpful in saying "yes" to one another in those instances where a collaborative effort is proposed, a little extra is asked of us, or an opportunity too good to pass up is in the balance. Sometimes we say yes simply based on who is doing the asking. Knowing when to say "yes" and when to say "no" can be the difference between a stressful, unsuccessful career in religious studies and a fruitful, enjoyable one. In any case, make the decisions in a timely way with clear-cut communication that signals a willingness to collaborate, or your inability or unwillingness to participate at this time. The worst answer can be no answer, but timely does not always mean immediate. If you are put on the spot, one effective strategy for women who are socialized to please others can be to say you need to consult your calendar, or review your current obligations. ("Let me check and get back to you.") When you reply, if the answer is no, it can be helpful to say that your current commitments prevent you from accepting even if those commitments are simply to your downtime.

ZEITGEIST

The Zeitgeist, that is, the spirit or attitude of a particular time, is changing in religious studies. Women, people of color, people from the wide range of religious traditions other than Christianity, folks from a wide range of sexualities and gender identities, and people living with disabilities are creating a new gestalt in religious studies. The study of religion itself increasingly corresponds more closely with the religious reality of a diverse and globalized world. You are part of it, and you give it new shape. Who you are and what you bring is a piece of it. We need you. Thank you.

American Academy of Religion
Sexual Harassment Policy

At its November 1996 meeting the AAR Board of Directors adopted a policy condemning sexual harassment in academic settings. Building upon the Equal Employment Opportunity Commission's definition of sexual harassment, the statement is designed to elevate member's awareness of the range of behaviors that can be described as sexual harassment, and to articulate the AAR's own commitment to ensuring that its own activities and operations are free from the pernicious effects of such behavior.

The AAR's Status of Women in the Profession Committee drafted the statement that also draws from statements by a number of other learned societies that have established similar policies. When asked why it was important for the AAR to put forward such a statement, Emilie Townes, a former chair of the AAR's Committee on the Status of Women in the Profession, said "... it is important to match the high standards the American Academy of Religion has for scholarship and research with a policy that calls forth the best of each of us professionally and interpersonally. It is important for AAR to make a clear and unambiguous statement against sexual harassment and provide all of the membership of the Academy resources for understanding and combating such dehumanizing behavior."

SEXUAL HARASSMENT POLICY FOR THE AMERICAN ACADEMY OF RELIGION

Introduction

The American Academy of Religion is committed to fostering and maintaining an environment of rigorous learning, research, and teaching in the field of religion. This environment must be free of sexual harassment. Sexual harassment is a discriminatory practice that is unethical, unprofessional, and threatening to intellectual freedom. It usually involves persons of unequal power, authority, or influence but can occur between persons of the same status.

Sexual harassment is illegal under Title VII of the 1980 Civil Rights Act and Title IX of the 1972 Educational Amendments. Sexual harassment is a gross violation of professional ethics comparable to plagiarism or falsification of research. It should be regarded and treated as such by members of the Academy. The policy of the American Academy of Religion is to condemn sexual harassment. Members of the Academy are encouraged to file complaints about sexual harassment with the appropriate administrative office of the institution where the harasser is employed or where he or she is enrolled, or with appropriate law enforcement authorities.

Background

The Equal Employment Opportunity Commission (EEOC) of the United States Government defines sexual harassment in the workplace or in the academic setting as:

"The use of one's authority or power, either explicitly or implicitly, to coerce another into unwanted sexual relations or to punish another for his or her refusal; or the creation of an intimidating, hostile or offensive working environment through verbal or physical conduct of a sexual nature."

Having friendships with students is common for teachers. It is also possible that teachers will experience attraction to students and experience students' sexual attraction to them. This cuts across gender and sexual orientation. Because of the inherent power differential between teacher and student, it is imperative that members of the Academy maintain the integrity of an environment that is not coercive, intimidating, hostile, or offensive.

The work of the Academy is best carried out in an atmosphere that fosters collegiality and mentoring. Sexual harassment can destroy or undermine this relationship. The impact of this on the life and future of the Academy cannot be belittled or ignored. When our actions are in violation of the dignity and integrity of another person, these actions are a profound violation of professional and human relationships. These are violations because they are exploitative and abusive.

Descriptions

Sexual harassment includes all behavior that prevents or impairs an individual's full enjoyment of educational or workplace rights, benefits, environments, or opportunities. These behaviors include but are not limited to:

1. sexist remarks, jokes, or behavior
2. unwelcome sexual advances, including unwanted touching
3. request for sexual favors
4. sexual assault, including attempted or completed physical sexual assault
5. the use of professional authority to inappropriately draw attention to the gender, sexuality or sexual orientation of an employee, colleague, or student
6. insults, including lewd remarks or conduct
7. visual displays of degrading sexual images or pornography
8. pressure to accept unwelcome social invitations

Sexual harassment occurs from these behaviors and other verbal or physical conduct of a sexual nature when any or all of the following conditions apply:

1. Submission to or rejection of such conduct by an individual is used, implicitly or explicitly, as a basis for employment decisions or academic decisions affecting such individuals; or
2. Such conduct has the purpose or effect of unreasonably interfering with an individual's work or academic performance or creating an intimidating, hostile, or offensive working or academic environment.

Such an atmosphere cannot and does not foster intellectual rigor or valuable, trusting human relationships. Both are necessary ingredients for good scholarship and professional excellence. The impact on the victim of sexual harassment can be profound. Studies on the effect of sexual harassment reveal disturbing consequences, such as loss of self-confidence, decline in academic performance, and inhibited forms of professional interaction. Sexual harassment has no place in the American Academy of Religion at any organizational level—formal or informal. It is behavior that we must seek to identify and eradicate.

RESOURCES

Baridan, Andrea P., *Working Together: The New Rules and Realities for Managing Men and Women At Work.* New York: McGraw-Hill, 1994.

Bouchad, Elizabeth, *Everything You Need to Know About Sexual Harassment.* New York: Rosen Publishing Group, 1990.

Grauerholz, Elizabeth, ed., *Sexual Coercion: A Sourcebook on Its Nature, Causes, and Prevention.* Lexington, MA: Lexington Books, 1991.

Paludi, Michele A., *Ivory Power: Sexual Harassment on Campus.* Albany: State University of New York, 1990.

Sexual Harassment on the Job: A Guide for Employers. Washington, DC: U.S. Commission on Civil Rights, 1982. Available at https://www.aarweb.org/node/145. By permission of the American Academy of Religion (*www.aarweb.org*).

American Academy of Religion Sexual Harassment Grievance Procedure

At its November 1996 meeting the AAR Board of Directors adopted a policy condemning sexual harassment in academic settings. At its April 1998 meeting the Board approved a Sexual Harassment Grievance Procedure.

The AAR's Status of Women in the Profession Committee formulated the procedure. In announcing the procedure for the membership, Emilie Townes, chair of the Committee, said "The Sexual Harassment Policy of the American Academy of Religion is designed to foster and maintain an environment of rigorous scholarship and professional excellence. Such an environment cannot be achieved when sexual harassment is present. The Policy is a clear and unambiguous statement against sexual harassment and it also provides resources for understanding and combating unprofessional and dehumanizing conduct. The Sexual Harassment Grievance Procedure provides an equitable mechanism to implement the sexual harassment policy of AAR. The Procedure seeks to provide confidentiality and a fair procedure for all parties involved. It, along with the Sexual Harassment Policy, provides the membership of AAR with a clear statement concerning sexual harassment, resources that are educational in helping combat it, and a procedure for the Academy to address any cases that may arise from official activities of AAR. Together, the Policy and Grievance Procedure, help AAR create and maintain the highest standards of professional conduct and academic freedom in our mutual pursuit of excellence in scholarship."

Introduction

The Grievance Committee has primary responsibility for interpretation of the AAR Sexual Harassment Policy, for the evaluation of complaints brought under it, and for recommendations to the Board of Directors pertinent to such complaints. The Grievance Committee will review those cases arising out of formally constituted activities of the AAR and for which it is the most appropriate forum, if it considers the matter important to the profession, and if it deems the AAR's resources to be adequate to yield a fair judgment. The Grievance Committee will not accept complaints it deems capricious or principally vindictive, and, except in unusual circumstances, it will not pursue a case while the dispute is pending in another forum. Review of a complaint by the Grievance Committee should not be regarded as substitute for legal action.

Composition of the Grievance Committee

The Grievance Committee should have direct lines of accountability to the AAR Board of Directors and the membership. It should be representative of the diversity of the member of AAR and avoid unnecessary bureaucratization.

1. President
2. President Elect
3. Vice President
4. SWP Chair
5. Secretary or Student Director in cases that involve a student

The Executive Director serves as the investigating officer.

No person who has been accused in the complaint will participate in the investigation or resolution of the complaint.

1. If any member of the Grievance Committee is named in the complaint, he or she is replaced by an appointment from the President. If the President is named in the complaint, the President Elect appoints a replacement for the President.
2. If someone comes forward with a complaint against the Executive Director, that complaint should be directed to the AAR President

who will replace the Executive Director in her/his role as investigator and/or member of the Grievance Committee.

COMPLAINT PROCEDURE

1. The complainant should present the complaint as promptly as possible with the Executive Director after the alleged harassment occurs. Failure to present a complaint promptly may preclude recourse to legal procedures beyond the jurisdiction of the AAR should the complainant decide to pursue such action at a later date.

   a). The initial discussion between the complainant and the Executive Director should be kept confidential, with no written record.

   b). The Executive Director has the authority to make a good faith effort to resolve the complaint through informal processes at this stage. There may be cases that can be resolved through efforts of mediation and for which the alleged offender apologizes for her/his actions.

   c). If the complainant, after the initial discussion with the Executive Director, decides to proceed, the complainant should submit a written statement to the Executive Director.

   d). The Executive Director then informs the alleged offender of the allegation and of the identity of the complainant in writing. A copy of this is sent to the complainant. Efforts should be made to protect the complainant from retaliatory action by the person(s) named in the complaint.

1. The Executive Director alerts the Grievance Committee that a complaint has been filed and promptly calls a meeting of the Committee. Each member of the Committee shall receive a copy of the written statement of the complaint. The Executive Director alerts the Grievance Committee that a complaint has been filed and promptly calls a meeting of the Committee. Each member of the Committee shall receive a copy of the written statement of the complaint.

2. The Grievance Committee may vote to either accept the complaint for full review or decline to consider the complaint. The Grievance Committee will base its decision on its judgment of its

capacity to handle the matter in light of its resources and competence; the seriousness of the complaint; the degree to which the complaint alleges specific violations of the AAR Sexual Harassment Policy; the likelihood that the AAR will be able to make a positive contribution to resolving the problem; the availability of a more suitable forum, such as a university grievance procedure or the AAUP. If the Committee decides to decline consideration of the complaint, it will submit an explanation in writing to the complainant and the alleged offender.

3. The Executive Director will gather all facts pertinent to the allegations of the complaint.
   a). The investigation will be conducted promptly and objectively.
   b). The investigation will include statements by the complainant(s), person(s) accused, and others as necessary.

1. The Grievance Committee has the following options:
   a). If the Committee concludes that on the basis of the investigation insufficient evidence of harassment exists to warrant any action, may close the investigation and so notify the complainant and alleged offender in writing.
   b). If the Committee concludes on the basis of the investigation that sexual harassment has occurred the following disciplinary actions may be taken:
      I.   Letter of reprimand to the offender.
      II. Training and education regarding sexual harassment and appropriate and inappropriate behaviors with documentation to the Committee that this training has been completed. Failure to comply may result in the rescinding of membership.
      III. Rescinding of membership in the AAR for a duration deemed appropriate by the committee.
      IV. Repeat offenders are subject only to disciplinary action 3.

1. Every effort will be made to maintain confidentiality throughout the process, but total confidentiality cannot be guaranteed. The Grievance Committee will protect the privacy of both the complainant and persons accused in every way possible during the process of the complaint and thereafter.

2. The AAR prohibits any form of retaliation against any member or employee of AAR filing a complaint against a member. Any retaliatory action of any kind taken against a complainant under this procedure is prohibited and will be the basis for a separate complaint subject to disciplinary action by the Grievance Committee.

3. If, after investigating a complaint the Grievance Committee determines that a complainant knowingly made a false complaint or knowingly provided false information regarding a complaint, the Committee may decide that disciplinary actions, as above, are warranted.

The decision of the Grievance Committee is final.

Available at *https://www.aarweb.org/node/190.*
By permission of the American Academy of Religion (www.aarweb.org).

Society of Biblical Literature (SBL) Ethics Statement

The members of the SBL constitute a community of scholars dedicated to promoting the critical investigation of biblical, religious, and theological literature and history, together with other related literature, by the exchange of scholarly research both in published form and in public forum.

While freedom of inquiry is at the heart of this enterprise, such freedom carries with it the responsibility of professional conduct. As a learned society, the SBL requires professional and intellectual conduct of its members as they exchange scholarly research in SBL publications or at SBL annual, regional, or committee meetings wherever they are held.

Professional and intellectual conduct includes, but is not limited to, conduct which is based on respect for others and which does not in any way exploit power and/or status differences such as those that exist between faculty and students or between senior and junior colleagues. Professional and intellectual conduct is free of all forms of harassment and discrimination.

Discrimination means a distinction, whether intentional or not, relating to personal characteristics of an individual or group, which has the effect of imposing burdens, obligations, or disadvantages on such individual or group not imposed on others; or which withholds or limits access to opportunities, benefits and advantages available to other members of the SBL.

Harassment means vexatious comment or conduct in relation to a person or group of persons which has the effect or purpose of creating a hostile or intimidating environment when such treatment abuses the power that one person holds over another or misuses authority; or such treatment has the effect or purpose of offending or demeaning a person or group of persons on the basis of race, ancestry, place of origin, color, ethnic group, citizenship, sex, sexual orientation, disability, creed, age, or marital/family status.

Sexual harassment includes any unwanted sexual attention or behavior by a person who knows or ought reasonably to know that such conduct is unwanted; or any implied or expressed promise of reward for complying with a sexually orientated request; or any implied or expressed threat of reprisal, in any form either of actual reprisal or the denial of opportunity for the refusal to comply with a sexually orientated request; or any inappropriate verbal or physical conduct that has a focus on sexuality or sexual identity in what reasonably may be perceived as a hostile or intimidating environment.

The SBL is committed to the creation and maintenance of a discrimination- and harassment-free environment in all of its sanctioned activities. The professional conduct of all members who participate in such activities is essential to the achievement of this standard.

Available at https://www.sbl-site.org/careercenter/policystatements. aspx.
By permission of the Society of Biblical Literature (http://www.sbl-site. org/).

Making Your Presentations Disability Friendly

ACCESSIBLE FACILITIES

- Clear aisles of any obstacles to individuals with mobility impairments.
- Remove chairs at the end of rows for those using wheelchairs, scooters, or guide dogs so they are not forced to sit in the front, back, or in an aisle.
- Seating should be made available in the front row for those who use assistive listening devices, who use sign language interpreters, or who lip-read.
- If it is possible to regulate the lighting, lights should be adjusted to meet the individual needs of those with visual impairments. (Note: This could mean dimming lights as well as raising them depending on the nature of the impairment.)
- Speakers and interpreters should be well lit for attendees who read lips or use sign language.

ACCESSIBLE MATERIALS

- Provide copies of all handouts in 16–18 point font.
- Provide copies of handouts in electronic format (e.g., .txt, .rtf, or .doc).
- Provide hard copies of overheads and PowerPoint presentations.
- Read and describe overheads, PowerPoint, or any visual information for those with visual or learning disabilities.
- Allow time for location and review when referring to visual materials.

ACCESSIBLE PRESENTATIONS

- Speak clearly and distinctly with a rate of speed and volume usually considered appropriate for public speaking.
- Use a microphone when provided. Microphones should be held at a distance from the mouth such that it will pick up your voice while not muffling the sound.
- Repeat all questions and comments from the audience into the microphone.
- Presenters should speak one at a time.
- Do not turn away from the audience while you are speaking.
- Speakers should identify who they are for those with visual impairments.
- Do not communicate key information solely in gesture or visual reference.
- Turn off overhead projectors and other equipment when not in use to decrease distracting noises.
- Eye contact and comments should be directed to the person who is deaf and not to the sign language interpreter.
- Comments should be addressed directly to participants with disabilities and not to their companions.
- Allow sessions not being taped through the taping service to be taped by participants with disabilities.
- Allow ample time for questions and answers.

Available at https://www.aarweb.org/annual-meeting/guidelines-for-accessible-presentations.

By permission of the American Academy of Religion (www.aarweb.org).

APPENDIX V

"Be Brief, Be Witty, Be Seated"

Mary E. Hunt

The following is a set of presentation tips that the Women and Religion Section has circulated to its presenters.

1. Be Brief. It takes about 20 minutes to read 10–12 double spaced pages. Allow a little time for introductory remarks and to repeat for emphasis what you really want to get across. Err on the side of too little material rather than too much. Your audience will thank you. Studies show that the average attention span for spoken words is slightly over 10 seconds. A few good ideas with a clear introduction and concise conclusion will stay with your listeners longer than a convoluted argument. Allow time for questions as it is another opportunity, usually more listener friendly than being read to, to communicate your ideas.

2. Be Witty. Every religious studies scholar is not Whoopi Goldberg or Lily Tomlin, but it is important to think of an academic audience as people first and foremost. A touch of humor is always appreciated. It keeps the audience alert. Think of the presentation as needing the clarity of a picture, the precision of an article, the flow of a conversation and the satisfaction of a good meal. Humor adds levity and makes your remarks memorable. Anecdotes and examples will give you a chance to lighten what might otherwise be a deadly dull performance.

3. Be Seated. Honor the time constraints because they assure that everyone will have an equal opportunity to speak. It is boorish

not to, a sure sign of inexperience. Practice speakers finish up with a bang on or a little ahead of the time. Novices start out strong but end up fumbling because they try to speed read a 30-page paper in twenty minutes. When they realize that their time is rapidly coming to a close they often exclaim, "Oh, heavens, I am just going to skip the next ten pages and read you the conclusion," or desperate words to that effect as if the content they are leaving aside has no bearing on the argument. To avoid this faux pas, keep your presentation to the time allowed. But if you do not manage that:

- acknowledge the time keeper with a nod so as not to distract your audience
- summarize your remaining material without reference to the time problem
- move smoothly to your conclusion like a practiced speaker and nobody will be any the wiser...except you, the next time.

Delivering a paper is learned behavior. It is like preaching a sermon, teaching a class or giving a lecture anywhere else. You can get it right with practice. Bad things can happen—the microphone can go dead, your PowerPoint presentation can freeze, you might even have an attack of nerves that will cause you enormous stress. But for the most part it will be a good, even an enjoyable experience. You can enhance it by offering a warm thank you to your introducer and by thanking your audience at the end, Miss Manners would suggest. A quick email thank you to the presider and/or the person who chairs the section is a nicety that increases graciousness among us.

Available at https://www.aarweb.org/annual-meeting/be-brief-be-witty-be-seated.
By permission of the American Academy of Religion (www.aarweb.org).

Writing a Successful Annual Meeting Paper Proposal

By Kecia Ali

EXPLAIN WHY YOUR PAPER IS AN IMPORTANT SCHOLARLY CONTRIBUTION

The point of conference papers—indeed the point of scholarship—is to move the discussion forward. You must explain why your proposed paper has broad significance to larger debates in your field but be sure to spend *at least* one substantial paragraph outlining your original contribution. Which thinkers? Which texts? Which countries, which years, which cities, which methods, which questions? You get the idea. Any proposal is only as good as the paper it's based on. Think twice. Is this paper really a contribution or are you just eager to present something? If it's the latter, please reconsider.

HAVE A POINT AND ARTICULATE IT CLEARLY.

Your goal is to be understood by your colleagues. Tell them exactly what you plan to argue in one thesis sentence. (If you cannot sum up the point of your proposed paper in one sentence that is an indication that you need to scale back your project to fit the limitations of a conference presentation). Then tell them exactly how you plan to support that point.

KNOW THE LITERATURE.

As you outline your argument, you should refer to the existing literature or demonstrate that you are familiar with it. You don't have to rehash the contributions of every single author who's written on your topic. You don't even have to refer explicitly to any of them, though it can be helpful to do so. But be sure you have read them. Be sure you're not plodding along a well-defined path—especially not holding a flag and attempting to claim new territory (or, conversely, stumbling through the wilderness unaware that others have, for sound reasons, marked your chosen path as prone to rockslides). Just because an insight is new to you doesn't mean it's new to the people reading your proposal—and it won't necessarily be new to your audience.

TAKE GUIDELINES SERIOUSLY WHEN WRITING YOUR PROPOSAL AND ABSTRACT.

If you have a thousand words, you needn't use every single one of them. However, you should use most of them. Explain why your paper is essential. It is almost impossible to make a compelling case for your paper in five hundred words that will stand up against proposals of nine hundred and fifty words. (Unless, that is, the authors of those proposals commit some of the cardinal sins of proposal writing.)

As a corollary, follow *all* directions for submitting proposals. If the call for papers requires online submission, do not email or fax your proposal to the organizers. If it asks for your abstract in a specific font, or without diacritics, comply. Doing so won't earn you extra points, but failing to do so will get you noticed, and not in a good way.

PROOFREAD.

We all make mistakes. One or two typos will not automatically bar you from inclusion. But garbled sentences and more than a few even very minor mistakes will raise serious questions about your competence or commitment.

GET A SECOND OPINION.

Non-native English speakers should get their proposals checked for clarity of expression. If you do not communicate regularly in scholarly English have your proposal read by someone who does. It is usually fairly clear when proposals are by nonnatives. Reviewers make allowances for quirky sentence construction and occasionally awkward vocabulary. However, if the conference is going to be in English, they want to make sure your presentation will be intelligible. Having an intelligible proposal is the best start.

Even if English is your first language, ask a colleague, friend, or long-suffering spouse to read your proposal. If you're a student, ask your advisor. It's part of the job description.

NEVER CITE WIKIPEDIA.

You'd think this would go without saying. You'd be wrong.

REMEMBER THE TIME LIMIT AND TAILOR YOUR PROPOSAL ACCORDINGLY.

Most paper sessions restrict presenters to twenty minutes. Sometimes they grant twenty-five. (If your paper is accepted, you should ask.) This allows for no more than eight to ten double-spaced pages of material. Propose something you can reasonably present in that time frame. You can't compress your entire dissertation or monograph into one conference presentation. A focused proposal will lead to a focused paper.

If your paper is not based on a dissertation chapter or article, you may not have written your paper by the time you write your proposal. This is actually an advantage. Go ahead and write the paper you can present. If you've written a thirty-page seminar paper, you cannot present the whole thing. No, not even if you read it very quickly.

If you are presenting from a larger paper, you will need to make appropriate revisions in advance. The moment when you are writing your proposal is a good time to begin. Focus on the key parts of the argument. Select your strongest evidence to explore more fully, and allude briefly to the rest. Make it smooth. Think about the experiences you have had in conferences where speakers ramble about how they have to skip this section and that section, frantically putting pages aside to wrap up their presentations in the given time. If you plan ahead—starting with your proposal—you can avoid being that person. Having a manageable topic that fits the allotted time will let you have a more professional and memorable presentation. As a bonus, approaching your chapter or article this way may help you strengthen it for future publication.

Proofread.

Be aware of sweeping generalizations that will raise hackles.

With only a thousand words you can't hedge and nuance every single statement. You can, however, avoid phrases like "As everyone knows, orthodox Islam holds belief A." Or "All Christians believe X."

Choose a methodological voice and stick with it.

Think about whether you are proposing a constructive theological paper (i.e., you're speaking as a committed Lutheran in order to convince other Lutherans of a particular view about what Lutherans should believe or do) or a scholarly analytical paper (Why do Lutherans believe as they do? How did they come to believe it?) These are sometimes not completely separable, but you should have your perspective and your objective clear in your own mind before you write. And, if your paper is aimed primarily at your coreligionists, consider whether you are proposing it for an appropriate venue.

Proofread.

Pitch your paper to your audience.

If you are an Islamic Studies scholar proposing a paper for the more general consultation on religion and law, you will need to define the term *hadith* or use its English equivalent. If you are writing for an audience of specialists in Islam, you needn't do so. In fact, please don't. And you certainly don't have to give a recap of the first two centuries of Muslim history. Or tell your readers who the Prophet Muhammad was. Truly, it's not necessary.

This rule can also be summed up as: don't insult your reviewers' intelligence.

Have a descriptive title.

Your title should be specific enough that proposal reviewers, and eventually conference attendees consulting the program book, know what you'll be discussing. "African American Christianity" is not sufficiently descriptive. Neither is "Islamic Theology." On the other hand, just naming a thinker or text without some attention to your particular topic is not much better. As with the proposal itself, strive for a happy medium between big picture and specific focus.

Tailor your proposal to the conference.

Proposals should highlight those elements of your paper most relevant to the conference's or panel's theme.

If your proposal is for a conference that you attend regularly, go to the business meeting for your group or section. Surprisingly few people attend business meetings. If you go you will have a step up on your colleagues. You will know exactly what the group or consultation is looking for in paper sessions or prearranged panels for next year. Organize your work to address what the group wants to improve your chances of getting your paper accepted. Better still, propose a panel on your general topic. If accepted by the group, you would then organize a prearranged panel on that very topic.

Some additional guidance for proposing a paper panel:

Make sure the papers go together. This sounds obvious but it's not. Pay attention to methodological and topical coherence as well as breadth.

Be aware of diversity. In addition to being conscious of scholars' gender, racial, ethnic, and religious backgrounds, consider professional diversity. Try to engage at least one senior scholar and one graduate student. Consider the types of institutions people come from—small colleges, large research institutions, varied geographic locations. All of this will help make for a more lively session as well as give you a chance to connect with other scholars.

Once you have the panel approved, collaborate. The best panels are those in which there is the most coordination between panelists, including the chair. Correspond by email. Consider reading each other's papers in draft form along the way. Include the respondent for at least the latter part of the process. The more cohesive the panel, the more productive the scholarly exchange between presenters and audience, resulting in a genuine conversation rather than narrow questions to individual presenters. The most satisfying panels are ones in which one could imagine the papers published together as a coherent book or pamphlet.

If your proposal is accepted, read Mary E. Hunt's presentation guidelines "Be Brief, Be Witty, Be Seated" (**Appendix V**).

If your proposal is rejected, you may be able to get feedback to help you in future submissions. You can send a politely worded email asking for suggestions to the Program Unit co-chairs, although, depending on the number of submissions, you may not get a detailed response or even any at all. If you followed the advice above (in brief, have something important and relevant to say and say it clearly and succinctly), there's a good chance it was simply a matter of numbers. Most conferences receive far greater numbers of good proposals—not to mention indifferent or outright lousy ones—than they can include. Perhaps your paper didn't fit naturally into a panel with other submissions. It could also be that the proposal wasn't as strong as it could have been. Review your proposal, improve it, and resubmit it. Before reapplying to the major conference in your field, consider smaller venues such as regional meetings or graduate student conferences.

These guidelines have been immeasurably improved by corrections and suggestions offered by generous colleagues. Further comments welcome to Kecia Ali at ka@bu.edu.

Available at https://www.aarweb.org/node/204.
By permission of the American Academy of Religion (www.aarweb.org).

Resources

Please note that while URLs are up to date as of mid-2014, web addresses may change. You may need to visit a site's home page or use a keyword search to locate updated pages; if entire sites move, try using search engines. Additionally, new resources emerge regularly. This list is nowhere close to comprehensive; it is meant to provide a starting point for your explorations.

Academic life

Academe (http://www.aaup.org/reports-and-publications/academe) is the bulletin of the American Academy of University Professors that has articles of interest to women. *The Chronicle of Higher Education* (*The Chronicle*) is a weekly newspaper aimed at college and university faculty and administrators. It includes news, employment openings, and other materials related to the field. Paid subscriptions provide full access to the website, www.chronicle.com, or one can sign up for the free news-letter *"Academe Today."* Some of its materials, including most of its advice articles and the blog www.chroniclevitae.com, which focuses on hiring and employment, require no subscription. The site can be very useful in the job-hunting process and in keeping up with scholarly trends and ideas in and beyond the field of religious studies.

Karen Kelsky, a consultant, sells her services but also offers a wealth of information for free at www.theprofessorisin.com.

"On Diversity, Institutional Whiteness and Its Will for Change" by W. Anne Joh, Garrett-Evangelical Theological Seminary
https://www.aarweb.org/node/1967

AAR

American Academy of Religion resources include the REM Career Guide and online advice columns by some of its committees including SWP ("Ask Academic Abby") and LGBTIQ ("Ask the Diva"). You can navigate to these resources from the AAR home page (www.aarweb. org). Access to these pages requires an AAR membership.

Alt-ac resources

Not limited to but relevant to religious studies scholars, #Alt-Academy contains essays, lists, and reflections by people who have chosen "non-traditional" careers using their humanities skills.
http://mediacommons.futureofthebook.org/alt-ac/

Academic proletariat issues

"The Emergent Academic Proletariat and Its Shortchanged Students"
http://www.dissentmagazine.org/online_articles/the-emergent-academic-proletariat-and-its-shortchanged-students

Women in the field

"Gender and Career Progression in Theology and Religious Studies"
http://trs.ac.uk/wp-content/uploads/2013/11/Gender-in-TRS-Project-Report-Final.pdf
"Check the Box: Diversity and Hiring Practices in the University Setting" by Ivy Helman http://feminismandreligion.com/2013/11/10/check-the-box-diversity-and-hiring-practices-in-the-university-setting-by-ivy-helman/.

GRADUATE STUDENT CONCERNS

"How to Get the Mentoring You Want: A Guide for Graduate Students"
http://www.rackham.umich.edu/downloads/publications/mentoring.pdf
"Scholarly Pursuits: A Guide to Professional Development During the Graduate Years"
http://www.gsas.harvard.edu/current_students/scholarly_pursuits.php

FEMINIST JOURNALS AND BLOGS

A number of journals deal with feminist religious studies and theological scholarship, including the *Journal of Feminist Studies in Religion* (*JFSR*), which maintains a website (http://www.fsrinc.org/jfsr) and a blog (http://www.fsrinc.org/blog/). Another useful blog is www.feminismandreligion.com. Contributors to these sites often link to other web pages and scholarship; both sites also welcome posts from guest contributors. More general religious studies and ethics journals may include feminist content; other feminist journals may include religious studies content.

MEDIA

Religion Source (www.religionsource.org) maintains a database of scholars that journalists can use to find experts in their field. It also offers guidance for scholars about serving as expert sources.

RESOURCES ON FUNDING

Association of Theological Schools funding manual
http://www.ats.edu/uploads/resources/publications-presentations/documents/seeking-funding-a-manual-for-faculty-in-theological-education.pdf)

RESOURCES ON LEADERSHIP AND ADMINISTRATION

Association of Theological Schools listserv and conference for women in leadership
http://www.ats.edu/resources/current-initiatives/women-in-leadership
HERS Summer Institute for Women in Higher Education Administration,
http://hersnet.org/
Harvard Graduate School of Education http://www.gse.harvard.edu/ppe/programs/higher-education/

RESOURCES ON TEACHING

Wabash Center for Teaching and Learning in Theology and Religion (http://wabashcenter.wabash.edu) maintains a database of syllabi as well as a collection of articles and other resources for teaching. The Center publishes a journal (*Teaching Theology and Religion*) that provides helpful guidance and offers summer workshops.
"Feminists Launch Model for Online Learning"
http://womensenews.org/story/education/130814/feminists-launch-model-online-learning#.Uw5jL_RdWXQ.

BOOKS OF INTEREST

None of these books is addressed expressly to women in religious studies, but many of the issues surrounding parenting, race, and gender are similar to those confronted by other academics. The authors' perspectives vary—some are optimistic, some pessimistic; some address only tenure-track faculty, while others take a broader view.

Books about motherhood and academia include those built around personal narratives and others based on research, including surveys and longitudinal studies. We list a few recent titles; more will likely appear. Some contributors opt out of the academic path, feeling its pressures and structures are incompatible with active parenting, while others are sanguine about the possibilities for women's flourishing in academic work.

Mari Castañeda and Kirsten Lynn Isgro, eds., *Mothers in Academia* (New York: Columbia University Press, 2013) is theoretically informed, queer-inclusive, and attentive to race.

Kristen Ghodsee and Rachel Connelly, *Professor Mommy: Finding Work-Life Balance in Academia* (Lanhan, MD: Rowman and Littlefield, 2011) is coauthored by colleagues, one a married mother of four and the other a single mother of one. It is primarily concerned with tenure-track faculty, and includes sections for graduate students and mid-career and senior faculty.

Elrena Evans, Caroline Grant, and Miriam Peskowitz, *Mama, PhD: Women Write about Motherhood and Academic Life* (Rutgers, NJ: Rutgers University Press, 2008) provides nearly three dozen personal narratives, which are clear-eyed about practical and ideological difficulties confronting mothers in academic careers, including some from women who have opted out.

Kelly Ward and Lisa Wendel's *Academic Motherhood: How Faculty Manage Work and Family* (Rutgers, NJ: Rutgers University Press, 2012), and Mary Ann Mason, Nicholas H. Wolfinger, and Marc Goulden, *Do Babies Matter? Gender and Family in the Ivory Tower* (Rutgers, NJ: Rutgers University Press, 2013) are both research-based overviews with practical recommendations for individuals and institutions.

Other books focus on race in academia, sometimes attending carefully to gender. Important resources include:

Eleazar S. Fernandez, *Teaching for a Culturally Diverse and Racially Just World* (Eugene, OR: Cascade Books, 2014).

Gabriella Gutierrez et al. eds., *Presumed Incompetent: The Intersections of Race and Class for Women in Academia* (Ogden, UT: Utah State University Press, 2012).

Kerry Anne Rockquemore and Tracey Laszloffy, *The Black Academic's Guide to Winning Tenure—Without Losing Your Soul* (Boulder, CO: Lynne Rienner, 2008).

ABOUT THE EDITORS

Kecia Ali is associate professor of Religion at Boston University. Before joining the BU faculty in 2006, she held research and teaching fellowships at Harvard Divinity School and Brandeis University, where she also worked on the Feminist Sexual Ethics Project. Her books include *Sexual Ethics and Islam* (2006), *Marriage and Slavery in Early Islam* (2010), and *The Lives of Muhammad* (2014). She is active in the American Academy of Religion and currently serves as president of the Society for the Study of Muslim Ethics.

Mary E. Hunt is co-director of the Women's Alliance for Theology, Ethics and Ritual (WATER) in Silver Spring, Maryland. She is a feminist theologian who teaches online for Pacific School of Religion and is active on social justice issues. She blogs regularly on theology and ethics on the Feminism and Religion Forum, and writes for Religion Dispatches. Her publications include *New Feminist Christianity: Many Voices, Many Views* (2010), edited with Diann L. Neu; *Good Sex: Feminist Perspectives from the World's Religions* (2000), edited with Patricia Beattie Jung and Radhika Balakrishnan; and *Fierce Tenderness: A Feminist Theology of Friendship* (Crossroad, 1989).

Monique Moultrie is assistant professor of Religious Studies at Georgia State University in Atlanta, Georgia. She received her PhD from Vanderbilt University. She has worked as a consultant for the Ford Foundation and the National Institutes of Health, and is writing her first solo monograph while at Harvard University. She serves on the Status of Women in the Profession Committee of the American Academy of Religion.

Index

Main entries in *bold italics*

AAR (American Academy of Religion), 4–6, *9–11*, 35, 36, 38, 40, 41, 65, 66, 73, 77, 78, 88, 113, 114, 117, 131, 138–9, 146–7, 149, 158–9, 162, 173, 179, 183–7, 194, 200, 201

AAR Annual Meeting, 9, *11–14*, 15, 35, 36, 38, 70, 73, 74, 78, 100, 103, 125, 128, 130, 136, 137, 150–1, 162, 174, 175

AAR Regions, 9, *14–15*, 73, 130, 151, 200

ableism, 1, 7, *15*, 51, 78, 118, 131. *See also* disability

academic freedom and risk, *15–16*, 113, 147, 164, 183

activism, 4, 10, *16–17*, 24, 40, 47, 58, 66, 69, 89, 107, 118, 159, 175

administration, 7, 8, *17–20*, 26, 27, 30, 42, 43, 45, 47, 57–8, 63, 81, 90, 95, 98, 103, 108, 109, 116, 129, 132, 134, 139, 157, 161, 162, 172, 180, 201, 203

admissions, *20–1*, 72, 92, 141

advisor/advisee relationships, 12, *21–2*, 54, 61–2, 65, 72, 80, 116, 141, 145, 158, 166, 169, 197. *See also* mentoring

Affirmative Action, *22–3*, 28, 63, 82, 104, 139, 140

aging, *23–4*

allies, *24–5*, 39, 57, 92, 95, 97, 98, 104, 115, 116, 129, 133, 150, 151, 157, 174

alternative academic careers (Alt-Ac), 13, *25–6*, 71, 88, 202

appointments, adjunct, 10, 13, 15, *26–7*, 30, 31, 34, 42, 48, 60, 63, 81, 89, 90, 92, 107, 108, 118, 121, 134, 142, 147, 164, 170, 176

appointments, visiting, *27–8*, 43, 86, 107, 165

archives, **28**, 40, 147

benefits, domestic partner, *28–9*

benefits, leaves (family), *29*, 59, 80, 110–11, 123, 147

benefits, leaves (study), *30*, 123, 149, 162

benefits, medical, *30–1*, 105, 147

benefits, retirement, *31*, 105, 122, 124, 127

books, 12, 30, *31–3*, 49, 54, 58, 66, 68, 93, 96, 108, 132, 135, 136–8, 148–9, 203–4

children, 21, *33–5*, 63–4, 122

Christian hegemony, 3, *35–7*, 56, 94, 131, 143, 146, 153

Chronicle of Higher Education (The Chronicle), 19, 25, 201

class, socioeconomic, 1, 36, *37*, 45, 47, 51, 64, 67, 89, 92, 120, 130, 131, 139, 151, 171, 204

clothing options, *37–8*, 154

collaborative work, 1, 19, *38–9*, 68, 133, 158, 178, 199

coming out, *39–41*, 80–1, 156

Committee on the Status of Women in the Profession (CSWP of SBL), *41–2*, 74, 158–9

committees, 8, 10–11, 14, 23, 26, 40, 46, *42–3*, 73, 77, 81, 82, 83, 106, 113, 117, 139, 141–2, 146–7, 155, 158–9, 164, 174, 176, 179, 183–7

commuting, *43*, 83
competition, 43–4, 47, 72, 74, 102,
120, 137, 151
computers, 46, 49, 50, 102, 124, 132
confidence, *45–6*, 62, 148
confidentiality, *46–7*, 59, 80, 133, 141,
183, 185, 186
conflict, *47–8. See also* competition
contracts, 8, *48–9*, 59, 63, 81, 87, 105,
106, 123–5, 136, 137–8, 147, 149,
161–2. *See also* negotiations
counter offers, 106, 108, 149
curriculum vitae, 21, *49–50*, 58, 75,
103, 134, 136, 141, 172

debt, 24, *50–1*, 64, 120–3
disability, 13, 15, 20, 29, 30, *51–3*, 79,
84, 130, 191–2. *See also* ableism,
illness and disability
dissertation, 26, 31, *53–4*, 62, 64–5,
72, 107, 135, 175, 197

editing, *54–5*, 137
emerita, 2, 23, *55*, 109, 147
employment opportunities, 71, 91–2,
93, 103, 107, 150, 201
entrepreneurs, 25, *55–6*, 73–4, 95
ethnocentrism, *56–7. See* racism, classism
evaluations, annual, *57–9*, 132, 134,
155, 164
evaluations, peer, *59–60*, 108
evaluations, student, *60–1*, 160, 161
exams, qualifying/comprehensives/
generals, 44, 53, *61–2*

faculty club, *62–3*
faculty handbook, 22, *63*, 116, 166
family, 29, 33–5, 43, *63–4*, 142–3,
204. *See also* children, relationships
fellowships, graduate student, 20, 21,
53, *64–6*, 69
fellowships, professional, *66–7*, 69, 74,
91, 111, 141
feminist, 4, 6, 10, 17, 35, 55, *67–8*, 90,
97, 98, 109, 123, 150, 159, 161,
175, 202, 203
Festschriften, *68–9*, 147
files, 58, 134–5
forerunners, *69*, 174
fundraising, 56, *69–70*, 85, 90, 93, 95

globalization, 37, *70*, 87, 100, 144,
145–6, 178
graduate school, 20, 21, 44, 53, 64,
70–3, 120, 121, 169
Graduate Student Committee, 11, 14, *73*
grants, 9, 21, 65, 66, 67, 69, *73–4*, 91,
100, 122, 132
guest lectures, 58, *74–6*, 103, 111–12,
132, 152, 167

harassment, *76–7*
harassment, racial, *77–8*
harassment, sexual, 4, 77, *78–9*, 158,
179–87
health, 31, *79–80*, 84–5, 110, 151–3,
176. *See also* illness and disability,
self-care
heterosexism, *80–1*, 102, 118, 139,
142–3. *See also* coming out
hiring, 8, 23, 40, 48, *81–3*, 94, 127,
147, 166, 201, 202. *See also*
interviewing
housing, 43, *83–4*

illness and acquired disability, 22, 29,
51, 79, *84–5*
immigration, *85–7*, 100, 177
inclusive language, *87–8*, 159
independent scholars, 10, 11, 39, *88–9*,
109, 125
institutional analysis, *89–90*, 95, 135,
144, 155
institutional analysis (independent
centers or institutes), 89, *94–5*
institutional analysis (private), *92–4*
institutional analysis (public), 37,
91–2, 170
institutional analysis (religiously
affiliated colleges and
seminaries), *94*
institutional culture/politics, 58, 64,
71, 83, *95*, 116, 157. *See also*
institutional analysis
intellectual property, *96*, 173
interdisciplinarity, 19, 38, 66, 71, *96–9*,
102, 145, 165, 169–70, 174–5
international colleagues, 14, 70,
99–100, 126
international study, *100*, 121
internships, *101*, 107, 121

intersectionality, 98, *101–2*, 139, 204
interviewing, 4, 28, 37–8, 40, 78, 81–2, 85, *102–3*, 107, 115, 119, 124, 143, 150
isolation, cultural and religious, 9, 91, *103–4*, 176, 177

JAAR (*Journal of the American Academy of Religion*), 9, 109
JFSR (*Journal of Feminist Studies in Religion*), 55, 109, 202
job search, 92, *106–9*
job sharing, *104–5*
jobs, changing, *105–6*
journals, reading and writing, 59, 68, 70, 96, *109–10*, 132, 135, 136, 138, 148, 178

language requirements, 52, 87–8, 100, 150, 159, 191, 192
leaves of absence, 30, 79, 105, *110–11*, 123. *See also* benefits, leaves
lecture circuit, 75, *111–12*. *See* guest lecture
LGBTIQ, 11, 14, 39–41, 81, 82, 98, *112–13*, 117, 166, 201. *See* transgender
LGBTIQ Committee (Status of Gay, Lesbian, Bisexual, Intersex, and Queer Persons in the Profession), 11, 14, *113*, 117

media relations, *113–16*, 132, 135–6, 172–3, 203
mentoring, 2, 11, 14, 22, 41, 44, 45, 54, 72, 80–1, 92, 93, 104, 109, 113, *116–17*, 126, 139, 151, 155, 157, 158, 170, 174, 176, 180, 202. *See also* advisor/advisee relationships
micro-aggressions, 77, *117–18*, 139, 140
midcareer issues, *118–19*, 121, 165
money management, 24, *120–3*, 147. *See* debt
MOOCs, 2, 90, *120*, 162
mujerista, 35, 36, 62, 67, *123*, 175

negotiations, 7, 24, 27, 29, 48–9, 55, 76, 99, 104, 106, 108–9, 116, 121, *123–5*, 137, 143, 147, 148, 149, 155, 160, 162, 170. *See also* contracts; leaves of absence
networking, 41, 46, 50, 70, 113, *125–6*, 131–2, 133, 147, 158, 164, 173–4

ordination, 114, *126–7*, 156

postcolonialism, 97, 98, *127–8*
poster sessions, *128*
power, white and male, 45, 97, *129–30*, 131
presenting a paper, 74, 119, 128, *130*, 132, 193–4, 195–200
privilege, 16, 17, 31, 35, 37, 45, 52, 63, 67, 78, 117, *130–1*, 151, 166, 169, 177
professional associations, 44, *131–2*, 155
professional development, 20, 22, 73, 104, 119, 124, *132–3*, 134, 139, 153, 202
professional ethics, *133–4*, 143, 173, 180, 189–90
promotion, 22, 42, 59, 60, 63, 89, 91, 99, 106, 118, 119, *134–5*, 147, 156, 164, 165–6
public scholarship, *135–6*, 173
publishing, 7, 8, 21, 26, 31–3, 59, 89, 91, 107, 109–10, 135, *136–8*, 148–9. *See also* books; journals
PWD (Status of People with Disabilities in the Profession Committee), 11, 13, 117, *138–9*

racism, 39, 56–7, 77–8, 100, 117–18, 128, 131, 133, *139–40*, 156, 166, 177
references and recommendations, 20, 21, 26, 65–6, *140–2*, 164
relationships, 22, 47, 63–4, 72, 78, 133, *142–3*, 181
religious belief and observance, 76, *143–4*, 153
religious studies, 9, 17, 32, 35–6, 39, 41, 53, 55, 66, 70, 80, 89, 96, 107, 119, 125, 126–7, 135, 140, *144–6*, 153, 154, 156, 158, 159, 166, 173–4, 175, 178, 202

REM (Status of Racial and Ethnic Minorities in the Profession Committee), 11, 14, 77, 117, *146–7*, 158

retirement, 23, 27, 30, 31, 55, 68, *147–8*

reviews, book, 138, *148–9*, 155. *See also* publishing

sabbaticals, 30, 48, 67, 87, *149*, 162. *See* leaves, benefits

SBL (Society of Biblical Literature), 4, 9, 41, 73, 77, 78–9, 103, 114, *149–50*, 158, 189–90

SBL, Annual Meeting, 11, 41, 70, 73, 74, 103, 130, 136, *150*, 151, 158–9, 162, 174

SBL, international meeting, *150*

SBL, regional, *150–1*

self-care, 79–80, 111, *151–3*

sensitivity, religious, *153–4*

service, 14, 91, 93, 105, 115, 119, 131, 134–5, *155–6*, 160

sexism, 23, 79, 118, 128, 133, 139, *156–7*, 166, 181

sponsoring, 116, *157–8*

staff, 18, 25, 45, 47, 80, 86, 95, 118, 140, *157*

SWP of AAR (Committee on the Status of Women in the Profession), 4, 5, 6, 9, 10, 14, 41, 117, 125, *158–9*, 174, 176, 184, 201

syllabi, 32, 51, 58, 108, 119, *159*, 160, 161, 172, 203

teaching, 2, 26–7, 38, 39, 43, 48, 60–1, 67, 90, 91, 92, 93, 105, 108, 120, 132, 146, *159–62*, 203

teaching, assistantship/research assistantship, *163*

teaching, first year, 42, 160

teaching portfolio, 58, 108

tenure, 15, 20, 38, 42, 81, 93, 98–9, 108, 119, 121, 132, 138, 148, *163–5*, 204

tenure track jobs, 26, 30, 39, 48, 57–9, 86, 89, 91–2, 105, 107–8, 118, 134, 155–6, *165–6*, 204

tokenism, 36, 160, *166*. *See also* racism; sexism

transgender, 9, 39–41, 112, 113, 126, 156, *166–7*. *See* LGBTIQ

travel, 13, 35, 41, 43, 74, 75, 81, 99, 111, *167–9*

undergraduates, 2, 142, *169–70*

unions, 27, 118, 157, *170–1*

vacation, 124, 167, *171*

vocation, 19, 26, 127, 169, *171–2*

webpage, personal, *172–3*

womanist, 10, 35, 67, 123, 125, *173–4*

Women's Caucus, 4, 5, 6, 14, 125, 158, *174*

women's studies, 4, 19, 55, 66, 82, 97–9, 104, 146, 165, 170, *174–5*. *See also* interdisciplinarity

work/life balance, 151, 158, *175–6*

xenophobia, 100, *177*

yes and no, 111, 156, 158, 160, *177–8*

Zeitgeist, *178*